R. ... ... LIBRARY
100 Wellesley Street West
Toronto, Ontario
Canada M5S 2Z5

WITHDRAWN

THE ACHIEVEMENT OF

Hans Urs von Balthasar

An Introduction to His Trilogy

MATTHEW LEVERING

Foreword by Cyril O'Regan

RE... ...RARY
100 Wellesley Street West
Toronto, Ontario
Canada M5S 2Z5

The Catholic University of America Press

Washington, D.C.

BX
4705
B163
L48
2019

Copyright © 2019
The Catholic University of America Press
All rights reserved
The paper used in this publication meets the minimum
requirements of American National Standards for
Information Science—Permanence of Paper for Printed
Library Materials, ANSI Z39.48-1984.

∞

Cataloging-in-Publication Data available from
the Library of Congress
ISBN 9780813231754

To Antonio López, FSCB

RE   :   :   :   RARY
100 Wellesley Street West
Toronto, Ontario
Canada M5S 2Z5

CONTENTS

In this book, Matthew Levering has written an unusual introduction to the famous trilogy of Hans Urs von Balthasar. In terms of
texts, he prioritizes the first volume of each part of the trilogy of
The Glory of the Lord, *Theo-Drama*, and *Theo-Logic*—in fact fifteen volumes in the English translation—and in terms of conversation and argument, he prioritizes von Balthasar's discussions
with Immanuel Kant, Georg W. F. Hegel, and Friedrich Nietzsche,
respectively.

In focusing on these three conversations as opening up the
introductory volumes of von Balthasar's trilogy, Levering aims
to provide a series of red threads whereby one does not get lost
in the labyrinth of the seven thousand pages of von Balthasar's
theological aesthetics, theological dramatics, and theo-logic.
Levering's uplifting of the philosophical does not mean to dis-
credit the view that other kinds of conversation occur in von
Balthasar's trilogy, but it is intended to offer the advisory that in
line with Aquinas and the entire modern Catholic tradition, theology's dialogue with philosophy holds a central position. It is
not even imaginable that Levering, a committed Thomist, would
be inclined to downplay in general the influence of the classical
tradition of philosophy that begins in wonder and is constituted by eros. It is simply that, on the one hand, in line with *Fides et Ratio*, Levering recognizes that philosophy is plural (even
if one can speak of Aquinas as first among equals) and, on the

Cyril O'Regan is Huisking Professor of Theology, University of Notre Dame.

other, that while there is much in modern philosophy that has gone awry (with skepticism and relativism holding hands with materialism and scientism), there are forms of modern philosophy that offer Catholic philosophy and theology opportunities for thinking more deeply about the nature of thinking, its scope, its dynamic, and its ends. In his interpretation of von Balthasar, Levering is neither supporting syncretism nor enjoining a policy of unrestricted openness to modern philosophical forms of reason, not to mention instrumental or ideological forms of reason, or reason operative in the more narrow fields of inquiry of the natural and social sciences with their predilection for metrics and repeatable results. What he is discouraging is the blanket condemnation of modern forms of philosophy; what he is recommending is encounter with a select number of forms of philosophy that, however compromised, demonstrate definite signs of grasping that passionate and rigorous inquiry is incapable of being satisfied by a finite object that resides on the immanent plane.

His book also represents an eloquent plea for unity between the contending parties of ressourcement theology and Thomism that have riven Catholic theology in the past two decades, and catastrophically so, since Catholicism finds itself in an entirely weakened state—having to face challenges not only from without but also increasingly from within. Not surprisingly, the main challenge from within is the doctrinal, ethical, and spiritual attenuation of Catholicism that is a byproduct of its desire to accommodate Catholic faith to the modern world. But another challenge is the failure to find a deeper unity in the presence of theological disagreement. With its evenness of tone (which is at once both firm and charitable), clarity of style, pastoral sense, and theological substance, this intervention simultaneously into von Balthasar studies and the Thomist-ressourcement rivalry seems to have as its basic inspiration the mandate of listening that opens *The Rule of St. Benedict* and as its basic template the theological performance of Benedict XVI, who seems to speak from and toward the unity of the wisdom of the church.

Justifying the Choices of Hegel, Kant, and Nietzsche

The basic intuition that serves as the raison d'être of this book is that not only introductory books on von Balthasar but also von Balthasar studies in general have failed to think through the importance of the volumes that introduce each part of the trilogy.[1] This focus by no means subserves an overly methodological penchant. Levering is convinced that theology is second-order reflection on revelation and its historical reception, and that while, as a good Thomist, he believes there is a place for methodological reflection, in the end it is counterproductive to consume a career with reflections on the condition of the possibility for practicing the "craft of theology," to use Avery Dulles's terms. Higher than possibility is actuality, and the best way forward in theology is to practice it with energy, discerning, unlearning bad habits, and acquiring good ones. Nonetheless, he feels it possible to sustain this conviction against methodologism—one shared by von Balthasar, who more than occasionally had critical things to say about modern forms of theology that took this tack—while proceeding to pull red threads from each of the opening volumes of the trilogy. The three prolegomena, he is convinced, deserve

---

1. Deep appreciation is shown by Levering for the many and varied introductions to von Balthasar's sprawling corpus that have been produced over the past few decades, even as he singles out Edward Oakes's book and Aidan Nichols's three-volume commentary on von Balthasar's trilogy for special praise. At the same time, Levering makes it clear that his volume is not only different in being much narrower in scope but also different in kind. In consequence, he judges that his text should not be thought to bear a competitive relation to those of Oakes and Nichols as well as other volumes that attempt to give an overview of the central concepts of von Balthasar's theology, spell out the Swiss theologian's appropriation of the theological tradition, outline the breadth of theological encounter with culture, and track genealogical observation, all of which are typical of ressourcement theology.

our attention, not only because there is much to be learned from them *in se* but also because they serve as forms of orientation that incite theological reflection without determining outcomes and activate and make truly present the Catholic tradition. On his account, then, the three prolegomena do not constitute a form of fundamental theology, even one that would have to be regarded as different in style and substance than important Catholic and Protestant versions produced in the modern period. If each of these volumes can rightly be considered to be exercises in apologetics, Balthasarian apologetics is, broadly speaking, ad hoc although far more capacious and theologically pertinent than this mode of apologetics usually is, for example, in the case of Barth whom, it is well-known, von Balthasar deeply admired. Levering is in no doubt that in these prolegomena, as in the subsequent volumes in each part of the trilogy, von Balthasar shows himself to be an intrinsically dialogical theologian. At once a strength and weakness in each of the three texts under examination is that there are both multiple conversations afoot and different kinds of conversations. Certainly, a patent difference between Aquinas and von Balthasar is that in the trilogy, philosophy is not the only discussion partner. In terms of dialogue, there is not only conversation with philosophical figures throughout but also a long and protracted account of the relation between Christian theology and the history of drama in *Theo-Drama* volume 1 and, at the very least, an implied conversation of Catholic theology with Goethe in *The Glory of the Lord* volume 1 and with Rilke in *Theo-Logic* volume 1. Without denying the presence of the conversation with literature, Levering focuses on the philosophical conversations and asks the simple but deep question of whether there is in each of the three introductory volumes in the trilogy a philosophical interlocutor sufficiently first among equals that around this philosophical figure other dialogue partners constellate and that von Balthasar's dialogue with this thinker establishes nothing less than the fundamental horizon of the text and a point of orientation with respect to the further volumes in theological aesthetics, theo-dramatics, and theo-logic.

Levering's selections of major dialogue partners are as a whole striking and not in all cases intuitively obvious. Levering suggests that the three crucial philosophical interlocutors are, in order, Kant, Hegel, and Nietzsche, or more specifically Kant as specified by the *Critique of Judgement*, Hegel as specified by his philosophy of religion as this receives its clearest and most comprehensive treatment in *Lectures on the Philosophy of Religion*, and Nietzsche as specified broadly by his articulation of the ecstatic erotic self throughout his genre-bending prophetic and apocalyptic works, but perhaps preeminently in *Thus Spoke Zarathustra*. Perhaps only in the case of *Theo-Drama* is there anything like an interpretive consensus concerning the primary philosophical interlocutor. Hegel both as a single figure and as synecdoche for German idealism has regularly come up in German, French, Italian, and English commentary and criticism. Given the prominence of Hegel and his epigones as foils throughout *Theo-Drama* volumes 4 and 5, and more than a few intimations of Hegel in *Theo-Drama* volume 2, an astute reader may return to the fifteen pages or so devoted in the first volume of *Theo-Drama* to Hegel's discussion of art and religion as a clue buried in its exhaustive presentation of the history of drama. Prospectively, however, it is much harder to know what to think. As with each of the prolegomena, at first it seems as if one is dealing with a case of "Where's Waldo?" Still, even if in terms of interpretation there is a back and forth between the prolegomenon and the later texts, the choice of Hegel in and for *Theo-Drama* volume 1 seems both relatively intuitive and interpretively justified. Yet, for Levering, in line with a number of other interpreters, including the writer of this foreword, Hegel is important to von Balthasar in positive but also decidedly negative ways. Hegel's self-consciously modern thought shows itself to be open to Christian thought in ways unimaginable in the Enlightenment of the philosophes.Thus, on Levering's account, the productive nature of von Balthasar's dialogue with Hegel and his refusal of the blacklisting of modern philosophers by Catholic thinkers that was ongoing since the latter half of the nineteenth century. The dialogue between the Catholic thought of von Balthasar and Hegel's philosophy of religion, however, must also be critical. While Hegel's endorsing of Christianity is trilling, in fact Hegel's reason functions imperialistically and effectively colonizes Christian faith. The "drama" of faith in a transcendent God who gives us salvation in Christ, who is the privileged exemplar of obedience and surrender, is eclipsed in a philosophy that speaks against gratuity, mystery, and obedience.

Levering's selection of a primary interlocutor in the case of *The Glory of the Lord* volume 1 and *Theo-Logic* volume 1 is somewhat less intuitively obvious. With respect to *The Glory of the Lord* volume 1, as a Thomist, Levering knows better than most just how dependent on medieval aesthetics von Balthasar is in this volume, and in particular on Aquinas and Bonaventure. And it is more than likely that he would accede to D. C. Schindler the positive and productive presence of Goethe, whom von Balthasar thinks translates the medieval aesthetics of divine beauty into a form that more nearly recommends itself to secular modernity. Levering's selection of Kant suggests that two interpretive principles are involved, the first having to do with the actual influence of Kant, the second having to do with the necessity of contesting him. Kant's philosophy once again is important for positive and negative reasons. According to Levering, Kant's turn to the self-constituting subject, whose legitimate epistemic function is inextricably tied to the bounds of sense, constitutes a crisis of Catholic thought to which there are at once highly optimistic (Blondel, Rousselot) and equally negative responses (Garrigou-Lagrange). Attempting to steer between these rival Catholic responses to Kant, von Balthasar refuses to prioritize the *Critique of Pure Reason*. Rather he favors the Kant of the *Critique of Judgement* who attempts to bind together the beautiful and the moral after the model of the ancient *kalokagathon*. Importantly, even in the dimension of the aesthetic in which the subject cannot apply the categories of understanding, von Balthasar rejects as well as accepts. Kant's emphasis on the subjective dimension of aesthetics is appropriate, but it risks making the aesthetic coordinate with the perceiving and knowing finite subject, and thereby fails to take adequate account of what is given, which remains free to transcend the order of finitude. What Kant gets wrong as well as what he gets right is constitutive of his selection as the prime interlocutor in the introductory volume in theological aesthetics that attempts to unite the objective and subjective dimensions of aesthetics while in the end going against Kant in tilting the balance in favor of the former over the latter.

Finally, when we get to the introductory volume of *Theo-Logic*, there is the somewhat startling choice of Nietzsche as the primary interlocutor. While there has not been enough discussion of this volume, which represents a recycling of von Balthasar's *Wahrheit*, written in 1947, to the degree to which a name has surfaced as the primary interlocutor, it has most often been Martin Heidegger. This is as true in English commentary and criticism as it is in German and French. Levering does not harrow this text, which is unusual in von Balthasar's canon in being almost totally without references. Rather what impresses him is that in the first volume of *Theo-Logic*, von Balthasar seems to be offering a phenomenological reading of the self-transcending self, which, while grateful for Nietzsche's insistence of the erotic nature of the subject, refuses to install and sustain a horizon of nothing rather than God. It seems to be von Balthasar's basic intuition, one he shared with a number of Catholic thinkers, that Catholicism need not be afraid of the kind of deep questioning posed by Nietzsche. Such questioning was, after all, the habitus of the great thinkers of the tradition, not excepting Augustine and Aquinas. This is not to say, however, that one should accept Nietzsche's insistence, on the one hand, that there is too much answer and correlatively too little question in Christianity and, on the other, that Christianity's answer is entirely wrong. In *Theo-Logic* volume 1, Levering sees a von Balthasar unafraid to take on Nietzsche's nihilism and anxious to put Christian will to love in opposition to Nietzsche's will to power and allow a phenomenological philosophy to decide the relative merits of each. As was the case with Przywara in *Analogia Entis*, von Balthasar was confident of a Catholic victory. Levering is subtle as well as compelling in articulating the relationship between von Balthasar and Nietzsche. But if one were to summarize, it would be to say that however counterintuitive the elevation of Nietzsche as von Balthasar's prime interlocutor in *Theo-Logic* volume 1 may appear to be at first blush, on reflection it comes across as an inspired choice. At the time in von Balthasar's career in which *Wahrheit* was written, Heidegger and Nietzsche essentially folded into each other. And the recycling of the 1947 text as the first volume of *Theo-Logic* in the early eighties suggests that Nietzsche continues to be relevant and has come to be regarded as a something of a "father" to Heidegger.

The Virtues of Matthew Levering and This Book

Anyone who reads this book will discover what Jean-Pierre Torrell and others have found in reading Aquinas, that is, the presence of a master teacher. This should not surprise. Levering has been producing book after book on topic after topic, whether scripture, the doctrines of revelation, creation, Christ and resurrection, the Holy Spirit, Mary, the relation between Christianity and Judaism, or the theology of Augustine, that illustrate the very same charism. The aim is always to meet the reader along the way and bring him or her to and through the circuit of Catholic tradition to establish the horizon for a rich present and a replete future. Here Levering teaches von Balthasar in much the same way as he would teach Augustine or Aquinas: Find an entrance point into the opus of a thinker that does justice to the complexity and richness of his work while maximizing that communicability born out of love for the reader who is presumed to have loved the truth first. The pedagogy is undertaken with extraordinary humility and self-effacement, whose literary trace is the simplicity of style and the perfect lucidity of the prose.

All of these virtues are evident in the tracking of relations between the introductory volumes of von Balthasar's trilogy and the philosophies of Kant, Hegel, and Nietzsche. Levering retires entirely behind the presentation of others' thoughts. One particularly interesting aspect of the performance is that Levering does not attempt to explain the thoughts of von Balthasar's interlocutors, instead allowing them to speak for themselves by providing in all three cases an eminently accessible presentation of their thoughts and laying it down alongside that of von Balthasar's thought. By so doing, Levering draws attention away from how much he actually knows and generously invites the far less learned reader to be a co-traveler on a voyage of discovery. This is a far more Thomistic than Balthasarian pedagogy. While there is nothing in von Balthasar's work or life to suggest that he desired to impress, his encyclopedic level of cultural and philosophical reference has from time to time oppressed the reader who, if awed by the range of reference, feels somewhat left out. Levering pays homage to von Balthasar's best intentions by pushing aside the erudition that functions in a loop to authorize the author. The irony is that as Levering makes a space for von Balthasar alongside Aquinas in modern thought with the view that in the broad *Catholica* it is better to have both than to have one, Aquinas remains very much present in spirit if not necessarily substance. Levering refuses any Thomistic colonization of von Balthasar whereby von Balthasar is translated into a Thomistic idiom. Yet he avails of a Thomistic pedagogy to provide his own *Gestalt* of what is originating as well as original in von Balthasar's trilogy.

While there are other Thomists who display almost equal generosity to von Balthasar, if I cast the net more widely for a modern or contemporary template for what I see manifest in Levering's form of interpretation, the theological figure to whom I continually return is Benedict XVI. Benedict is at once a public theologian who over a period of sixty years pointed to the crises of knowledge, authority, and reception in the church while being the church's most comprehensive, incisive, and subtle catechist. One finds in Levering both intervention and catechesis, and one finds both expressed with a simplicity and translucency that show marvelous confidence in reason despites its tendency to lose its fundamental transcendent aim, to fracture and splinter, and to become opaque.

My last point is about the second aim of the text of overcoming fracture among theologians and the theologically literate. If the first aim is to understand von Balthasar's great trilogy by uncovering the dynamics and fundamental orientation of its three introductory volumes, the second primary aim is a reconciliation between contending theological parties in contemporary Catholic thought that has something of the mark of a scandal. It is true that some healing is required. Too often ressourcement thinkers in their effort to supply another theological good were singularly uncharitable with respect to Thomism. In retrospect, it is not a sufficient excuse to specify that the target was really Neo-Thomism rather than Thomism, for if the distinction can easily be made nominally, it is not self-evident where one ends and another begins. It speaks to his generosity of spirit that in this book Levering effectively performs this reconciliation from the side of Thomism. Having recently read Dante again, when I think of this kind of reconciliation, I cannot help recalling the scene in "Paradiso" where the wounds between the Franciscans and Dominicans are healed by mutual blessing. Reconciliation is an eschatological act. It is also realized in the overpowering charity of Christ in history. Reconciliation need not be infinitely deferrable. In writing this book on von Balthasar, Matthew Levering, a Thomist by election and habit, has lovingly embraced a proximate but separated other. The embrace promotes repetition on the Thomist side as it calls for an answer on the Balthasarian side. And I'll end this foreword that speaks along with the writer to the future with a question: What lovers of von Balthasar will respond to the calls of this text to embrace their proximity to their separated other?

ACKNOWLEDGMENTS

This book began as an S.T.L. seminar at Mundelein Seminary on "The Theology of Hans Urs von Balthasar." I wish to thank the wonderful students—including two doctoral students from Wheaton College—who led the discussions in the seminar and taught me a great deal: Fr. Valery Akoh, Fr. Anthony Joseph Alles, Fr. Seth Brown, Daniel Hill, Fr. John Michael Morgan, and Kevin Wong.

After I had written a draft of the epilogue of this book, Fr. Thomas Joseph White, OP, gave me helpful corrections to it. Matthew Minerd shared his philosophical erudition by carefully commenting on an early draft of the whole book. Michele Schumacher offered crucial corrections for the introduction to the book. Jennifer Newsome Martin graciously took an interest in the manuscript when I met her at a conference at the University of St. Thomas in Minnesota. She read a late draft of the entire manuscript, and she made a number of comments and corrections that improved the manuscript significantly. Two anonymous reviewers for the Catholic University of America Press offered very helpful comments and corrections. John Martino, the estimable theology acquisitions editor for the Catholic University of America Press, not only supported the manuscript from the outset but also patiently bore with me as I kept sending him new drafts. My friend and research assistant David Augustine, currently in his third year of the doctoral program at the Catholic University of America, prepared the bibliography with his usual skill, and he made corrections to the introduction and epilogue.

Cyril O'Regan helped me discern when my revisions had sufficiently improved the text, and he also vetted my exposition of Kant, Hegel, Nietzsche, and von Balthasar when I emailed him drafts of the manuscript. Cyril generously offered to write a foreword to this book. His foreword is better than my book, and I am thrilled to have it. Reading a draft of his foreword enabled me to make some final clarifications regarding why I engage von Balthasar's trilogy from this distinctive, though in certain ways quite limited, angle.

Like a number of theologians I know, I was converted to the Catholic faith by reading the work of von Balthasar. He gives persuasive testimony to the beauty, goodness, and truth of Catholicism, and I am deeply grateful for his powerful and intensely personal witness.

I dedicate this book to a very good friend, Fr. Antonio López, FSCB. He and I met in fall 1996 as first-year doctoral students at Boston College who shared a love of von Balthasar's writings. The course we had together that semester, however, was on St. Thomas Aquinas. I recall Fr. Antonio helping me in my first steps in learning how to read Aquinas. My prayer for you, Fr. Antonio, is that our Lord will place you eternally among his "sons of light" (Jn 12:36), because, by the grace of his Holy Spirit, you have faithfully obeyed his commandment of love—not least in your friendship and generosity toward me.

THE ACHIEVEMENT OF

Hans Urs von Balthasar

Introduction

In *Balthasar at the End of Modernity*, Lucy Gardner, David Moss, Ben Quash, and Graham Ward make the simple point that "to criticize modernity and its philosophies cannot involve any un-problematic return to the pre-modern."[1] Without doubt, this expresses the perspective of Hans Urs von Balthasar. On the one hand, he holds that the preeminent modern philosophers have helped to blind us moderns—all of us whose worldviews have been shaped, whether consciously or not, by modern anthropocentrism, modern technology, and modern politics and economics—to the beauty, goodness, and truth of Jesus Christ. From the very beginning of his career, von Balthasar showed profound concern about "the rise of German idealism and its highly problematic aftereffects" (in the words of Andrew Prevot).[2] But on the other hand, rather than simply returning to the premodern—though he certainly engaged in multiple retrievals of the premodern—he considered that the path forward would require discerning what in the preeminent modern philosophers has proven so attractive and has, by its real insight, abetted the culpable modern forgetfulness of Christ. Whatever real insight there is should enrich Catholic faith and practice. As Bruce Marshall observes with regard to the Second Vatican Council, "Given the Church's deep and ancient impulse to embrace truth and good-

---

1. Lucy Gardner, David Moss, Ben Quash, and Graham Ward, *Balthasar at the End of Modernity* (Edinburgh: T&T Clark, 1999), vii.

2. Andrew L. Prevot, "Dialectic and Analogy in Balthasar's 'The Metaphysics of the Saints,'" *Pro Ecclesia* 26, no. 3 (2017): 261–77, at 273.

ness wherever she finds it, the benefits of modernity had to be sought out and assimilated.... Everything depended upon the Church, when the time had arrived, truly coming to grips with modernity on her own terms, and not on the terms modernity inevitably sought to impose."[3] This was the work to which von Balthasar's trilogy sought to contribute in its creative retrievals and reconstructions of the Catholic tradition in light of the most influential thinkers of modernity.

Obviously von Balthasar's engagement with philosophical modernity is so extensive that one cannot sum up his critical acquisitions very easily. But I propose in this book that most importantly—though far from exclusively—his trilogy engages critically with the three preeminent German fathers of modernity: Immanuel Kant, Georg W. F. Hegel, and Friedrich Nietzsche.[4] By means of this threefold engagement, von Balthasar aims to

---

3. Bruce D. Marshall, "The Church, the Modern World, and the Spirit of Vatican II," *Nova et Vetera* 15, no. 4 (2017): 999–1,012, at 1,008. Marshall has in view the Second Vatican Council's achievements.

4. Apologies to Friedrich Schelling and Martin Heidegger, whose influence also spans the whole trilogy. For Schelling, see Jennifer Newsome Martin, *Hans Urs von Balthasar and the Critical Appropriation of Russian Religious Thought* (Notre Dame: University of Notre Dame Press, 2015); Stephen van Erp, *The Art of Theology: Hans Urs von Balthasar's Theological Aesthetics and the Foundations of Faith* (Leuven: Peeters, 2004), 195–227. For Heidegger, see Cyril O'Regan, "Hans Urs von Balthasar and the Unwelcoming of Heidegger," in *Grandeur of Reason: Religion, Tradition, and Universalism*, ed. Conor Cunningham and Peter Candler (London: SCM, 2010), 264–98. O'Regan is currently completing the definitive study of von Balthasar's engagement with Heidegger, a companion volume to O'Regan's study of von Balthasar's engagement with Hegel. Heidegger is comprehensible only in relation to Kant, Hegel, and Nietzsche, just as Schelling is in constant interaction with Kant and Hegel. Jennifer Martin argues that "for Balthasar it is Schelling rather than Hegel who represents the culmination of German Idealism" (*Hans Urs von Balthasar and the Critical Appropriation of Russian Religious Thought*, 11), and she demonstrates that Schelling has a strong influence on von Balthasar and his Russian sources, notwithstanding von Balthasar's often sharp critique of Schelling. As Martin notes, "Schelling's thought contains unequivocally and irremediably dark seeds that run counter to the mainline theological project, not least of which is a deeply rooted materialism and the inheritance of Böhme's irrational, ungrounded abyss of an originary will. Schelling's philosophical aesthetics cannot be thought otherwise than a secular 'aesthetic theology,' which cannot be welcomed as it stands as an authentic (and thoroughly Balthasarian) theological aesthetics of 'glory'" (ibid., 15).

overcome modernity's false choice, in Rodney Howsare's words, "between revelational positivism and anthropological reductionism."[5]

By introducing von Balthasar's trilogy in dialogue with these three figures, I hope to display his achievement along lines that will be somewhat new even for expert Balthasarians and that will serve to introduce students and scholars to some of the richness of his trilogy. My strategy for introducing von Balthasar's trilogy seeks to get around the ongoing aftereffects of the lamentable mid-twentieth-century Catholic struggle between the *nouvelle théologie* (or *ressourcement* theology) and neo-scholastic theologians. Although I will describe this struggle more fully in the book's epilogue, here let me note that far too often the choice demanded by theological "schools of thought" is *all or nothing*. Thus, for some contemporary Thomists—and my own theological approach is grounded deeply in the theology of Aquinas—the fact that von Balthasar gets important things wrong is enough to justify not reading him at all or reading him only with distaste and derogation. Likewise, for some contemporary Balthasarians, theologians who rely heavily upon Aquinas are historians at best and more likely reactionaries, unworthy of a significant place in the discipline of contemporary Catholic systematic theology.

By means of the present book, I wish to resist this "all or nothing" mentality and to encourage others who are resisting it. As Randall Rosenberg observes, "The relationship between emerging forms of Thomism and the *ressourcement* tradition, however, has not been an altogether polemical affair. They have at times exhibited similar aims as found, for example, in the *Ressourcement* Thomism project."[6] As a graduate student, I read

5. Rodney A. Howsare, *Hans Urs von Balthasar and Protestantism: The Ecumenical Implications of His Theological Style* (London: T&T Clark International, 2005), 133.

6. Randall S. Rosenberg, *The Givenness of Desire: Concrete Subjectivity and the Natural Desire to See God* (Toronto: University of Toronto Press, 2017), 40. Rosenberg cites the very helpful observation of William F. Murphy Jr.: "Catholic intellectual life has begun—and will need to continue—a more thoughtful encounter between these

both von Balthasar and Aquinas with joy, and I continue to do so today. While I do not think that von Balthasar should replace Aquinas in graduate theological training—it seems to me that serious and extended reading of Aquinas is necessary for graduate students in theology because Aquinas's theology not only has superb balance and insight but also helps one to go up and down the ladder of the twenty centuries of Catholic theological and philosophical reflection—I hold that reading von Balthasar's trilogy provides an extraordinary education in many of the pathways of Catholic theology, filled with important insights that cannot be found elsewhere. It is mournful when theologians, dismayed by a mistake or lacuna in the thought of von Balthasar or Aquinas, war with each other to the death, forgetting their more fundamental agreements on doctrine and morals.[7]

Let me describe the genesis of this book. Recently, I taught a course on the thought of von Balthasar in which I assigned the introductory volume of each part of von Balthasar's trilogy. As I was

---

two overlapping streams [*ressourcement* and neo-scholasticism] of the tradition, a dialogue that ... was unfortunately sidelined when Thomism was widely abandoned in the postwar years and even more in those following the council, at least partially due to a backlash against the official imposition of some aspects of it in the antimodernist era" (Murphy, "Thomism and the *Nouvelle Théologie*: A Dialogue Renewed?," *Josephinum Journal of Theology* 18, no. 1 [2011]: 4–36, at 6). See also Anthony Sciglitano, "Leaving Neo-Scholasticism Behind: Aspirations and Anxieties," *Josephinum Journal of Theology* 18, no. 1 (2011): 216–39; Aidan Nichols, OP, "Thomism and the Nouvelle Théologie," *The Thomist* 64, no. 1 (2000): 1–19; Thomas Joseph White, OP, "The Precarity of Wisdom: Modern Dominican Theology, Perspectivalism, and the Tasks of Reconstruction," in *Ressourcement Thomism: Sacred Doctrine, the Sacraments, and the Moral Life*, ed. Reinhard Hütter and Matthew Levering, 92–123 (Washington, D.C.: The Catholic University of America Press, 2010); Christopher Ruddy, "*Ressourcement* and the *Enduring* Legacy of Post-Tridentine Theology," in *Ressourcement: A Movement for Renewal in Twentieth-Century Catholic Theology*, ed. Gabriel Flynn and Paul D. Murray, 185–201 (Oxford: Oxford University Press, 2012).

7. In conversation with Balthasarians or Thomists, it is not uncommon to find that each regards the other with suspicion, as a source of rationalistic and immanentist theological liberalism or modernism. In making this charge, they are simply repeating what the *nouvelle théologie* theologians and the neo-scholastics said about each other in the 1940s. I will discuss this a bit further in the epilogue, but for now I note that this is an instance of forming a "circular firing squad," where theologians turn their theological firepower against each other rather than against their real shared foe.

rereading these three volumes, two things struck me. First, I realized that what I find most impressive in von Balthasar is the way that his argument unfolds slowly in brilliant and exciting conversation with a marvelous ecumenical array of important poets, philosophers, and theologians. Von Balthasar draws the reader into the task of theology in a manner that deeply enriches one's mind by contact with such a range of perspectives and insights. Second, I realized that the three volumes offer a critical and constructive engagement with Kant, Hegel, and Nietzsche, respectively.

This experience formed the approach of my book on von Balthasar. This rationale for my approach is threefold: contemporary theologians will greatly benefit from "thinking with" the amazingly rich and wide-ranging conversations present in von Balthasar's trilogy; the first volume of each part of the trilogy offers an entrance point that enables one to appreciate (even if not in an all-encompassing manner) the achievement of the whole; and the trilogy is fruitfully read as a constructive and critical response to Kant, Hegel, and Nietzsche.

In Kant, I suggest, von Balthasar finds a real insight into the perception of the beautiful form and into the fact that "the beautiful is the symbol of the morally good," via a universally valid aesthetic judgment that nonetheless is "incognizable by means of any universal concept."[8] He finds in Kant's transcendental apperception a modern justification for seeking a ground of all this-worldly forms—which, for von Balthasar, is Christ crucified, the form of the beauty of all things, revealing that all beings make manifest the beauty of self-surrendering love. In Hegel, von Balthasar finds a real insight into how evolving spirit encounters and resolves contradictions in its infinite quest to know: "Every *aliud* [otherness] must be posited in the Absolute in order to be integrated (*aufgehoben*: transcended while being preserved)."[9]

8. Immanuel Kant, *Critique of Judgement*, trans. James Creed Meredith, ed. Nicholas Walker (Oxford: Oxford University Press, 2007), 180–81.
9. Hans Urs von Balthasar, *The Glory of the Lord: A Theological Aesthetics*,

He also finds help for the task of appreciating the value of history despite all the travails that history entails. This serves to deepen his reflection upon Christ crucified and more generally upon the sufferings that mark God's world so that the goodness of history is revealed in self-surrendering love. In Nietzsche, he finds a real insight into the rationalistic pretensions of the human knower. He also finds striking evidence of the relationship of truth-claims to our desire for growth in life, health, and power. This enriches his appreciation of truth's relation to life-giving love—ultimately the self-surrendering love who is Christ crucified.

Given what Ben Quash terms von Balthasar's "aim of shaking modernity from pursuit of its tidier and more hubristic 'ends'," von Balthasar engages with these modern philosophical insights *from the inside* and seeks to expose their fruitfulness when stripped of their erroneous aspects. Specifically, he explores spiritual perception and the judgment of faith (*Theological Aesthetics*), history and spirit (*Theo-Drama*), and truth and love (*Theo-Logic*) in a manner that takes up and boldly redirects the influential modernity of Kant, Hegel, and Nietzsche.[10] Taking up Kant's insight in his *Theological Aesthetics*, von Balthasar employs Kant's understanding of aesthetics as a theory of perception (or judgment) of the beautiful form and Kant's notion of transcendental apperception in order to show that beings reveal or "surrender" themselves to subjective perception, and that there is a unifying ground of all phenomena—namely, Christ's self-surrendering love.

Taking up Hegel's insight in his *Theo-Drama*, von Balthasar

---

vol. 5, *The Realm of Metaphysics in the Modern Age*, trans. Oliver Davies, Andrew Louth, Brian McNeil, CRV, John Saward, and Rowan Williams, ed. Brian McNeil, CRV, and John Riches (San Francisco: Ignatius Press, 1991), 574.

10. Quash, "Drama and the Ends of Modernity," in *Balthasar at the End of Modernity*, 139–71, at 141. Todd Walatka points out that von Balthasar is "explicitly countering Kant" by following the order beauty, goodness, and truth. Kant begins with truth and ends with beauty in his *Critique of Pure Reason*, *Critique of Practical Reason*, and *Critique of Judgement*. See Todd Walatka, *Von Balthasar and the Option for the Poor: Theodramatics in the Light of Liberation Theology* (Washington, D.C.: The Catholic University of America Press, 2017), 81.

employs Hegel's dramatic theory and Hegel's account of the unfolding of infinite spirit in history (via a Trinitarian and Christological pattern) in order to show that the intra-Trinitarian processions, with their fruitful self-surrender and personal "distance," ground all finite difference in history, including the incarnate Son's self-surrendering love for the sake of the world's salvation. The Son bears in himself the contradictions and alienations that so deeply disfigure our histories, and he redeems the whole world through his self-surrendering in love for us sinners to the Father through the Spirit.[11] Taking up Nietzsche's insight in his *Theo-Logic*, von Balthasar employs Nietzsche's emphasis on truth as grounded in the will-to-power as a path for revealing that truth is actually self-surrendering love, or the will-to-love.

Thus, to a modern world forgetful of God and Christ, von Balthasar wishes to proclaim the beauty of beings, the goodness of history, and the truth of love. He wishes to help us remember that "God is love" (1 Jn 4:8), that God has "destined us in love to be his sons through Jesus Christ" in history (Eph 1:5), and that we must now live "according to the measure of Christ's gift" (Eph 4:7). Antonio López and David L. Schindler have rightly suggested that von Balthasar seeks to overcome modernity's forgetfulness of the (self-)gift of love.[12] As Pascal Ide observes in his insightful study of von Balthasar's trilogy, "The theology of Hans

11. Kenneth Oakes has pointed out, "One of the primary semantic difficulties of this way of speaking is that the Father has no 'self', either to give or to have or to empty or to surrender, in isolation from the Son and Spirit. However, this semantic difficulty is shared by any account of the divine persons when they are signified by substance or form rather than by relation or act, as von Balthasar himself was aware: 'The Father must not be thought to exist "prior" to this self-surrender (in an Arian sense): he is this movement of self-giving that holds nothing back.'" See Oakes, "Gathering Many Likenesses: Trinity and Kenosis," *Nova et Vetera* (forthcoming), fn 77, citing Hans Urs von Balthasar, *Theo-Drama: Theological Dramatic Theory*, vol. 4, *The Action*, trans. Graham Harrison (San Francisco: Ignatius Press, 1994), 323.

12. See Antonio López, *Gift and the Unity of Being* (Eugene, Ore.: Cascade, 2013); David L. Schindler, "Modernity and the Nature of a Distinction: Balthasar's Ontology of Generosity," in *Ordering Love: Liberal Societies and the Memory of God* (Grand Rapids, Mich.: Eerdmans, 2011), 350–82.

Urs von Balthasar is a theology of love," and "the essence of love is identified as gift."[13]

Introducing von Balthasar

Given that my focus in this introductory book is on only the first volume of each part of the trilogy, in light of Kant, Hegel, and Nietzsche, respectively, I inevitably simplify some of von Balthasar's contributions and neglect others. Insofar as possible, I have sought to avoid reductive oversimplification by setting forth in painstaking detail the concrete arguments that von Balthasar makes in the programmatic first volume of each of his trilogy's three parts. These concrete arguments provide a taste of the distinctive range and breadth of his theology. The specific lens—Kant, Hegel, and Nietzsche—through which I approach the first volume of each part of the trilogy is intended to illumine his achievement, not to encompass it.

Introductory books on von Balthasar can help to focus one's reading of his vast corpus, and they can identify and illumine certain keys to his project. Obviously, however, no introductory book can rise to the intellectual and rhetorical level of von Balthasar's actual trilogy. If it is not the height of foolishness to attempt an introductory book on the achievement of von Balthasar, then it is perilously close to this height. In a real sense, von Balthasar's work cannot be introduced. Cyril O'Regan makes this clear when he remarks, "Given his interest in rescuing the traditions of Christian discourse and forms of life from their genealogical internment in the Hegelian system, which goes hand in hand with [Hegel's] correction of the meaning of major Christian doctrines and symbols, Balthasar acts as if there is no choice

---

13. Pascal Ide, *Une théologie de l'amour. L'amour, centre de la* Trilogie *de Hans Urs von Balthasar* (Brussels: Lessius, 2012), 246. See also Ide's massive and rewarding *Une théo-logique du don. Le don dans la* Trilogie *de Hans Urs von Balthasar* (Leuven: Peeters, 2013).

but to submit Hegel's thought ... to genealogical trial."[14] I agree
with O'Regan that von Balthasar engages Hegel in this way. It
should be clear that it is impossible to survey or introduce a "genealogical trial" in all its dimensions.

Briefly, let me enumerate some of the paths that would be
necessary to traverse in any full-scale introduction to von
Balthasar's trilogy. Given von Balthasar's repeated attestations
to the significance of Adrienne von Speyr's mystical writings for
his work, an introductory book on von Balthasar's trilogy should
attend carefully to von Speyr's writings and their relation to von
Balthasar's. An introductory book should also examine the evident influence of Sergius Bulgakov and other Russian thinkers
upon von Balthasar. Then there would be the task of introducing von Balthasar's large debts to Greek and Roman literature
and philosophy, Dante, Pedro Calderón de la Barca, William
Shakespeare, Johann Wolfgang von Goethe, Friedrich Schiller,
Friedrich Hölderlin, Charles Péguy, Fyodor Dostoevsky, Gerard
Manley Hopkins, Georges Bernanos, Reinhold Schneider, and
so on. An introductory book on von Balthasar's trilogy should
also evaluate von Balthasar's indebtedness to, and criticisms of,
historical-critical biblical interpretation. Von Balthasar's interaction with Karl Barth also deserves attention, as does his relationship to the thought of Søren Kierkegaard, Erich Przywara, Karl
Rahner, Origen, Irenaeus, Maximus, Thomas Aquinas, Martin
Buber, and many others.[15]

14. Cyril O'Regan, *The Anatomy of Misremembering: Von Balthasar's Response
to Philosophical Modernity*, vol. 1, *Hegel* (New York: Crossroad, 2014), 51.

15. See, for example, Michele M. Schumacher, *A Trinitarian Anthropology: Adrienne von Speyr and Hans Urs von Balthasar in Dialogue with Thomas Aquinas* (Washington, D.C.: The Catholic University of America Press, 2014); Martin, *Hans Urs von
Balthasar and the Critical Appropriation of Russian Religious Thought*; Christopher D.
Denny, *A Generous Symphony: Hans Urs von Balthasar's Literary Revelations* (Minneapolis, Minn.: Fortress Press, 2016); Cecilia Inés de Palumbo, *La literatura en la estética de Hans Urs von Balthasar. Figura, drama y verdad* (Salamanca: Secretariado
Trinitario, 2002); Michael Patrick Murphy, *A Theology of Criticism: Balthasar, Postmod-
ernism, and the Catholic Imagination* (Oxford: Oxford University Press, 2008); W. T.
Dickens, *Hans Urs von Balthasar's* Theological Aesthetics: *A Model for Post-Critical*

In any full introduction to von Balthasar's achievement, moreover, various specific theological topics would need treatment, among them—with apologies for simply offering a list—his ethics, his relationship to liberation theology, his eschatology, his doctrine of analogy, his contributions to ecumenism, his understanding of Christ's filial obedience, his account of the drama of finite and infinite freedom, his theology of the saints, his theology of the Virgin Mary, his theology of the divine Father, his theology of Holy Saturday, his theology of mission, his theology of the Eucharist, his understanding of the relationship of love and truth, his view of the spiritual senses, his contributions to Jewish-Christian dialogue, his appreciation of Christian apophaticism and prayer, his theology of the Church, his Christology, his theology of Christ's Passion in light of the relation of the immanent and economic Trinity, his theological anthropology, and his theology of history.[16]

Biblical Interpretation (Notre Dame: University of Notre Dame Press, 2003); Matthew A. Rothaus Moser, Love Itself Is Understanding: Hans Urs von Balthasar's Theology of the Saints (Minneapolis, Minn.: Fortress Press, 2016); Joshua Furnal, Catholic Theology after Kierkegaard (Oxford: Oxford University Press, 2016), chap. 4; D. Stephen Long, Saving Karl Barth: Hans Urs von Balthasar's Preoccupation (Minneapolis, Minn.: Fortress Press, 2014); Benjamin Dahlke, Karl Barth, Catholic Renewal, and Vatican II (London: Bloomsbury, 2012), chap. 6–9; John Thompson, "Barth and Balthasar: An Ecumenical Dialogue," in The Beauty of Christ: An Introduction to the Theology of Hans Urs von Balthasar, ed. Bede McGregor, OP, and Thomas Norris, 171–92 (Edinburgh: T&T Clark, 1994); Martin Bieler, "Die kleine Drehung: Hans Urs von Balthasar und Karl Barth im Logik der Liebe und Herrlichkeit Gottes: Hans Urs von Balthasar im Gespräch. Festgabe für Karl Kardinal Lehmann zum 70. Geburtstag, ed. Walter Kasper, 318–38 (Ostfildern: Matthias-Grünewald-Verlag, 2006).

16. See, for example, Christopher W. Steck, SJ, The Ethical Thought of Hans Urs von Balthasar (New York: Crossroad, 2001); Melanie Susan Barrett, Love's Beauty at the Heart of the Christian Moral Life: The Ethics of Catholic Theologian Hans Urs von Balthasar (Lewiston, N.Y.: Edwin Mellen, 2009); Nicholas J. Healy, The Eschatology of Hans Urs von Balthasar: Being as Communion (Oxford: Oxford University Press, 2005); Junius Johnson, Christ and Analogy: The Christocentric Metaphysics of Hans Urs von Balthasar (Minneapolis, Minn.: Fortress Press, 2013); Henriette Danet, Gloire et croix de Jésus-Christ: L'analogie chez H. Urs von Balthasar comme introduction à sa christologie (Paris: Desclée, 1987); Eva-Maria Spiegelhalter, Objektiv Evident? Die Wahrnehmbarkeit der Christusgestalt im Denken Hans Urs von Balthasars und Hansjürgen Verweyens (Freiburg: Herder, 2013); Steffen Lösel, Kreuzwege: Ein ökumenisches

Additionally, the contributions made by his numerous shorter books and his collections of essays require analysis in their own right.[17] And lastly, although Aidan Nichols has pro-

Gespräch mit Hans Urs von Balthasar (Paderborn: Schöningh, 2001); Dietrich Oettler, *Sauerteig der Einheit: Der Beitrag der Theodramatik Hans Urs von Balthasars für die evangelisch-katholische Oekumene nach der Gemeinsamen Erklärung zur Rechtfertigungslehre* (Würzburg: Echter, 2011); Michel Beaudin, *Obéissance et solidarité: Essai sur la christologie de Hans Urs von Balthasar* (Montreal: Fides, 1989); Thomas G. Dalzell, SM, *The Dramatic Encounter of Divine and Human Freedom in the Theology of Hans Urs von Balthasar* (Bern: Peter Lang, 1997); Hilda Steinhauer, *Maria als dramatische Person bei Hans Urs von Balthasar: Zum marianischen Prinzip seines Denkens* (Innsbruck: Tyrolia, 2001); Breandán Leahy, *The Marian Principle in the Church according to Hans Urs von Balthasar* (New York: Peter Lang, 1996); Margaret M. Turek, *Towards a Theology of God the Father: Hans Urs von Balthasar's Theodramatic Approach* (New York: Peter Lang, 2001); Helmut Dieser, *Der gottähnliche Mensch und die Gottlosigkeit der Sünde: Zur Theologie des* Descensus Christi *bei Hans Urs von Balthasar* (Trier: Paulinus, 1998); Alyssa Lyra Pitstick, *Light in Darkness: Hans Urs von Balthasar and the Catholic Doctrine of Christ's Descent into Hell* (Grand Rapids, Mich.: Eerdmans, 2007); Hans-Peter Göbbeler, *Existenz als Sendung. Zum Verständnis der Nachfolge Christi in der Theologie Hans Urs von Balthasars. Unter besonderer Berücksichtigung der Gestalt des Priestertums und von Ehe und Familie* (St. Ottilien: EOS Verlag, 1997); Georg Bätzing, *Die Eucharistie als Opfer der Kirche* (Einsiedeln: Johannes Verlag, 1992); D. C. Schindler, *Hans Urs von Balthasar and the Dramatic Structure of Truth: A Philosophical Investigation* (New York: Fordham University Press, 2004); Michael Albus, *Die Wahrheit ist Liebe: Zur Unterscheidung des Christlichen nach Hans Urs von Balthasar* (Freiburg: Herder, 1976); Mark McInroy, *Balthasar on the Spiritual Senses: Perceiving Splendour* (Oxford: Oxford University Press, 2014); Anthony C. Sciglitano Jr., *Marcion and Prometheus: Balthasar against the Expulsion of Jewish Origins from Modern Religious Dialogue* (New York: Crossroad, 2014); Raymond Gawronski, SJ, *Word and Silence: Hans Urs von Balthasar and the Spiritual Encounter between East and West* (Grand Rapids, Mich.: Eerdmans, 1995); Ioan Moga, *Kirche als Braut Christi zwischen Kreuz und Parusie: Die Ekklesiologie Hans Urs von Balthasars aus orthodoxer Sicht* (Münster: LIT, 2010); Joseph Fessio, SJ, *The Origin of the Church in Christ's Kenosis: The Ontological Structure of the Church in the Ecclesiology of Hans Urs von Balthasar* (Regensburg: Pustet, 1974); Mark A. McIntosh, *Christology from Within: Spirituality and the Incarnation in Hans Urs von Balthasar* (Notre Dame: University of Notre Dame Press, 1996); Giovanni Marchesi, *La cristologia di Hans Urs von Balthasar: La figura di Gesù Cristo espressione visibile di Dio* (Rome: Gregorian University Press, 1977); Marchesi, *La cristologia trinitaria di Hans Urs von Balthasar. Gesù Cristo pienezza della rivelazione e della salvezza*, 2nd ed. (Brescia: Queriniana, 2003); Philippe Dockwiller, *Le temps du Christ: Coeur et fin de la théologie de l'histoire selon Hans Urs von Balthasar* (Paris: Cerf, 2011).

17. See, for example, among others, Hans Urs von Balthasar, *Thomas von Aquin: Besondere Gnadengaben und die zwei Wege des menschlichen Lebens: Kommentar zur Summa Theologica II-II, 171–182*, vol. 23, *Die Deutsche Thomas-Ausgabe*, ed. H. M. Christmann (Vienna: Pustet, 1958).

vided an overview of von Balthasar's first major publication, his three-volume expanded doctoral dissertation *Apocalypse of the German Soul*,[18] this major early work demands a thorough examination for its account of such thinkers as Kant, J. G. Fichte, F. W. J. Schelling, Goethe, Hegel, Arthur Schopenhauer, Friedrich Hebbel, Richard Wagner, Nietzsche, Max Scheler, Martin Heidegger, Rainer Maria Rilke, and Barth.

Despite the daunting nature of the task, a number of praiseworthy introductions to von Balthasar's achievement have been written. At various points in his life, von Balthasar himself published short reflections on his work, which were compiled after his death as *My Work: In Retrospect*.[19] Four years before his death, he published a lengthy survey of his extensive practical and theological collaboration with Adrienne von Speyr.[20] Important biographical work has been done by Manfred Lochbrunner in his *Hans Urs von Balthasar als Autor, Herausgeber und Verleger* and *Hans Urs von Balthasar und seine Theologen-kollegen*, the latter of which treats von Balthasar's relationships with Przywara, Rahner, and Barth, among others.[21] Philippe Barbarin's *"Théologie et sainteté": Introduction à Hans-Urs von Balthasar* in-

18. Aidan Nichols, OP, *Scattering the Seed: A Guide through Balthasar's Early Writings on Philosophy and the Arts* (Washington, D.C.: The Catholic University of America Press, 2006).

19. Hans Urs von Balthasar, *My Work: In Retrospect* (San Francisco: Ignatius Press, 1993).

20. Hans Urs von Balthasar, *Our Task: A Report and a Plan*, trans. John Saward (San Francisco: Ignatius Press, 1994).

21. Manfred Lochbrunner, *Hans Urs von Balthasar als Autor, Herausgeber und Verleger: Fünf Studien zu seinen Sammlungen (1942–1967)* (Würzburg: Echter Verlag, 2002); Lochbrunner, *Hans Urs von Balthasar und seine Theologen-kollegen: Sechs Beziehungsgeschichten* (Würzburg: Echter Verlag, 2009). See also Lochbrunner, *Hans Urs von Balthasar und seine Philosophenfreunde: Fünf Doppelporträts* (Würzburg: Echter Verlag, 2005); Lochbrunner, *Hans Urs von Balthasar und seine Literatenfreunde: Neun Korrespondenzen* (Würzburg: Echter Verlag, 2007). See also the surprisingly undetailed biographical sketch offered by von Balthasar's friend Elio Guerriero, *Hans Urs von Balthasar* (Milan: Edizioni Paoline, 1991). For his collaboration with von Speyr in founding the Community of St. John, see Daniela Mohr, *Existenz im Herzen der Kirche: Zur Theologie der Säkularinstitute in Leben und Werk H. Urs von Balthasars* (Würzburg: Echter Verlag, 2000).

sightfully roots von Balthasar's writings in his childhood in Lu-
cerne, Switzerland, as the son of a notable architect and his wife,
the daughter of a Hungarian baroness.[22] As Barbarin points out,
von Balthasar's Hungarian cousin, Bishop Vilmos Apor, died in
1945 defending refugees from Soviet soldiers and was beatified in
1997 by Pope John Paul II.

In three volumes of manageable size, Aidan Nichols has ably
summarized the entire trilogy.[23] His goal is simple summary, but
at the same time he adds his own charm and insight to what von
Balthasar has written. Similarly displaying cultural erudition
and rhetorical flair, Edward T. Oakes's 1994 *The Theology of Hans
Urs von Balthasar* reflects the excitement that many, including
me, experienced in first reading von Balthasar in the mid-1990s.
Oakes begins with the positive influences on von Balthasar's
thought, including Przywara, Barth, Goethe, Nietzsche, and
the Church Fathers. The final eight chapters of Oakes's book
treat the trilogy, with the weakest section being the one on the
Theo-Logic, due to Oakes's surprisingly sparse quotations from
the *Theo-Logic*.[24]

---

22. Philippe Barbarin, *Théologie et sainteté: Introduction à Hans-Urs von
Balthasar* (Paris: Parole et Silence, 2017).

23. Aidan Nichols, OP, *The Word Has Been Abroad: A Guide Through Balthasar's
Aesthetics* (Washington, D.C.: The Catholic University of America Press, 1998); Nich-
ols, *No Bloodless Myth: A Guide Through Balthasar's Dramatics* (Washington, D.C.:
The Catholic University of America Press, 2000); Nichols, *Say It Is Pentecost: A Guide
Through Balthasar's Logic* (Washington, D.C.: The Catholic University of America
Press, 2001). See also the excellent brief summary of these three volumes: Nichols,
A Key to Balthasar: Hans Urs von Balthasar on Beauty, Goodness, and Truth (Grand
Rapids, Mich.: Baker Academic, 2011). For a complementary study, see Thomas Nor-
ris, "The Symphonic Unity of His Theology: An Overview," in *The Beauty of Christ:
An Introduction to the Theology of Hans Urs von Balthasar*, ed. Bede McGregor, OP,
and Norris, 213–52 (Edinburgh: T&T Clark, 1994).

24. Edward T. Oakes, SJ, *Pattern of Redemption: The Theology of Hans Urs von
Balthasar* (New York: Continuum, 1994), 242. See also Angelo Scola's *Hans Urs von
Balthasar: A Theological Style* (Grand Rapids, Mich.: Eerdmans, 1991). Scola's emphasis on the personal piety and ecclesial mission of the theologian, his or her existential commitment to the fullness of Catholic truth and to a specific participation in
the triune God's gift of self-surrendering love, strikes me as central to what it means
to follow von Balthasar (or indeed to be a theologian at all). Scola addresses the

Among recent introductions to von Balthasar, Michael
Schulz's 2002 *Hans Urs von Balthasar begegnen* is notable in that
fully half the book discusses von Balthasar's life: his early studies in German literature, his entrance into the Jesuits, his Basel
chaplaincy, his meeting von Speyr and their work together, his
dialogue with Barth, his tensions with Rahner, and so forth. In
his book, Schulz analyzes the first volume of von Balthasar's
Theo-Logic, in light of the influence of Maurice Blondel.[25] Schulz
carefully examines how von Balthasar develops his Christological path to the Trinity in the *Theo-Drama*, and how the *Theo-
Drama* describes the world and salvation coming forth from the
intra-Trinitarian life of kenotic love. He highlights the bridal
church, which can in no way be divorced from Christ and which
reflects von Balthasar's understanding of Christian anthropology and ethics.[26]

basis for legitimate theological pluralism: the mystery of Christ is so great that it can
be viewed from many angles without exhausting it, so long as the dogmatic truth
remains intact.

25. See also Peter Reifenberg, "Blondel and Balthasar—eine Skizze," in *Logik
der Liebe und Herrlichkeit Gottes*, ed. Walter Kasper, 176–203. For helpful background to Blondel, including the point that "the encyclical *Pascendi* in its discussion
of apologetics appeared to condemn not so much Loisy as Blondel" (despite Blondel's
aversion to theological modernism), see Avery Dulles, SJ, *A History of Apologetics*
(San Francisco: Ignatius Press, 2005), 272–79.

26. Michael Schulz, *Hans Urs von Balthasar begegnen* (Augsburg: Sankt-
Ulrich-Verlag, 2002). Rodney A. Howsare's *Balthasar: A Guide for the Perplexed* (New
York: T&T Clark International, 2009) is distinguished especially by attention to the
ongoing reception of von Balthasar, which is the topic of Howsare's final chapter
and which is prepared for by a first chapter that locates von Balthasar in relation
to his own contemporaries and thereby in relation to ongoing debates. Karen Kilby's *Balthasar: A (Very) Critical Introduction* (Grand Rapids, Mich.: Eerdmans, 2012),
while important, is less an introduction than it is a short monograph offering a critique of von Balthasar's project. I briefly discuss her book in my epilogue. For two
other studies that function in certain ways as introductions, see Mario Saint-Pierre,
Beauté, bonté, vérité chez Hans Urs von Balthasar (Paris: Cerf, 1998); and Wolfgang
Klaghofer-Treitler, *Gotteswort im Menschenwort: Inhalt und Form von Theologie nach
Hans Urs von Balthasar* (Innsbruck: Tyrolia, 1992). See also Vincent Holzer, *Hans
Urs von Balthasar, 1905–1988* (Paris: Cerf, 2012). Holzer sketches the development
of von Balthasar's theological thought over the decades, engaging especially with
the *Theological Aesthetics*, and then he ranges across the central themes of the
Theo-Drama, with some attention also to the *Theo-Logic*. In a third part of his book,

Most introductory readers, I expect, will want to turn to these more traditional introductions to von Balthasar's writings before attempting to follow my more focused approach. From Barbarin, Oakes, Schulz, and others, one gains a sense of von Balthasar's whole project, his collaborators and interlocutors, and his background and central interests. Nichols offers a summary of all the volumes of the trilogy, not solely the three volumes that I survey through my specific lens.

Why then have I added my book to the pile of introductions to von Balthasar? In addition to thinking that my approach offers a helpful way of entering into von Balthasar's trilogy, I have written this book for theologically educated readers who mistrust von Balthasar *or* who mistrust von Balthasar's critics. I hope to show that von Balthasar's critics can and should benefit both from the rich and wide-ranging conversations that mark his trilogy and from the critical and constructive engagement with German philosophical modernity offered by the trilogy. I also hope to show that those who *mistrust* von Balthasar's critics need to be more Balthasarian in their response to criticisms of the Swiss theologian.

In this introductory book, I focus on the first volume of each part of the trilogy for two main reasons. First, this approach exhibits the main lines of his trilogy in a way that allows for an introductory volume of manageable size. Second, this approach avoids the more controversial volumes, such as volumes 4 and 5 of the *Theo-Drama* and volume 2 of the *Theo-Logic*. Reading von Balthasar with the goal of engaging his more controversial views is certainly justifiable, and I have done it myself elsewhere. But in an introductory book, the danger is that some readers could miss the forest due to their opposition to some of the trees. In the present book, therefore, one will not find as much of von Balthasar's

---

Holzer examines von Balthasar's engagements with Barth and Rahner. Unlike many experts on von Balthasar, Holzer also knows Rahner's corpus well, and so this third part is particularly rewarding.

sharp paradox, speculative surprise, and controversial boldness
as one would find if I treated all the volumes of the trilogy.

As already indicated, I hope to contribute to the healing of the
internecine conflicts that, since the 1930s or earlier, have pitted
ressourcement theologians and Thomistic theologians against
each other with grave consequences for the health of Catholic
theology. Despite sharing a strong belief in the faithful mediation
of divine revelation through scripture and the church, many Catholic theologians today find themselves at loggerheads with each
other, while classically liberal Catholic theologians often enjoy
unanimity with each other and, in the current academic climate,
proceed relatively unopposed. Easily forgotten by the *ressourcement* and Thomistic combatants is their shared commitment to the
theo-aesthetic beauty, theo-dramatic goodness, and theo-logical
truth of Christ's revelation of Trinitarian self-surrendering love
as our source and supernatural goal, and their shared rejection
of philosophical modernity's immanentism, historicism, and
power-centered voluntarism.[27] They also share what O'Regan
calls the costly and constructive willingness "to say no to the secular culture that says no to Christianity," without falling either
into "endless concession to secular culture" or into the paralysis
of reactionary nostalgia.[28] The present book seeks to highlight
these shared commitments, while leaving room for disagreement
about von Balthasar's specific positions and approaches.

27. In his "Gathering Many Likenesses: Trinity and Kenosis," Kenneth Oakes
defends the application to the Trinitarian Persons of the terms "self-giving" and
"self-surrendering." As Oakes remarks, these terms should not be taken to mean
that one is affirming that each Person has a distinct "self" or that the Trinity is a vol-
untarist reality (solely "will"). All terms applied to the Trinity are at best analogous
in their signification and need to be clarified lest they be misunderstood in one way
or another; for example "Person" needs to be clarified in order to not imply a distinct
center of consciousness. Oakes notes that Aquinas encourages the use of many analogies or likenesses to express the Trinitarian mystery, even though Aquinas gives a
primary place to the analogy (drawn from Augustine) of the mind and its powers.

28. Cyril O'Regan, *Theology and the Spaces of Apocalyptic* (Milwaukee, Wisc.:
Marquette University Press, 2009), 26, 128. O'Regan has apocalyptic theology in view
here.

My Task

Above I presented my view that von Balthasar's trilogy can rightly be understood as a dialogic response to the modernity of Kant, Hegel, and Nietzsche. Without imposing a narrow framework upon the richness of von Balthasar's project, I hope that the cumulative effect of each chapter will enable readers to perceive that his trilogy does indeed operate as a "Kantian" critique of Kant, a "Hegelian" critique of Hegel, and a "Nietzschean" critique of Nietzsche.

Arguably, an overarching aim of von Balthasar's *Theological Aesthetics* is to offer a Kantian critique of Kant. It is most importantly a *critique* of Kant, since von Balthasar strongly rejects Kant's epistemology and insists upon the self-revelation of beings, upon a realist metaphysics, and upon scriptural particularity. He rejects all "aesthetic theologies" that show the influence of Kantian immanentism. Yet, by drawing certain significant elements from Kant, *Theological Aesthetics* also stands as a "Kantian" critique of Kant. In his *Theological Aesthetics*, von Balthasar finds that contemporary (neo-scholastic) Catholic apologetics and fundamental theology have a good deal to learn from Kant, even if he suggests that Pierre Rousselot (to whom his own understanding of faith and apologetics is indebted) may have adopted a bit too much from Kant.

Von Balthasar's *Theo-Drama* is undoubtedly a Hegelian critique of Hegel. The influence of Hegel, and von Balthasar's explicit critique of Hegel, can be seen throughout the *Theo-Drama*, as all commentators recognize. This does not mean that Hegel is not found in major ways in the other parts of the trilogy, since of course he is. Nor does it mean that von Balthasar's vast *Theo-Drama* engages only with Hegel, a claim that would be absurd. But it does mean that von Balthasar's *Theo-Drama* is shaped in preeminent ways by its engagement with Hegel, an engagement that is first and foremost a critique.

Lastly, von Balthasar's *Theo-Logic* offers a Nietzschean critique of Nietzsche.[29] The critique of Nietzsche's understanding of truth as the will-to-power is central to the *Theo-Logic*'s unfolding of the truth of creation and redemption, even though many other sources contribute to the wide-ranging volumes of the *Theo-Logic*. Von Balthasar recognizes the value of Nietzsche's emphasis that truth is not merely a matter of getting facts or propositions right, because truth also involves the movement of the will (self-surrendering love), which directs us toward truth as good for us and which helps to fuel our quest for truth. Matthew Moser sums up von Balthasar's critique of both Hegel and Nietzsche: "countering the drive that funds Hegelian titanism, Balthasar offers the saints as those whose understanding of truth rises from the obedient receptivity of their love. The titanic will-to-power that aims for the intellectual mastery of Being is replaced by the saintly will-to-surrender that apprehends truth through the nuptial delight of contemplative union with God."[30]

It is the beauty, goodness, and truth of Christ's self-surrendering love that von Balthasar wants us to remember. Kant tells us that we are the (Promethean) source of our own morality and of our hope for peace on earth;[31] Hegel tells us that we are the (Titanic) source of absolute Spirit's perfect unfolding; Nietzsche tells us that we can be the (Dionysian) source of our own life. All three deny that the *transcendent* God's radical self-surrendering love is salvifically revealed in the particularity of Jesus Christ. This denial has seeped into popular consciousness, to the point where in many parts of Western culture today the very notion of "God" is treated as though one were speaking about an impos-

29. I note that it is also a critique of Heidegger. Although I give a primary place to von Balthasar's constructive critique of Nietzsche, I recognize the central importance of Heidegger in the *Theo-Logic* (and indeed throughout the trilogy).

30. Moser, *Love Itself Is Understanding*, 291–92.

31. See Immanuel Kant, *Grounding for the Metaphysics of Morals*, trans. James W. Ellington, 3rd ed. (Indianapolis, Ind.: Hackett, 1993); Kant, *Religion with the Limits of Reason Alone*, trans. Theodore M. Greene and Hoyt H. Hudson (New York: Harper and Row, 1960).

sible and unintelligible myth, a source of human violence rather than of human flourishing. My task is to show that from within philosophical modernity, von Balthasar combats our forgetfulness of the beauty, goodness, and truth of Christ and the Christian tradition.

My approach to von Balthasar's trilogy accords with an observation made by Rowan Williams some years prior to his becoming archbishop of Canterbury. Williams remarked that von Balthasar's "objection to Rahner is in fact an objection not so much to one contemporary theologian ... as a protest against the whole tradition of European 'mainstream' philosophy between Kant and Heidegger."[32] In the mainstream tradition of modern (German) philosophy, von Balthasar found a deep "anthropocentrism, the commitment to the standpoint that the correct interpretative principle for the whole of reality is the subjectivity of the person."[33] The choice for the future of Catholic theology was clear to von Balthasar: "either the God of Jesus Christ in perfect discipleship or his substitution and elimination by man-made secondary realities."[34]

In dialogic love rather than with mere condemnation, von Balthasar sought to respond to this situation. He followed the counsel given by Jean Daniélou in his 1946 manifesto for *ressourcement*: "Catholic thinkers ... must not hesitate to follow the representatives of these alien philosophers onto their own home ground, the better to respond to them."[35]

32. Rowan Williams, "Balthasar and Rahner," in *The Analogy of Beauty: The Theology of Hans Urs von Balthasar*, ed. John Riches, 11–34 (Edinburgh: T&T Clark, 1986), at 23.

33. Norris, "The Symphonic Unity of His Theology," 246.

34. Ibid.

35. Nichols, "Thomism and the Nouvelle Théologie," 4. See Jean Daniélou, SJ, "Les orientations présentes de la pensée religieuse," *Études* 249 (1946): 5–21. David L. Schindler has observed that von Balthasar's response to modernity "is one that shares the assumptions neither of modernity nor of postmodernity—or better, one that adopts the assumptions of both modernity and postmodernity but only as it transforms these." Von Balthasar's response to modernity is neither simply "modern" nor simply "anti-modern." Schindler has ontology specifically in view,

Each of my three chapters starts with an exposition of relevant writings of Kant, Hegel, or Nietzsche. Chapter 1 surveys the first volume of the *Theological Aesthetics*; chapter 2, the first volume of the *Theo-Drama*; and chapter 3, the first volume of the *Theo-Logic*. I hope that this approach will enable both his admirers and his critics (while *remaining* admirers or critics, since in my view both admiration and criticism are warranted) to advance *together* into the core of his achievement. Francesca Aran Murphy notes that von "Balthasar's admirers and detractors have become ... fixated with the daring passages in his writings."[36] A more sensitive lens is needed to introduce von Balthasar's achievement as a theological contribution that can be valued by admirers and critics alike, so long as they share in von Balthasar's firm rejection of the "demythologisation of the Gospel" by classically liberal thinkers who assume that "whatever there is of form in the Gospel possesses the same limited structure as the mythical form of any other man-made religion."[37]

Von Balthasar's Task

A provocative criticism of von Balthasar's trilogy has been advanced by R. R. Reno in "The Paradox of Hans Urs von Balthasar." Von Balthasar's task in his trilogy can be illumined by reflecting on and responding to this criticism.

Reno praises von Balthasar at some length. Nonetheless,

---

and his crucial insight is that von Balthasar, with his "catholic ontology of generosity," meets modernity dialogically from within its assumptions while critiquing and transforming them. See David L. Schindler, "Modernity and the Nature of a Distinction: Balthasar's Ontology of Generosity," in *How Balthasar Changed My Mind: 15 Scholars Reflect on the Meaning of Balthasar for Their Own Work*, ed. Rodney A. Howsare and Larry S. Chapp, 224–58 (New York: Crossroad, 2008), at 253.

36. Francesca Murphy, "Truth Grounded in Love: Hans Urs von Balthasar's *Theo-Logic* and Christian Pedagogy," in *How Balthasar Changed My Mind*, 123–34, at 133.

37. Hans Urs von Balthasar, *The Glory of the Lord: A Theological Aesthetics*, vol. 1, *Seeing the Form*, trans. Erasmo Leiva-Merikakis, ed. Joseph Fessio, SJ, and John Riches (San Francisco: Ignatius Press, 1982), 177–78.

Reno argues that von Balthasar's "virtuosity" and "faithful creativity" do not give sufficient place to the church's need to possess "a standard theology," rooted in "the broad agreement to accept the general framework of a theological system."[38] For Reno,
it will prove impossible to turn von Balthasar's theology into a
unifying theological discourse for the church, in part because
of von Balthasar's creativity and distaste for systematizing, and
also in part because of von Balthasar's general refusal to engage
with the neo-scholastic theologies of his day. Reno remarks, "Instead of a sustained engagement with previous patterns of Catholic theology, Balthasar's habit was to launch out in new directions with little regard for the official, mainstream theologies. He
made his counterthrusts against Rahnerian theology, but he never offered a patient diagnosis of what went wrong in this influential form of post-Vatican II theology."[39] The result, Reno thinks,
was the neglect by von Balthasar of the crucial ecclesial need "to
sustain a functional, communally accepted and widely taught
mode of analyzing, explaining, and defending doctrine."[40]

Again, Reno has many positive things to say about von
Balthasar's theology. He argues that von Balthasar makes superb
contributions to the connection between theology, prayer, and
obedience to Christ (especially important given the rise of lay
theologians without deep spiritual formation); to confidence in
Jesus Christ as the alpha and omega and as the key to unlocking
the true insights of all thinkers; and to appreciation for the primacy of scripture in its concrete and explosive particularity. At
the same time, Reno adds that Rahner won the immediate postconciliar period because "he worked hard to show how his transcendental theology could be molded into a teachable textbook
system, preserving the scaffolding of Heinrich Denzinger while

38. R. R. Reno, "The Paradox of Hans Urs von Balthasar," in *How Balthasar
Changed My Mind*, 172–90, at 176–77.
    39. Ibid., 179.
    40. Ibid., 180.

hollowing out the force and import of traditional doctrine," even if "today the failure of Rahner's misbegotten post-Kantian Scholasticism is plain to see."[41] What Reno calls for is "a genuine, fuller form of *Ressourcement*," a "textbook theology" with the "systematic clarity and comprehensiveness of the neo-Scholastic synthesis," that will provide introductory students with "a cogent account of how the Tridentine categories and convictions of Catholic theology gave rise to and were enriched by the two great councils of the modern era, Vatican I and Vatican II."[42]

In my view, Reno is correct that the task of measuring von Balthasar's achievement ultimately cannot mean attempting to boil down the insights of his trilogy to the systematic form of a textbook. Systematizing von Balthasar's trilogy into the form of a textbook theology could be done, but it would come at a significant cost to a thinker whose "theological method"—as Jennifer Martin appreciatively remarks—"is, rather like Origen's, fundamentally daring and experimental."[43] Had von Balthasar wanted to offer a new system to stand as the church's theology, he could have done so, but his project was a different one. In a striking passage cited by Martin, he states, "It is not our concern to get a secure place to stand, but rather to get sight of what cannot be securely grasped, and this must remain the event of Jesus Christ; woe to the Christian who would not stand daily speechless before this event! If this event truly is what the Church believes, then it can be mastered through no methodology."[44] Existentially, his trilogy's constructive and critical grappling with modernity

---

41. Ibid., 188. On the theological textbooks that Rahner's writings replaced, see Jared Wicks, SJ, "A Note on 'Neo-Scholastic' Manuals of Theological Instruction, 1900–1960," *Josephinum Journal of Theology* 18, no. 1 (2011): 240–46.

42. Reno, "The Paradox of Hans Urs von Balthasar," 188.

43. Martin, *Hans Urs von Balthasar and the Critical Appropriation of Russian Religious Thought*, 3.

44. Hans Urs von Balthasar, *The Glory of the Lord: A Theological Aesthetics*, vol. 7, *Theology: The New Covenant*, trans. Brian McNeil, CRV, ed. John Riches (San Francisco: Ignatius Press, 1989), 10, cited in Martin, *Hans Urs von Balthasar and the Critical Appropriation of Russian Religious Thought*, 2.

serves the purpose of enabling us to perceive the awe-inspiring event of Jesus Christ, his self-surrendering love.

Like Reno, O'Regan feels free to criticize von Balthasar and rejects efforts to "reproduce" von Balthasar's thought as though it were an easily packageable entity.[45] In a profound way, however, O'Regan appreciates von Balthasar as a theologian who sought to "respond to modernity characterized by forgetting."[46] In this response, von Balthasar insists upon the necessity of two-way dialogue. He does not come at philosophical "modernity" with a hammer to pound it into submission or to show its unadulterated falsity.[47] Yet he thinks that twentieth-century modernity, as informed by Kant, Hegel, and Nietzsche (among other influences), has forgotten the source and summit of all reality: the beauty, goodness, and truth of Christ's self-surrendering love. Thus it can no longer perceive the true form of Christ; it cannot perceive that the incarnate Son, in his self-surrendering love, is the form that undergirds and unifies all phenomena. It cannot recognize the ultimate goodness of history because it no longer sees the transcendent self-surrendering love of the Trinitarian Persons sustaining all creaturely difference (including the difference of finitude) and because it no longer sees the incarnate Son and the Holy Spirit entering into the world's history, taking up the world's sin and alienation, and embracing and overcoming this alienation within the goodness of infinite self-surrendering love. It can no longer know the truth of the world, which it mistakes as merely the will-to-power rather than appreciating that truth is grounded in self-surrender and that the truth of reality is triune self-surrendering love that enables us, fallen but redeemed, to

45. See Cyril O'Regan, "I Am Not What I Am Because of …," in *How Balthasar Changed My Mind*, 151–71, at 157, 159 and 170.

46. Ibid., 165.

47. For various more recent accounts of and responses to "modernity," see Colin Miller, "Ivan Illich, Catholic Theologian (Part I)," *Pro Ecclesia* 26, no. 1 (2017): 81–110. "Modernity" is such a complex reality that a wide variety of Christian responses will be needed and appropriate.

participate in its self-surrendering love and thereby to be what divine love knows us to be.

If modernity has forgotten all this, why not simply say a pox on philosophical modernity and get on with the business of Christian theology? Because, according to von Balthasar, a "response" that will be in any way adequate—a "response" that will be in any way itself an act of self-surrendering love—must be a response that listens to and hears modern concerns, that takes up what is insightful in philosophical modernity while correcting its forgetting by placing it in a deeper dialogue with the main sources of the Christian tradition. For von Balthasar, the Christian tradition itself will emerge from this dialogue positively affected, since in its human elements the Christian tradition always stands in need of some reform and renewal as well. But it is ultimately modernity itself that will be healed: as Moser says, von "Balthasar ultimately sees the saints as the *positive* fulfillment of the questions and concerns of modernity."[48]

After completing his trilogy, von Balthasar published an *Epilogue* to it in 1987, the year before his death. One might imagine that this *Epilogue* draws together the main points of his trilogy into an accessible summary. But in fact, it is if anything more intricate and dense than the trilogy itself! In the *Epilogue*, von Balthasar points once more to the "self-showing" (aesthetics), "self-giving" (dramatics), and "self-saying" (logic) that is Christ's "death of ultimate surrender to the Father and to us, consummated from within the surrender of his (Holy) Spirit exhaled in death and inhaled into the world at Easter."[49] Although his *Epilogue* does not function as a synopsis of the trilogy, it does unfold once more the central theme of all his work, namely the particulari-

48. Moser, *Love Itself Is Understanding*, 292.

49. Hans Urs von Balthasar, *Epilogue*, trans. Edward T. Oakes, SJ (San Francisco: Ignatius Press, 2004), 122.

ty of Christ's self-surrendering love for us sinners, a love that is grounded in the eternal triune self-surrendering love.[50]

When this central theme is kept in view, we can see that von Balthasar's dialogically critical engagement with Kant, Hegel, and Nietzsche, in his unfolding of Christ's self-showing, self-giving, and self-saying, has a simple but radical goal: to invite us moderns, shaped inevitably by Kant, Hegel, and Nietzsche (among others), into the absolute self-surrender in love to God and neighbor that has been made possible by Christ's absolute self-surrender in supreme love for us, through the Spirit who draws us into the ever-greater love of triune beauty, goodness, and truth.

Let me therefore conclude this introduction with words from von Balthasar himself. "God's love is ever greater; we can never catch up with it.... In his 'kenosis' [self-emptying] God shows man that, right from the outset, he (man) is constructed according to a kenotic principle. It is precisely in this self-emptying and poverty that he will become—and already is—rich and glorious."[51] Or, as St. Paul says, "Love never ends" (1 Cor 13:8).

---

50. See Hans Urs von Balthasar, *Heart of the World*, trans. Erasmo S. Leiva (San Francisco: Ignatius Press, 1979 [German edition 1954]); von Balthasar, *Love Alone Is Credible*, trans. D. C. Schindler (San Francisco: Ignatius Press, 2004 [German edition 1963]); von Balthasar, *Convergences: To the Source of the Christian Mystery*, trans. E. A. Nelson (San Francisco: Ignatius Press, 1983 [German edition 1969]); von Balthasar, *Light of the World: Brief Reflections on the Sunday Readings*, trans. Dennis D. Martin (San Francisco: Ignatius Press, 1993).

51. Hans Urs von Balthasar, *In the Fullness of Faith: On the Centrality of the Distinctively Catholic*, trans. Graham Harrison (San Francisco: Ignatius Press, 1988), 31, 115. As Jason A. Fout remarks, "For von Balthasar ... it is the love present in and among the Three of the Trinity, which overflows in expressions of God's glory, a love which is more than a declaration, a love which touches and draws in the creation to the Trinitarian relations. Moreover, this love has a particular shape which flows out of von Balthasar's interpretation of Christ and his mission. For von Balthasar the specific shape of God's love is expressed through the self-giving and self-emptying on the cross" (*Fully Alive: The Glory of God and the Human Creature in Karl Barth, Hans Urs von Balthasar and Theological Exegesis of Scripture* [London: Bloomsbury, 2015], 112).

1 ⌖ *Theological Aesthetics*

A KANTIAN CRITIQUE
OF KANT

Vincent Holzer, a French expert on the theology of Hans Urs von Balthasar, has observed that Immanuel "Kant is very present in the first volume of the *Aesthetics*."[1] Drawing upon von Balthasar's short book *The Moment of Christian Witness*, Holzer notes that von Balthasar's engagement with Kant in the *Theological Aesthetics*—both in its first volume and in later volumes—is generally critical, due to Kant's failure to give place to the "givenness of being," existence's character as a gift.[2] Quite rightly, interpreters of von Balthasar often comment upon his explicit preference for the concrete path of Johann Wolfgang von Goethe over the transcendental path of Kant.[3] But in his *Epi-*

1. Vincent Holzer, *Hans Urs von Balthasar, 1905–1988* (Paris: Cerf, 2012), 92.

2. Ibid. See also Hans Urs von Balthasar, *The Moment of Christian Witness*, trans. Richard Beckley (San Francisco: Ignatius Press, 1994), 61–76.

3. Von Balthasar remarked in 1976, "There is a book by Simmel called *Goethe und Kant*. Rahner has chosen Kant, or if you will, Fichte, the transcendental approach. And I have chosen Goethe, my field being German literature. The form (*Gestalt*), the indissoluble unique, organic, developing form—I am thinking of Goethe's poem 'The Metamorphosis of Plants'—this form, which Kant does not know what to do with, even in his aesthetics.... One can walk around a form and see it from all sides. One always sees something different, and yet one sees the same thing." See Peter Henrici, SJ, "The Philosophy of Hans Urs von Balthasar," in *Hans Urs von Balthasar: His Life and Work*, ed. David L. Schindler, 149–67 (San Francisco: Ignatius Press, 1991), at 154, citing "Geist und Feuer. Michael Albus: Ein Gespräch mit Hans Urs von Balthasar," *Herder-Korrespondenz* 30 (1976): 75–76.

logue to the trilogy, von Balthasar makes the following remark in describing the task of the *Theological Aesthetics*: "The fact ... that the image points to a real essence being expressed in them can only be grasped on the basis of the unity of what Kant called 'transcendental apperception', which alone does full justice to the full concept of *Gestalt*."[4] Since *Gestalt* is a crucial concept in von Balthasar's *Theological Aesthetics*, the positive reference to Kant here is significant. Von Balthasar suggests that Kant's concept of "transcendental apperception" helps us to appreciate that "*Gestalt* is more than image; it is the unity encountering the perceiver that is also simultaneously manifest in the experience of self ... so that the object encountered and the 'I'—in spite of the variety of our ever-unique essences—truly communicate in the all-one depth of reality (*esse*)."[5] This will have Christological implications, since it (namely the transcendental apperception that grounds the encounter of subject and object that is found in the true *Gestalt*) characterizes what Balthasar calls the "transcendental epiphany of the entirety of the world's Being."[6]

In the first volume of the *Theological Aesthetics*, von Balthasar again refers to Kant in a positive way. He argues that "theological aesthetics must properly be developed in two phases, which are: 1. *The theory of vision* (or fundamental theology): 'aesthetics' in the Kantian sense as a theory about the perception of the form of God's self-revelation. 2. *The theory of rapture* (or dogmatic theology): 'aesthetics' as a theory about the incarnation of God's glory and the consequent elevation of man to participate in that glory."[7] Recall that according to Kant's *Critique of Judgement*, "*Beauty* is the form of *purposiveness* in an object, so far as this is perceived

4. Hans Urs von Balthasar, *Epilogue*, trans. Edward T. Oakes, SJ (San Francisco: Ignatius Press, 2004), 62–63.

5. Ibid.

6. Ibid.

7. Hans Urs von Balthasar, *The Glory of the Lord: A Theological Aesthetics*, vol. 1, *Seeing the Form*, trans. Erasmo Leiva-Merikakis, ed. Joseph Fessio, SJ, and John Riches (San Francisco: Ignatius Press, 1982), 125.

in it *apart from the representation of an end*"—that is, apart from
mere usefulness.[8] Kant held that "the beautiful is the symbol of
the morally good, and only in this light (a point of view natural
to everyone, and one which everyone demands from others as
a duty) does it give us pleasure with an attendant claim to the
agreement of everyone else."[9]

In these two positive references to Kant, von Balthasar indicates Kant's significant place in the work of the *Theological
Aesthetics*. Obviously, however, von Balthasar is no Kantian.[10]
Not only does he sternly refute Kant's immanentism, Kant's correspondingly reductive view of the transcendentals, and Kant's
distance from "Thomas's major creative achievement—his definition of *esse* and its relation to essences,"[11] but also he cannot
accept Kant's aesthetics as a whole. For Kant, as Francesca Aran
Murphy points out, beauty ultimately refers back not to the beautiful thing but to "the depths of the subject," even if Kant in a
certain way "links the formal representation of beauty to the
thing in itself."[12] Murphy explains that Kant's "aesthetic has two
thrusts. The first focuses so intently on the formal qualities of art
that it loses sight of beauty's participation in reality.... Kant's
second thrust locates the validity of judgements about art in the

8. Immanuel Kant, *Critique of Judgement*, trans. James Creed Meredith, ed.
Nicholas Walker (Oxford: Oxford University Press, 2007), 66.

9. Ibid., 180.

10. For a succinct outline of his strong critique of Kant, see the chapter on "The
Anthropological Reduction" in Hans Urs von Balthasar, *Love Alone Is Credible*, trans.
D.C. Schindler, 31–50 (San Francisco: Ignatius Press, 2004). *Love Alone Is Credible*
summarizes von Balthasar's project in his *Theological Aesthetics*.

11. Hans Urs von Balthasar, *The Glory of the Lord: A Theological Aesthetics*, vol. 4,
The Realm of Metaphysics in Antiquity, trans. Brian McNeil, CRV, Andrew Louth, John
Saward, Rowan Williams, and Oliver Davies, ed. John Riches (San Francisco: Igna-
tius Press, 1989), 393.

12. Francesca Aran Murphy, *Christ the Form of Beauty: A Study in Theology and
Literature* (Edinburgh: T&T Clark, 1995), 28. Murphy cites Robert Zimmerman, "Kant:
The Aesthetic Judgement," in *Kant: A Collection of Critical Essays*, ed. Robert Paul
Wolff (London: Macmillan, 1968); Theodore Edward Uehling Jr., *The Notion of Form
in Kant's Critique of Aesthetic Judgement* (The Hague: Mouton, 1971).

judging community."[13] By contrast, although von Balthasar appreciates Kant's emphasis upon perceiving the form and upon communal judgment of the beauty of the form, von Balthasar opposes "Kantian formalism" by recognizing that the transcendentals, including beauty, "are part of the fabric of being. It is only thus that a beautiful image can contain and transmit the call of the good, the affirmation of the true and the 'is-ing' of being."[14]

The key for my purposes in this chapter will be how von Balthasar engaged Kant in positing a "transcendental epiphany of the entirety of the world's Being."[15] For von Balthasar,

13. Murphy, *Christ the Form of Beauty*, 29.

14. Ibid., 31. In the first volume of his *Apocalypse of the German Soul*, von Balthasar addresses Kant's *Critique of Pure Reason*. Aidan Nichols sums up von Balthasar's findings: for Kant "the very 'to-and-fro' of the understanding (*Verstand*) in its dealings with nature, the 'to-and-fro' in which spirit comes to know itself as limited, points to a ground of unity which itself renders possible valid criticism (*Kritik*) and therefore genuine knowledge" (Nichols, *Scattering the Seed: A Guide through Balthasar's Early Writings on Philosophy and the Arts* [Washington, D.C.: The Catholic University of America Press, 2006], 51). For Kant, this ground of unity is our consciousness, and Kant is not able to identify any more fundamental ground from the perspective of "pure reason." Yet the knowing self is contingent, subject to mortality, and unable truly to unify all things. See Hans Urs von Balthasar, *Apokalypse der deutschen Seele: Studien zu einer Lehre von letzten Haltungen*, vol. 1, *Der deutsche Idealismus* (Salzburg: A. Pustet, 1937); Kant, "The End of All Things" (1794), published in English in *Immanuel Kant: Religion and Rational Theology*, ed. Allen W. Wood and G. de Giovanni (Cambridge: Cambridge University Press, 1996), 221–31.

15. Von Balthasar, *Epilogue*, 62–63. For Kant, transcendental apperception entails apprehending that one's own mental state or representation is indeed *one's own*. Since Kant holds that we do not know things as they are in themselves but rather know them as they are cognized in accord with the categories of our minds, it is crucial that in some way we can know our minds, since things have their ground not in themselves but in our minds. Thus, the transcendental or a priori apperception of one's own self-consciousness plays a crucial unifying and grounding role. D. C. Schindler adds the point that "the manifestation of the unconditioned unity of self-consciousness" does not mean, for Kant, "any knowledge of the soul in itself" (Schindler, *Hans Urs von Balthasar and the Dramatic Structure of Truth: A Philosophical Investigation* [New York: Fordham University Press, 2004], 102–3). I note also that in volume 5 of the *Theological Aesthetics*, in his lengthy discussion of "The Metaphysics of Spirit" according to modern (mainly German) philosophy, von Balthasar pushes back against Kant's view, on the grounds that Kant's "'purification' of philosophy from all empirical experience turns transcendentalism into an unadulterated formalism" (von Balthasar, *The Glory of the Lord: A Theological Aesthetics*, vol. 5, *The Realm of Metaphysics in the Modern Age*, trans. Oliver Davies, Andrew Louth,

the unifying ground of all phenomena (every "epiphany ... of the world's Being") is found in perceiving the *Gestalt* of Christ's self-surrendering love. In its focus on the revelation and perception of divine beauty in Christ (and in all things as created by Christ), the *Theological Aesthetics* aims to transform theological apologetics and fundamental theology.[16]

The present chapter surveys the *Theological Aesthetics*'s programmatic first volume, *Seeing the Form*. My hope is to show how von Balthasar's Kantian critique of Kant emerges within a wide-ranging conversation that accomplishes an extraordinary retrieval of large swaths of the Christian tradition and other intellectual conversations as well. To prepare for this reading of *Seeing the Form*, I will first devote some attention to Kant's *Critique of Pure Reason* and *Critique of Judgement*.

Contributions from Immanuel Kant's *Critique of Pure Reason* and *Critique of Judgement*

In this section, I first survey Kant's notion of "transcendental apperception" in his *Critique of Pure Reason*. So as to provide some background for this notion, I begin here with Kant's examination of the "Transcendental Analytic," where he is seeking "an ana-

---

Brian McNeil, CRV, John Saward, and Rowan Williams, ed. Brian McNeil, CRV, and John Riches [San Francisco: Ignatius Press, 1991], 496).

16. In the first half of the twentieth century, this domain was divided in the Catholic world between those who wanted to take some insights from Kant (e.g., Blondel, Rousselot) and those who wanted to reject Kant entirely (e.g., Gardeil, Garrigou-Lagrange). See Maurice Blondel, *The Letter on Apologetics and History and Dogma*, trans. Alexander Dru and Illtyd Trethowan (Grand Rapids, Mich.: Eerdmans, 1994); Pierre Rousselot, SJ, *The Eyes of Faith*, trans. Joseph Donceel, SJ (New York: Fordham University Press, 1990); Ambroise Gardeil, OP, *La crédibilité et l'apologétique*, 4th ed. (Paris: Gabalda, 1928); Réginald Garrigou-Lagrange, OP, *De revelatione per Ecclesiam catholicam proposita*, 2 vols., 3rd ed. (Rome: F. Ferrari, 1929). See also Henri de Lubac, SJ, "Apologétique et théologie," *Nouvelle revue théologique* 57 (1930): 361–78, which has appeared in English as "Apologetics and Theology," in de Lubac, *Theological Fragments*, trans. Rebecca Howell Balinski (San Francisco: Ignatius Press, 1989), 91–104.

lytic of concepts."[17] This discussion is found toward the beginning of his dense and massive *Critique of Pure Reason*.

By the phrase "analytic of concepts," Kant meant not analyzing the content of concepts but analyzing "the faculty of understanding itself."[18] He wanted to discover whether "*a priori* concepts"—"pure concepts of the understanding" that are not rooted in empirical phenomena but that precede such phenomena (due to being rooted solely in the mind itself)—are possible.[19] He aimed to seek such pure concepts "only in the understanding as their birthplace," where, he explained, "they lie ready, until with the opportunity of experience they are finally developed and exhibited in their clarity by the very same understanding, liberated from the empirical conditions attached to them."[20]

The first chapter of his "Transcendental Analytic" or "Analytic of Concepts" bears the title "On the Clue to the Discovery of all Pure Concepts of the Understanding."[21] He begins with the notion that the faculty of knowing exhibits, in the course of thinking, a variety of concepts or categories of understanding. These concepts are the underlying conditions for the possibility of experience. The task of what Kant calls "transcendental philosophy" is to understand the connection and indeed the unity of these "pure concepts of understanding." Thus, transcendental philosophy aims to understand the unifying principle that ensures that "the place of each pure concept of the understanding and the completeness of all of them together can be determined *a priori*."[22]

In undertaking this ambitious task, Kant first offers a reflection on the mind, the "non-sensible faculty of cognition."[23] He

17. Immanuel Kant, *Critique of Pure Reason*, trans. and ed. Paul Guyer and Allen W. Wood (Cambridge: Cambridge University Press, 1998), 202.
18. Ibid.
19. Ibid., 199, 202.
20. Ibid., 202–3.
21. Ibid., 204.
22. Ibid.
23. Ibid.

distinguishes understanding from intuition, since the latter requires sensibility or the capacity of receiving sense impressions. Intuition differs from conceptual cognition, which rises above sense impressions. When we understand things, we do so discursively through concepts. Kant states, "Concepts are therefore grounded on the spontaneity of thinking, as sensible intuitions are grounded on the receptivity of impressions."[24] In thinking, we make judgments on the basis of concepts. These concepts, Kant notes, are separate from empirical objects; intuition alone has direct contact with empirical objects through sense impressions. A concept can be related either to another concept or to an intuition. What a judgment is, then, is the attainment of a "concept that holds of many, and that among this many also comprehends a given representation, which is then related immediately to the object."[25]

For example, one might make the judgment that the phenomena that one perceives—a table, books, a computer—are divisible. This judgment would be a judgment that "all bodies are divisible."[26] This judgment, it is clear, is a concept that relates to other concepts, some of which relate to phenomena that one intuits. Kant explains that "the concept of the divisible is related to various other concepts; among these, however, it is here particularly related to the concept of body, and this in turn is related to certain appearances that come before us."[27] Through the concept of divisibility, we may draw many concepts into one; our thinking therefore leads to the higher concepts that pertain to a judgment.

Kant distinguishes various kinds of logical judgments: universal, particular, and singular judgments (quantity); affirmative, negative, and infinite judgments (quality); categorical,

24. Ibid., 205.
25. Ibid.
26. Ibid.
27. Ibid.

hypothetical, and disjunctive judgments (relation); and problematic, assertoric, and apodictic judgments (modality). On this
basis, he identifies three "moments" in thinking: "One first judges something problematically, then assumes it assertorically as
true, and finally asserts it to be inseparably connected with the
understanding, i.e., asserts it as necessary and apodictic."[28] He
argues that it would be a mistake to think of this logical movement as grounded in empirical phenomena. Rather, the essential
ground is the categories or pure concepts of the mind.

Kant describes the process of "synthesis," by which different
"representations" are put together and comprehended "in one
cognition."[29] Synthesis takes place both in intuition and in judgment, because in both cases the unification of different "representations" is necessary. Among the "pure concepts of synthesis
that the understanding contains in itself *a priori*," he lists unity,
plurality, and totality (quantity); reality, negation, and limitation
(quality); inherence and subsistence, causality and dependence,
and community (relation); and possibility and impossibility, existence and nonexistence, and necessity and contingency (modality).[30] He thinks that these synthetic categories are "the true
ancestral concepts of pure understanding."[31] He contrasts these
original a priori concepts with what he terms derivative concepts, or "predicables" such as (for example) force, action, and
passion under the category of causality.[32]

Understanding himself to be updating and improving upon
Aristotle, Kant is moving toward the fullness of his "plan for
the whole of science insofar as it rests on *a priori* concepts."[33]
He addresses the transcendental properties of beings, which, as
he notes, Aristotle does not include among the ten Aristotelian

28. Ibid., 210.
29. Ibid.
30. Ibid., 212–13.
31. Ibid., 213.
32. Ibid., 213–14.
33. Ibid., 214.

categories. These transcendental properties are being, one, true, and good. In Kant's view, however, these classical transcendental properties have been profoundly misinterpreted by metaphysicians. They have been taken as really inhering in things, or, as Kant says, as properties "belonging to the possibility of things itself."[34] In fact, they "are nothing other than logical requisites and criteria of all cognition of things in general," or in other words purely formal elements of the "logical requirements for every cognition."[35] On this view, the four classical transcendentals have to do with thought about things, not with the things in themselves. Kant explains this point: unity or oneness has to do with the concept's unity; truth has to do with the "true consequences [that flow] from a given concept"; and goodness or perfection has to do with all the aspects of a concept "being traced back to the unity of the concept" so as to ensure the concept's completeness.[36]

The second chapter of his "Transcendental Analytic" is titled "On the Deduction of Pure Concepts of the Understanding." Well aware that the human mind employs countless concepts, he argues that some concepts are "destined for pure use *a priori* (completely independent of all experience)."[37] But how can concepts be used that have no root in experience? Kant explains that the task of empirical deduction consists in exploring how experience and reflection lead to the production of a concept, whereas the task of "transcendental deduction" is to show how the use of concepts can be justified in cases where their relation to objects has no basis in empirical experience.[38] Earlier, Kant distinguished between two kinds of concepts that relate to objects in a completely a priori way, and he reiterates that distinction here: "the concepts of space and time, as forms of sensibility, and the cat-

34. Ibid., 217.
35. Ibid.
36. Ibid.
37. Ibid., 220.
38. Ibid.

egories [surveyed above], as concepts of the understanding."[39]
The categories of the understanding are not deduced empirically; they precede the influence of empirical experience and their
use cannot depend upon experiential justification. Kant thereby
rules out Locke's effort to find in sense experience the causes of
the generation of concepts of the understanding, even though
Kant does not doubt that we can "ascend from individual perceptions to general concepts."[40] The point is that the use of a priori
concepts or categories of the understanding cannot be justified
on experiential grounds because a priori concepts and categories
of our minds do not arise from experience. How, then, can their
use be justified vis-à-vis phenomena?

Kant points out that space and time are easier to defend as
"pure intuitions that contain *a priori* the conditions of the possibility of objects as appearances."[41] Nothing can appear to someone's sensible intuition unless it appears within the categories of
space and time. The categories of understanding are more difficult to defend, since objects *can* appear without being explicitly
related by the mind to the categories (such as, for example, the
category of causality). The categories of our understanding must,
however, be defended as objectively valid, or in other words as
necessarily providing "the conditions of the possibility of all
cognition of objects."[42] In undertaking this defense, we cannot
appeal to experience, since the deduction of a priori categories
cannot appeal to a posteriori experience. Kant takes seriously
the possibility, therefore, that we might have a priori categories
of understanding that belong to our thinking but do not in fact
relate to experiential phenomena. The question is how to bridge
this gap through a properly transcendental (a priori) deduction.
If it cannot be bridged, then we cannot say that the concept of

39. Ibid.
40. Ibid., 221.
41. Ibid., 222.
42. Ibid.

causality (for example) is necessary and universal in our under-standing of experiential phenomena. Empirically, as Hume says, we can show only that effects *regularly* arise from causes. It is impossible to prove empirically that the concept of causality *necessarily* is related to all phenomena.

In response to this difficulty, Kant argues that "the objective validity of the categories, as *a priori* concepts, rests on the fact that through them alone is experience possible (as far as the form of thinking is concerned)."[43] But if we cannot demonstrate that it is impossible to understand phenomena without the categories, then the latter would not be objectively valid in their use in rela-tion to objects of the mind. Thus, if the categories do not concep-tually "supply the objective ground of the possibility of experi-ence," we could not be justified in holding that they apply to every phenomenon.[44] Kant cites Locke's and Hume's efforts to address the problem, and he comments that the weak point in Hume's ap-proach (which appeals to custom rather than to demonstration) is that "it never occurred to him that perhaps the understanding itself, by means of these concepts, could be the originator of the experience in which its objects are considered."[45] This view that the (a priori) categories of understanding originate our experience is Kant's solution to Humean skepticism.

To make his point, Kant finds that he needs to explore "the subjective sources that comprise the *a priori* foundations for the possibility of experience."[46] He identifies three sources: intu-ition, imagination, and conceptualization. With respect to intu-ition, he notes that it depends on the a priori categories of time and space. With respect to imagination, he remarks that "appear-ances are not things in themselves, but rather the mere play of our representations," which again requires the categories of time

43. Ibid., 224.
44. Ibid., 225.
45. Ibid.
46. Ibid., 227.

and space.[47] With respect to conceptualization, he emphasizes that "we cognize the object if we have effected synthetic unity in the manifold of intuition," and this requires "a rule that makes the reproduction of the manifold necessary *a priori* and a concept in which this manifold is united possible."[48] This "rule" must impose necessity (as for example "the concept of body makes necessary the representation of extension"), and "every necessity has a transcendental condition as its ground."[49]

Why, however, must a necessity be grounded by a transcendental condition? Again, the answer is that if there were no a priori ground, then we would be compelled to hold either Locke's or Hume's position. Either we would have to argue that a necessary connection between our categories and phenomena could be proven on the basis of experience (Locke's position, which Hume disproves) or we would have to hold to custom and Humean skepticism.

We are now approaching the point that von Balthasar, in his *Epilogue*, cites as crucial for the project of his *Theological Aesthetics*. As noted above, von Balthasar remarks that "the fact ... that the image points to a real essence being expressed in them can only be grasped on the basis of the unity of what Kant called 'transcendental apperception', which alone does full justice to the full concept of *Gestalt*."[50] For Kant, this "transcendental apperception" is the transcendental ground of the necessity of the relation between our a priori concepts of pure understanding and the objects (appearances or phenomena) of these concepts. My task, therefore, is to describe what "transcendental apperception" means in the context of Kant's *Critique of Pure Reason* and to identify why transcendental apperception has such significance for von Balthasar's *theological* aesthetics.

47. Ibid., 230.
48. Ibid., 231.
49. Ibid., 232.
50. Von Balthasar, *Epilogue*, 62–63.

Kant argues that just as intuition (linked with synthetic apprehension) and imagination (linked with synthetic reproduction) rely for their connection with their objects upon the a priori categories of space and time, so also synthetic recognition through conceptualization relies for its connection with its object upon "transcendental apperception." He differentiates this from "empirical apperception," or the empirical and variable consciousness of oneself.[51] What undergirds all of the understanding's conceptualization is a "unity of consciousness that precedes all data of the intuitions, and in relation to which all representation of objects is alone possible."[52] This unity of consciousness, since it precedes any empirical data, stands as "pure, original, unchanging."[53] It provides the basis for all unity of concepts, including the unity "of the *a priori* concepts (space and time)."[54] Kant calls it "transcendental apperception." It is an "apperception" that, in its utter unity and priority as consciousness, "grounds all concepts *a priori*, just as the manifoldness of space and time grounds the intuitions of sensibility."[55]

The value of this a priori unity of consciousness might not yet be clear. Given that consciousness grounds the unity of concepts, Kant emphasizes that it grounds the synthetic unity of all phenomena. He states that "the original and necessary consciousness of the identity of oneself is at the same time a consciousness of an equally necessary unity of the synthesis of all appearances in accordance with concepts."[56] The phrase "in accordance with concepts" makes clear the scope of the synthetic unity of all phenomena. The a priori concepts or categories of understanding establish the "rules" that justify us in holding that phenomena are regular not simply because custom tells us but because the

51. Kant, *Critique of Pure Reason*, 232.
52. Ibid.
53. Ibid.
54. Ibid.
55. Ibid., 233.
56. Ibid.

phenomena are "necessarily connected" and constitute a determinate "object."[57] This "object" is not something behind the phenomena but rather is "the concept of something in which they are necessarily connected."[58]

All possible appearances or phenomena, then, are a unity because of the transcendental or a priori "unity of apperception."[59] Transcendental apperception attests to the unity of consciousness and the unity of the phenomena in our concepts. The mind perceives here the "identity" of its own act of understanding, in which all phenomena are connected with each other necessarily due to the rules of the mind's a priori categories or concepts of pure understanding. If we had no unchanging consciousness, we could not conceive of any necessary connections of phenomena in our concepts. But given transcendental apperception and the unity it establishes, we can have a concept of "objective reality."[60] We can know that "all appearances, insofar as objects are to be given to us through them, must stand under *a priori* rules of their synthetic unity."[61]

Transcendental apperception therefore gives an a priori ground for the unity of all experience. Kant states that although there are different spaces and times and different experiences, in fact all space and time and all experience constitute a unity, as we know from the transcendental apperception of the a priori unity of consciousness in ourselves. He remarks, "The thoroughgoing and synthetic unity of perceptions is precisely what constitutes the form of experience, and it is nothing other than the synthetic unity of the appearances in accordance with concepts."[62]

For my purposes here, the key point is that transcendental apperception grounds the synthetic unity of all appearances, all

57. Ibid.
58. Ibid.
59. Ibid.
60. Ibid.
61. Ibid.
62. Ibid., 234.

phenomena, in our concepts. It is what enables us to have an integrated experience and to know that our concepts or categories are not useless when used in relation to phenomena. For Kant, the whole of "nature," as we know it, is "a sum of appearances," and "nature" can be known because of transcendental apperception; we could not know "nature" as an object of necessary and universal knowledge if "it were given in itself independently of the primary sources of our thinking."[63] But due to transcendental apperception—the pure and unchanging unity of consciousness that underlies our experienced self-consciousness—we can know all appearances, all phenomena, as a unity.

In arguing that transcendental apperception "alone does full justice to the full concept of *Gestalt*," von Balthasar explains that this is because transcendental apperception allows "the encountered and the 'I'" to "truly communicate in the all-one depth of reality."[64] It is crucial to note that the terms that von Balthasar associates with transcendental apperception—which is for Kant the unchanging ground of all understanding and intuition, enabling "nature" to be perceived as a unity—are terms that are at the very heart of von Balthasar's theological aesthetics, which seeks through reflection upon *Gestalt* to penetrate into the deepest, unchanging, and unifying ground of communion in "the all-one depth of reality." For von Balthasar, the "transcendental apperception" that is "the original and necessary consciousness of the identity of oneself" and is "a consciousness of an equally necessary unity of the synthesis of all appearances in accordance with concepts"[65] cannot stop with human consciousness. Transcendental apperception must instead seek the pure and unchanging *divine* ground of human consciousness. The "unity of the synthesis of all appearances" (all forms, figures, images, and thus each *Gestalt*) is to be found in divine consciousness—under-

63. Ibid., 236.
64. Von Balthasar, *Epilogue*, 63.
65. Kant, *Critique of Pure Reason*, 233.

stood more precisely as divine self-surrendering triune love as revealed by the *Gestalt* of Jesus Christ.

Here we should also recall that von Balthasar, in the first volume of his *Theological Aesthetics*, holds that a proper theological aesthetics must include a "theory of vision" or "'aesthetics' in the Kantian sense as a theory about the perception of the form of God's self-revelation."[66] In the *Critique of Judgement*, as noted above, Kant defines beauty as "the form of *purposiveness* in an object, so far as this is perceived in it *apart from the representation of an end*."[67] Kant shows an appreciation for a "purposiveness" that is sheer overflowing generosity, and that therefore is beautiful. He also comments that "only when sensibility is brought into harmony with moral feeling can genuine taste assume a definite unchangeable form," because "the beautiful is the symbol of the morally good."[68] This connection between true beauty and moral goodness is crucial for aesthetics. Less promisingly, Kant holds that the beautiful and the good are "relations of representations to the feeling of pleasure and displeasure."[69] On the positive side, this position emphasizes the importance of the interiority of the person perceiving the beautiful object, in a way that accords with von Balthasar's emphasis on interiority (love, the eyes of faith). But on the negative side, as von Balthasar makes clear, it fails to appreciate the objectivity of the beautiful thing's self-manifestation.

In his *Epilogue*'s summary of the intention of his *Theologi-*

66. Von Balthasar, *Seeing the Form*, 125.

67. Kant, *Critique of Judgement*, 66; cf. ibid.,177, for Kant's rejection of "a realism of the purposiveness of nature" and insistence that "it is we who receive nature with favour, and not nature that does us a favour." Von Balthasar critiques these aspects of Kant's theory.

68. Ibid., 180, 183. For Kant, however, "all our knowledge of God is merely symbolic; and one who takes it ... to be schematic, falls into anthropomorphism, just as, if he abandons every intuitive element, he falls into Deism which furnishes no knowledge whatsoever—not even from a practical point of view" (ibid., 180). By "symbolic," Kant means "a *mode* of the intuitive" (ibid., 179).

69. Ibid., 41.

cal Aesthetics, von Balthasar states that "from this transcendental epiphany of the entirety of the world's Being we can already catch a glimpse of the structures of revelation, that revelation of the absolute reality in whose midpoint stands the figure of Christ."[70] He makes clear that Christ is the revelation of the primal ground that unifies all appearances. Along these lines, he comments that "since Christ (as a human being who submitted himself to the intraworldly structures of ground and appearance) at the same time presents himself as the true interpretation of (supraworldly) absolute Being, this makes him utterly unique, so that the worldly structures of 'form and light' (beauty) themselves serve as an epiphany of this above-mentioned structure of the Absolute."[71] Christ alone is the perfect *Gestalt*, and Christ makes possible our communion, through his Spirit, in the "all-one depth of reality." Since the divine consciousness is triune self-surrendering love, it makes sense that radical surrender has a central place in Christ's *Gestalt*. Thus, von Balthasar notes that "the 'de-formity' of Christ's death on the Cross and God's abandonment of him on Golgotha occupy a central place in this total form."[72]

In his *Epilogue*, von Balthasar adds that in order to ensure that Christ's appearance not be counted as merely one among the appearances that comprise "nature," the risen Christ ascends to the right hand of the Father. He states in this regard that "it is necessary that the appearance *dis*appear, so that it is finally made clear that Christ's appearance really was the revelation of the *Absolute*."[73] The outpouring of the divine Spirit makes clear that Christ's appearance, his *Gestalt*, has not disappeared. The Holy Spirit interprets Christ to the world and thereby reveals that the *Gestalt* of Christ is "the uniquely definitive appearance of the

70. Von Balthasar, *Epilogue*, 63.
71. Ibid., 65.
72. Ibid.
73. Ibid.

Absolute now dwelling in Church and world."[74] By revealing the love of the Father, Christ reveals the divine consciousness that grounds the unity of all appearances and contains (analogously) difference in itself. The Trinitarian "difference in the Absolute (which transcends even the meaning of difference) becomes apparent in God's identity."[75]

Hans Urs von Balthasar's Kantian Critique of Kant: *Seeing the Form*

In the remainder of this chapter, I restrict myself to the first volume—*Seeing the Form*—of von Balthasar's seven-volume *Theological Aesthetics*. In this programmatic first volume, von Balthasar makes clear that his project is preeminently, though far from exclusively, a Kantian critique of Kant. As we will discover in *Seeing the Form*, von Balthasar's theology of revelation and faith extracts some good from Kant (here unlike the predominant nineteenth- and early twentieth-century Catholic responses) while also sharply critiquing Kant (here unlike Catholic liberalism or modernism).

When von Balthasar explicitly mentions Kant in *Seeing the Form*, he makes both positive and negative observations. Of the three positive observations, the first comes when von Balthasar is explaining that "as a totality of spirit and body, man must make himself into God's mirror and seek to attain to that transcendence and radiance that must be found in the world's substance if it is indeed God's image and likeness—his word and gesture, action and drama."[76] In this sense, the human being is a form that, whether more or less perfectly, reflects analogously the form of the Creator. The human spirit does this through the human body. Von Balthasar notes that Friedrich Schiller, who

74. Ibid.
75. Ibid.
76. Von Balthasar, *Seeing the Form*, 22.

borrows from Kant, describes "the spirit's splendour in the beauty of form."[77] Later, von Balthasar repeats this point in a more detailed fashion. He states that "the soul manifests itself in the body in various degrees of relationship which Kant and Schiller have described in a strict sense as beauty and as 'the sublime' in the sense of gracefulness and dignity."[78] Lastly, von Balthasar approvingly cites Kant's view that the beautiful is marked by "disinterestedness" in the sense that we cannot control it or use it for our own purposes, although at the same time he remarks that Kant presents this position "somewhat misleadingly."[79]

The other explicit references to Kant in *Seeing the Form* are negative. Von Balthasar points out that Johann Georg Hamann, whose work von Balthasar greatly admires, writes in opposition to Kant.[80] Similarly, the romantic thinker Johann Gottfried Herder receives praise for standing against Kant's dry "formalism."[81] According to von Balthasar, such formalism contributes to a split between existential faith and historical reason, since for "Kantian formalism ... nothing exists but the 'material' of the senses which is then ordered and assimilated by categorical forms or by ideas."[82] Von Balthasar faults even Rousselot, who is one of the heroes of *Seeing the Form*, for remaining "too close to the Kantianism he is trying to surpass," inasmuch as Rousselot speaks of "signs" rather than "form," and overestimates (with regard to faith's synthetic knowledge) "the active-constructive synthetic power ... to the detriment of God's own power, which expresses and imposes itself in the historical witness."[83]

Seeing the Form challenges Kant's limitations in three overarching ways. First, von Balthasar continually insists upon theo-

---

77. Ibid.
78. Ibid., 118.
79. Ibid., 152.
80. See ibid., 81.
81. Ibid., 84.
82. Ibid., 174–75.
83. Ibid., 177.

centrism, the absolute priority of God and of divine action. Second, he insists that we can know (without exhausting) the *esse* of beings, rather than being able only to know the *appearances* of beings in our own concepts or categories. Third, he insists upon the priority of Christ and the Holy Spirit in every Christian reality, rather than seeing Christianity as fundamentally arising from human religious impulses and inventions. In all three of these ways, his account of the "seeing the form" distances itself sharply from Kant. Let me now turn to my section-by-section survey of von Balthasar's *Seeing the Form*.

Von Balthasar's Introductory Reflections

In *Seeing the Form*, von Balthasar begins by observing that he wishes to "[confront] the whole truth—not only man's truth and that of the world, but the truth of a God who bestows himself on man, the truth not only of the historical Gospel and of the Church that preserves it, but the truth of the growing Kingdom of God."[84] This is no small task! To confront the whole truth, von Balthasar argues that it is beneficial to begin with beauty. This is because truth is not merely an abstraction but rather "a transcendental property of Being" and "the living bond between God and the world."[85] The transcendentals confront us with the full dimensions of the whole of Being, and beauty has a particularly important role because it helps us to retain and to integrate the true and the good. In Western culture, which has become an economically and politically focused "world of interests," beauty has been neglected and ignored—even by Christianity—due to the fact that beauty is intrinsically "disinterested."[86] Here we see a Kantian note guiding von Balthasar's discussion from the outset, mingled with patristic-medieval notes that, with regard to the transcendentals and to history, explode Kant's immanent horizon.

84. Ibid., 17.
85. Ibid., 18.
86. Ibid.

Without beauty, von Balthasar argues, Christianity withers away. Prayer and love require that we perceive the world as "penetrated by God's light" rather than simply as mere matter.[87] Without recognizing beings as beautiful, we cannot truly value them as good or appreciate them as true, and the lure of evil becomes strong. Stripped of its transcendental beauty, existence seems to lack depth and sacred mystery; even though the existence of anything is wondrous, we no longer treat it with wonder. Furthermore, in the beautiful thing, we see a "uniting" of diverse aspects within "the one thing which now manifests and expresses itself," joined by a free self-expression or self-outpouring.[88] Von Balthasar argues that the unity of diverse aspects is crucial: for example, body and soul are not divided in the one human being. He criticizes Kant and all others who give us the false problem of "how the soul can break out of its interiority and enter the so-called 'exterior world'."[89]

In speaking about beauty, von Balthasar says, it is necessary to speak about "form" (German: *Gestalt*), figure, and shape. The Latin word for beautiful (*formosus*) derives from the Latin word for shape (*forma*). We also speak of "splendour." Von Balthasar states that "we are confronted simultaneously with both the figure and that which shines forth from the figure."[90] At the same time, nothing finite can generate its own form or splendor or overcome the seeming transience of both. Von Balthasar rejects any notion of Kantian autonomy or self-sufficiency: "Man must realize that he is not lord over himself. Neither does he rule his own being in freedom so as to confer form upon himself, nor is he free in his communication. As body, man is a being whose condition it is always to be communicated."[91] Humans are not the source of Being or Beauty but its image, expression, response,

87. Ibid., 19.
88. Ibid., 20.
89. Ibid., 21.
90. Ibid., 20.
91. Ibid., 21.

mirror. The body-soul "form" that we are is conferred by Another, who grounds our freedom. Here von Balthasar refers to Schiller's account, indebted to Kant, of the way in which body and spirit are related in youth and in age, as well as of the way in which the aesthetic and the ethical are related.[92] Von Balthasar also cites Origen's insistence upon the unity of the moral and the spiritual meanings of divine revelation. There is no "beauty" or "form" that stands outside the ethical; thus, it is possible for us to besmirch our spiritual beauty.

Von Balthasar describes the human "form" not only in terms of body-soul unity but also in terms of a freely chosen and "uniquely personal" pattern of life.[93] To choose our pattern of life (our "form") well, however, we need eyes that can perceive the truth and goodness of life. We need "a vision for wholeness."[94] But in contemporary culture, we do not recognize paths to human wholeness; instead, life seems fragmentary and formless, destructive of real dignity. To find the now concealed unity, therefore, we need the eyes to perceive "primal form" once again.[95] This primal form is the unchanging ground of the unity of all phenomena, and indeed it is none other than divine (self-surrendering) love.

Von Balthasar describes this primal form as "a form which is identical with existence, a form beyond 'open' and 'closed', beyond 'I' and 'Thou' (since it, and it alone, encompasses both), a form which is even beyond autonomy and heteronomy since it unites God and man in an unimaginable intimacy."[96] He suggests that in today's culture, living as the "Gospel's Humiliated Fool"—in whose marred and despised visage love is hidden—may be our only path back to our true "form," and thus may be the

92. Recall Kant's insistence that "the beautiful is the symbol of the morally good" (Kant, *Critique of Judgement*, 180).
93. Von Balthasar, *Seeing the Form*, 24.
94. Ibid., 25.
95. Ibid.
96. Ibid.

path that Christians must follow as despised members of the modern world. Those who are opened by grace to follow this path of humiliation today are the ones who "behold the primal form of man-in-existence" and who in fact, despite their lowly place, "bear the weight of the whole on their shoulders."[97]

Von Balthasar unfolds his understanding of Christian life by means of the example of marriage, which provides a stable "form" into which the man and woman grow, indeed a form that (if it is not tossed aside) has the power to compel such growth. The "form" does not enslave but liberates: "All fruitfulness, all freedom is discovered within the form itself."[98] Likewise, the Christian life is a "form," given by God as "a part of the miracle of the forgiveness of sins, of justification, of holiness."[99] The priority and action are on the side of Christ and the Holy Spirit. Von Balthasar emphasizes that "the Christian will realise his mission only if he truly *becomes* this form which has been willed and instituted by Christ," a form that possesses "radiant beauty" and "is the most beautiful thing that may be found in the human realm."[100]

On this basis, von Balthasar states that the purpose of his *Theological Aesthetics* is to explore "the form of divine revelation in salvation-history, leading to Christ and deriving from him."[101] To see this form, we need to have received supernatural illumination (the eyes of faith), but we also need to have sharpened our natural eyes, since, rather than destroying nature, "God's Incarnation perfects the whole ontology and aesthetics of created Being."[102] As the incarnate Word, Jesus expresses God, whom Jesus is, but at the same time Jesus expresses the Father, whom Jesus is not. This combination of identity and difference,

97. Ibid., 26.
98. Ibid., 27.
99. Ibid., 28.
100. Ibid.
101. Ibid., 29.
102. Ibid.

von Balthasar says, "stands as the fountainhead of the Christian aesthetic, and therefore of all aesthetics."[103] Additionally, the promise-fulfillment relationship of Christ to the preceding history of salvation and to the whole cosmos indicates that in Christ we find the unity of the multidimensional "sub-forms" that preceded him.

Illumined in their eyes and in their pens by the Holy Spirit, the inspired authors conveyed "the Spirit's testimony concerning the Word, which springs from an indissoluble bond and marriage between the Spirit and those eyewitnesses who were originally invited and admitted to the vision"—with the result that scripture's testimony possesses "an inner form which is canonical simply by being such a form, and for this reason we can 'go behind' this form only at the risk of losing both image and Spirit conjointly."[104] The "form" of Jesus Christ and the form of Christ as expressed in the testimony of scripture are the same, which is why historical methods that break up or dissect this form never are able to "recapture the living totality of form."[105] For the interpretation of scripture to proceed in the same Spirit in which it was written, we must return to scripture's actual text, treating it along the lines of an "aesthetic contemplation that steadily and patiently beholds those forms which either nature or art offers to its view."[106] Indeed, if the "form" of Christ never comes into view, then there will be no way for "the ray of the Unconditional" to break "through, casting a person down to adoration and transforming him into a believer and a follower."[107]

Contemplating the beauty of the form of Christ, then, we see in it the unchanging ground of the unity of all phenomena (supernatural and natural); we see in it the perfection of the "ethical"; and we see in it the "purposiveness" of the free self-surrendering

103. Ibid.
104. Ibid., 31.
105. Ibid.
106. Ibid., 32.
107. Ibid., 33.

love that stands at the heart of God and all creation. Kant's positive contributions are present in all three of these aspects.

Aesthetic Theology versus Theological Aesthetics

Von Balthasar next addresses the question of the relationship of "God's revelation with its own form" to "this-worldly aesthetics."[108] There is an analogy, but the former must not be subordinated to the latter. While affirming a "theological aesthetics," von Balthasar warns strongly and at length against an "aesthetic theology."[109] For "theological aesthetics," says von Balthasar, much depends upon whether we affirm with the Fathers and medievals that beauty is a transcendental, thereby rooted in the doctrine of God, so that all shines with the splendor of the divine light. Theological aesthetics, however, must always keep in mind the radical distinction between "the transcendental beauty of revelation" and "inner-worldly natural beauty."[110]

Von Balthasar devotes attention to Protestant and Catholic efforts to eliminate aesthetics from theology, due to fear of a human- and world-centered theology (an "aesthetic theology") and to the desire to underscore the transcendent inbreaking of God's Word. As he says, "it appeared to Luther that the Death-and-Resurrection dialectic of the Christ-event had been replaced by the non-dialectical schemata of Neo-Platonic aesthetic metaphysics."[111] By and large, von Balthasar praises Luther's emphasis on God's free sovereignty in creation and grace, on Christ's descent into Godforsakenness for our salvation (to which the necessary response is trust), and on the hiddenness of God, especially in Christ's taking on of sin and acting through the power of weakness. Yet, von Balthasar observes, for Luther every intelligible "form," with respect to divine revelation, "must

---

108. Ibid., 37.
109. Ibid., 38.
110. Ibid., 41.
111. Ibid., 45.

disintegrate in the face of the 'contradiction', the concealment of everything divine under its opposite, the concealment, that is, of all proportions and analogies between God and man in dialectic."[112] Von Balthasar also examines Søren Kierkegaard's rejection of aesthetics due to its resurgence in liberal theology. Among Protestant theologians, the credit for restoring aesthetics to its proper place goes to Karl Barth, who recognizes the importance of contemplating God's glory and perceiving the light and "*real form* of God's objective act of revelation."[113] For Barth, God is Beauty (not least in his unity of opposites), and Barth powerfully responds to the unique form of God's glory, which is found in the beauty of the crucified Christ.[114] Von Balthasar considers that the key to the whole problem is recognizing that beauty is a transcendental, so that "its definition must be derived from God himself" and therefore from God's "self-revelation in history and in the Incarnation."[115]

In modern Catholic theology, influenced by modern philosophy that has denied the transcendentals and relegated theology to the study of historical facts, theological aesthetics has similarly been rejected. Von Balthasar urges that when fundamental theology, biblical studies, and even dogmatic and moral theology become simply or primarily domains of historical study, the connection with God becomes obscured, since God exceeds the empirical bounds of the historical method.[116] Once faith's graced

112. Ibid., 48.

113. Ibid., 53.

114. Von Balthasar also provides a lengthy discussion of Gerhard Nebel's theological aesthetics in Nebel's *Das Ereignis des Schönen* (Stuttgart: Klett, 1953). Toward the end of this discussion, von Balthasar concludes that "from the standpoint of Protestantism, beauty has to be transferred wholly to the sphere of event. For from the Protestant perspective, any kind of regularity, of immanence which is seen as perduring, inherent *qualitas*, as Being-in-repose, as *habitus*, as something that can be manipulated, is already by that fact identified with demonic corruption" (Von Balthasar, *Seeing the Form*, 67).

115. Von Balthasar, *Seeing the Form*, 69.

116. See ibid., 75. He states, "True theology begins only at the point where 'exact historical science' passes over into the science of faith proper" (ibid.). Note, however,

participation "in the intuitive saving knowledge of God himself and of the Church" is eliminated, no theological aesthetics is possible, because one has excised "the vision of the distinctively theological 'form' and its specific beauty."[117]

Von Balthasar seeks to clarify with precision what he means by "aesthetic theology," which is the opposite of true theological aesthetics and which therefore he strongly rejects. One particularly common kind of aesthetic theology consists in the effort to understand the whole of scripture as artistic or poetic narrative. Yet, von Balthasar does not wish to deny that there is "a genuine relationship between theological beauty and the beauty of the world."[118] He takes the Lutheran Johann Georg Hamann as a model of how to set forth such a relationship, in which "the total aspiration of worldly and pagan beauty is fulfilled while all glory is at the same time given to God in Jesus Christ."[119] For Hamann, God's glory and beauty are to be found in his *kenosis*, his self-surrendering love that leads him to come to us in the utter humility of the cross, so as to produce the unity of all (fallen) things in the (holy) Christ. But due to his opaque writing style, Hamann was not understood by his contemporaries, even by his student Johann Gottfried Herder.

While correctly critiquing Kant's formalism, Herder unfortunately produced an exemplification of aesthetic theology. For Herder, poetry and theology are one, the Bible being the purest and most noble form of poetry and Christ the purest Image. It is inevitable that such theology begins with human construction and is centered upon the human; the Bible is simply the communication of our highest human possibilities. The result is that Christianity is not God breaking into history through his free in-

---

his clarification: "The point here is not that the *habitus acquisitus scientiae* ought to be left behind and transcended by a *habitus infusus* and the *donum Spiritus*. The point is that these latter ought to be allowed to develop and unfold in the very midst of the most stringent scientific form" (ibid., 78).

117. Ibid., 76.
118. Ibid., 80.
119. Ibid., 80–81.

carnation and redeeming and glorifying fallen humankind, but rather Christianity is humankind ascending to the pinnacle and fulfillment of its own resources. The free divine descent of God's Word and Spirit to elevate humankind far beyond what created resources could attain becomes, in Herder, the free ascent of nature and culture to their highest possible points, so that Christianity becomes merely an optimistic humanism.

Another exemplar of aesthetic theology is the Catholic apologist René de Chateaubriand. Chateaubriand contrasts the Catholicism of dogma, ethics, and institution with the effects of Catholicism upon culture and the arts. He argues that the fact that Catholicism has produced the most beautiful cultural artifacts indicates that Catholicism is true. He likewise finds that Catholic dogma corresponds precisely to what human nature needs, as do the beautiful and inspiring forms taken by Catholic liturgy and life. In this approach, everything is measured by this-worldly form, this-worldly nature. This immanentism, insufficiently aware of the transcendence of God and the truly radical inbreaking of God's love for us in Christ, is an aesthetic theology.[120]

In critiquing aesthetic theology, of course, von Balthasar is critiquing one of the main theological ways of responding to Kantian immanentism—Kant's view that we can have no knowledge of God other than "symbolic" knowledge and that our knowledge of the world is solely a knowledge of the phenomena in our concepts. In general, aesthetic theology was encouraged by the Romantic reaction to Kant.

Von Balthasar chooses as a Catholic ally for his theological aesthetics Matthias Joseph Scheeben, who "did us the service of replacing the 'aesthetic theology' of Romanticism with the outlines of a methodologically founded 'theological aesthetics'."[121] Scheeben departed from aesthetic theology by insisting upon the

---

120. Von Balthasar also gives extensive attention to the Catholic theologian Alois Gügler as an exemplar of Romantic aesthetic theology.
    121. Ibid., 105.

utter transcendence of grace vis-à-vis created nature. He rejoiced
in the beauty and glories of the mysteries of grace, above all the
incarnation and cross, which reveal God's humility and fiery
love. For Scheeben, von Balthasar says, the mysteries of grace
are "the glories of God himself ... infinitely superior and more
sublime (*erhaben*) than natural beauty and dignity."[122] Scheeben celebrated the divinely willed marriage of nature and grace
in and through Christ, a marriage befitting the intra-Trinitarian
self-outpouring of the divine Persons. The only problem in
Scheeben's theological aesthetics, for von Balthasar, is that it remains somewhat ahistorical in execution, especially with regard
to its account of the impact of sin. On this view, Scheeben did not
fully grasp the depth of humility and humiliation to which Christ
descends on the cross, a depth of humility that fully reveals the
beauty of Christ's supreme form of self-surrender.

In light of these sources, von Balthasar sets forth the prin-
cipal elements that he thinks should belong to a renewed theological aesthetics. First, we need to appreciate that the beautiful
involves form (*Gestalt*) and splendor, or species and light. As
such, the beautiful is present in created things, though it is present according to the mode of a transcendental that points analogously to divine beauty. From Kant (and Schiller), von Balthasar
takes the view that the soul manifests itself through the body
in beautiful and sublime ways; and he also takes from Kant the
connection of the beautiful with the ethical (due, however, to a
profoundly different understanding of Being than Kant possesses). Von Balthasar states, "the appearance of the form, as revelation of the depths, is an indissoluble union of two things. It is
the real presence of the depths, of the whole of reality, *and* it is a
real pointing beyond itself to these depths."[123] Each "form," if we
properly contemplate it, reveals the whole, due to "its unity with

122. Ibid., 107.
123. Ibid., 118.

the depths that make their appearance in it."[124] The "depths" here refers to the whole of Being, and thus analogously refers to the triune God, who as the Creator of finite Being reveals himself through it. Here von Balthasar's theological deployment of the notion of transcendental apperception is at work.

The ultimate theophany, of course, is Christ, the incarnate Word. When we see Christ with eyes enlightened by grace, we see his beauty and we see the splendor of divine self-surrendering love that pours forth from his form. This beauty and splendor cannot "be equated with the other kinds of aesthetic radiance which we encounter in the world," but as the revelation of God's love it is intelligible to us, and it converts us in rapturous joy.[125] At the root of our ascending movement is God's descending kenosis, filled with self-surrendering divine Eros for his creatures whom he elevates beyond their natural capacities. Our human desire for beauty is fulfilled by our graced perception of the embodied self-surrendering love, or "form," of Christ. On these grounds—and against all aesthetic theology—von Balthasar argues that "just as we can never attain to the living God in any way except through his Son become man ... so, too, we ought never to speak of God's beauty without reference to the form and manner of appearing which he exhibits in salvation-history."[126] We cannot simply deduce God's beauty from the transcendentals, from the harmony of his divine attributes, or from the Trinitarian relations.

Von Balthasar proposes two inseparable steps that should be present in any theological aesthetics. The first step is the "theory of vision," or "'aesthetics' in the Kantian sense as a theory about the perception of the form."[127] This step, whose province is fundamental theology, focuses on the evidence of God's descending

124. Ibid., 119.
125. Ibid., 120.
126. Ibid., 124.
127. Ibid., 125.

in the visible form of Christ and on the Spirit who illumines our eyes. The second step is a "theory of rapture."[128] The province of this step is dogmatic theology, and it has to do with the incarnation of the Word and the graced elevation of human beings to share in God's life through Christ and the Spirit. With regard to the two steps, von Balthasar speaks of a "double and reciprocal *ekstasis*," or self-surrendering in love, namely, on the part of God and on the part of human beings.

The Light of Faith

Von Balthasar devotes eighty dense pages to analyzing the light of faith. He begins by noting that faith cannot be reduced to a simple act of the believing subject but rather is dependent on God's revelation and on the grace of the Holy Spirit. God makes himself known, both in Israel (the Old Testament) and in the New Testament. Faith is an "act of total self-surrender" that responds to God's making himself known through God's act of total self-surrender.[129] Knowledge of God in faith is not merely something that leads us to faith; it stays with us as continually nourishing us and pulling us further toward the divine light. Part of von Balthasar's point here is that both the liberal denigration of the place of knowledge in faith and the neo-scholastic "disincarnating of the act of faith from the real context of a man's life and spiritual development in which he encounters God" are a mistake.[130] Von Balthasar also provides an account of the authority on which the content of faith is believed: it is the authority of the glory of God's self-revelation and the light of divine Reason (Logos), and so it is only secondarily the authority of the church that faithfully mediates and proclaims the Gospel.

Von Balthasar discusses the relationship of biblical revelation to philosophy and myth; the self-revelation of God ful-

---

128. Ibid.
129. Ibid., 133.
130. Ibid., 139.

fills the latter two but cannot be deduced from them. He warns against dividing theology and philosophy in such a way that philosophy becomes a "formalism" (as in Kant) that no longer "can strive for the unconditionally Ultimate, True, Good, and Beautiful."[131] He argues that the form of revelation can be discerned by focusing on its historical contingencies, its words and signs known through the light of faith, or else by focusing on God's eternal truth that illumines everything ("the inwardness of absolute Being, the mystery of its life and love").[132]

Building upon Kant's point about the disinterestedness of the beautiful, von Balthasar explains that the attitude of faith is prepared for by "the quality of 'being-in-itself' which belongs to the beautiful, the demand the beautiful itself makes to be allowed to be what it is, the demand, therefore, that we renounce our attempts to control and manipulate it."[133] When Christ manifests himself, we cannot truly know his unique form if we do not perceive his divinity shining through his humanity, the infinite in the finite. We must receive him as one who possesses "a divine depth transcending all worldly nature," and we can do this only by God's grace.[134] Philosophy itself, however, prepares for this manifestation in the sense that—contra Kant, but extending Kant's investigation of transcendental apperception—true philosophical thinking discovers in itself "the opening up of infinity" as well as the "rapture" of perceiving "the fulness of this fountain which bestows itself."[135] Contra Kant, von Balthasar insists that "the spirit's horizon is not confined to worldly being (*ens univocum*), but extends to absolute Being (*ens analogum*), and only in this light can it think, will, and love."[136]

Von Balthasar thinks that there is a philosophical "faith,"

131. Ibid., 144.
132. Ibid., 148.
133. Ibid., 153.
134. Ibid., 154.
135. Ibid., 158.
136. Ibid.; cf. ibid., 164.

rooted in "love's gravitational pull" or "the gravitational pull of Being itself," that prepares for supernatural faith.[137] In the latter, Being is revealed concretely as self-surrendering love and humility, in a manner that fulfills and far exceeds the philosophic dynamism. For theology truly to be theology, it must arise from a real participation in this light of love, which builds upon and elevates the natural light of reason (itself an "openness to the light of Being").[138] We must become proportioned to "the dynamic identity of the Trinitarian light."[139] On this view, using Kantian terms, faith for von Balthasar is "an experiential apperception by the whole person," in union with the pure and unchanging ground of the unity of all things—and therefore constituted by "an ever more total surrender" and "ever more radical abandonment" to the triune God who is infinite self-surrendering love.[140]

In accord with this fulfillment of "apperception" by supernatural faith, von Balthasar speaks again in Kantian terms—but in a way that explodes Kant's immanentism—of the "religious *a priori*."[141] For von Balthasar, this ultimate a priori ground is not consciousness as such but rather consciousness's "ability to understand all existents in the light of Being, which is analogous to and points to God."[142] Moreover, for von Balthasar, the elevation of this a priori ground by grace is something that is offered to all humans and therefore is something that all humans have the choice of accepting or rejecting. In this context, however, von Balthasar warns against the sinful obscuring of "the expressive form of God's genuine light."[143] At issue, he thinks, is whether people in non-Christian religions choose to stand "in an attitude of pure self-surrender and abandonment to God" rath-

---

137. Ibid., 162. Von Balthasar adds, "It is not that we demand grace in virtue of our peculiar dynamism; it is grace which both claims and expropriates us" (ibid.).

138. Ibid., 165.

139. Ibid.

140. Ibid., 167.

141. Ibid.

142. Ibid.

143. Ibid., 169.

er than cleaving to some form of self-redemption by mastering certain techniques.[144] Using Kantian language to go far beyond Kant, von Balthasar describes the world as a realm of "appearances" and notes that it is only God who can provide the unity of the world's "total configuration," a unity of forms that is found concretely and historically in Christ as the center point of divine revelation.[145] Christ is the "measure, both in judgment and in redemption, of all other religious forms in mankind."[146]

Von Balthasar argues that finite yearning for the infinite can be understood only when the mystery of the Trinity is revealed in Christ. In the "form of Christ," he argues, "here and only here a form becomes visible in which everything makes sense for the light that beholds it."[147] Knowing the true form of Christ requires the light of faith, but it is not irrational. God's artistry has set forth the entire form of salvation history, and the light of faith enables the person to recognize its rightness, its beauty. What this form is—manifested fully in Christ—is nothing less than "the revelation of the inner depth of God," and thus it goes beyond what we can conceptualize.[148] Humans could not have invented this salvation-historical form, and this is why breaking down the form historical-critically into bits and pieces poses a problem. Von Balthasar links such dissection to "Kantian formalism, for which nothing exist but the 'material' of the senses which is then ordered and assimilated by categorical forms or by ideas."[149]

Against Kantian formalism, von Balthasar puts forward the insights of Pierre Rousselot, who drew upon Thomas Aquinas, Maurice Blondel, and John Henry Newman. Indebted to Kant's

144. Ibid., 170.
145. Ibid.
146. Ibid., 171.
147. Ibid.
148. Ibid., 172. Recall that for Kant, the faculty of aesthetic judgment is "a faculty of judging of forms without the aid of concepts, and of finding, in the mere judging of them, a delight that we at the same time make into a rule for everyone" (Kant, *Critique of Judgement*, 129).
149. Von Balthasar, *Seeing the Form*, 174–75.

quest for an a priori ground of the unity of appearances, while at the same time firmly rejecting Kant's immanentism, Rousselot held that the human spirit "must include in anticipatory fashion that point of convergence which makes the signs comprehensible."[150] This "point of unity," however, cannot be found "in the realm of the natural."[151] The rational quest for the a priori ground of the unity of appearances leads the human spirit upward to the point where the spirit recognizes that this ground can only be a supernatural one. The light of reason leads to the light of faith, which alone can synthetically perceive the unity and meaning of the "signs" or appearances.

Von Balthasar admits that "Rousselot, in his manner of expression and thought-habits, still remains too close to the Kantianism he is trying to surpass."[152] Rousselot rightly identifies the dynamic yearning of our spirit for fulfillment in the infinite, and von Balthasar holds that Rousselot is also correct that "the subjective conditions of the possibility of such illumination can be described in Kantian categories."[153] But von Balthasar thinks that somewhat lacking in Rousselot's work is an emphasis on God's power in his concrete descending in the Person of Jesus. Von Balthasar recognizes that when the subjective light of faith is exaggerated (beyond what Rousselot does), it will lead to modernism, for which interiority is everything. He neatly defines "modernism," or Catholic liberalism: "For modernism, dogmas are but crystallised forms of the existential faith-relationship to God, forms of vital religious intuitions and needs, valid as long as they foster the existential reality, but harmful once the life has gone out of them and they have stiffened into dead formulae."[154] Modernism's fundamentally Kantian perspective on dogma finds in the subject (the human being's interiority) the existential truth

150. Ibid., 175.
151. Ibid.
152. Ibid., 176.
153. Ibid., 177.
154. Ibid.

of dogma, whereas in fact dogma's existential truth is to be found in the realities to which it testifies.

Von Balthasar suggests that attending to the progress of the aesthetic act can be helpful at this stage. The aesthetic act begins with an assortment of objects generally deemed beautiful, to which the young person will respond with enthusiasm. Gradually, with time, the young person will learn discernment. In philosophy, too, the young person will begin with an enthusiastic desire for "totality of vision" and will need to "be trained in the disciplined contemplation of the Being of existents."[155] The same progress, then, happens in the realm of faith. We begin with an a priori desire for God, but we must seek with effort "the correct form" of what we are to believe, and we will find this form only outside ourselves, in God's own action in history (in the particular historical form of Christ, "*the* definitive and determinant form of God in the world") and through a supernatural interior light that we cannot give ourselves but that Christ gives us.[156] Ultimately, what is required is a graced self-surrender to Christ, through the power of Christ who has revealed the self-surrendering triune God to us.

Christ, of course, presents himself not as a mere teacher of wisdom but as wisdom itself, present in our midst. This wisdom is the form of divine revelation. Von Balthasar argues that Christ's "form" can be perceived as a unity, even though it is filled with seeming contradictions, such as "the distance of the man, the nearness and unity of the Son; the relationship between lord and servant, exaltation and humiliation: of exaltation in humiliation and humility in exaltation."[157] As we contemplate Christ, we realize that these seeming contradictions or tensions are in fact in the most profound balance and unity. We will find no inconsistency whatsoever in this form, no "insufficiency" or

155. Ibid., 179.
156. Ibid., 179, 182.
157. Ibid., 188.

"objective structural error which would bring to nought his claim to being the revealer of the Father."[158] Christ's form is the fulfillment and perfection of the covenant-form, through his "boundless self-surrender" in love.[159]

In Christ, we are called to this same self-surrender in love, to "the beatific shudder of self-surrender."[160] Indeed, faith-filled embrace of the form of Christ reveals to us that absolute Being is love and that humans have been created to be "elevated and incorporated into the Trinity's Being-as-Love."[161] The height of what Christ reveals is the intensely, infinitely personal self-surrender in love that is the Trinity. Reflecting at length upon the various elements of "Christ's total form," including his "whole interior life-form," von Balthasar states that "the trinitarian aspect alone encompasses every event of salvation-history as its essential ground and goal."[162] From this perspective, he explores prophecy, Christ's miracles, the unity of the Old and New Testaments in "the total form of revelation," and the relationship of dogma and God's Word.[163] Everything finds its pure and unchanging ground of unity in the glorious and radiant "act of the divine Eros which goes out of itself in order to become man and die on the Cross for the world."[164]

The Experience of Faith

In a section comprising over two hundred pages, von Balthasar takes up the topic of the experience of faith. His main point is that the interior act of faith, as a response to the beauty of Christ, "requires the reaction of the whole man" rather than a single, isolated act of the mind or will.[165] In faith, the whole of our ex-

158. Ibid., 189.
159. Ibid., 191.
160. Ibid., 193.
161. Ibid.
162. Ibid., 198, 203.
163. Ibid., 208.
164. Ibid., 216–17.
165. Ibid., 220.

istence must be attuned and configured to the self-surrendering love that characterizes the Trinity as revealed in Christ. This does not mean that faith should direct our attention to the experience of the believer. Rather, since "faith is the freely given participation in the perfect covenant-fidelity of Jesus Christ," in faith "I am made open and dispossessed of self."[166] As an "existence of self-surrender" (in and through Christ's perfect self-surrender), faith involves not self-congratulation but self-emptying in love of God and neighbor.[167] Faith is other-directed. True Christian experience consists in the experience of self-surrendering love, a weakness through which God's strength becomes manifest (see 2 Corinthians 12). Faith, when truly possessed, means the configuration of the whole person to the form of Christ by the Holy Spirit. As von Balthasar puts it, therefore, what Christians share "can be called 'faith', but it can also be called 'possession of the Spirit', and, because the Spirit is the Spirit of God and of Christ, it can also be called 'love'."[168]

Von Balthasar observes that this love represents an aesthetic. In the form of Christ, freely pouring himself out in love, we see the intradivine self-emptying love. Christ reveals "the pure light of divine love pouring itself out: in Christ the *species* and the *lumen* coincide—as manifest, personal love."[169] The aesthetic judgment unites the particular and the universal. Nothing accomplishes this union more perfectly than the form of Christ. For von Balthasar, the evangelist John understands "faith" as "a living handing over of self to God," and "such self-surrender to the incarnate Beloved is simply one and the same thing as love."[170] Christ's form and the form of faith are beautiful because they radiate the intradivine form of self-surrendering love—the form that is the pure and unchanging ground for the unity of

166. Ibid., 224.
167. Ibid., 225.
168. Ibid., 230.
169. Ibid., 235.
170. Ibid., 236.

all appearances and all nature. Everything shines, ontologically at least, with the reflection of this beautiful form of divine self-surrendering love.

When we see this form, the aesthetic and the ethical are inseparable (as in Kant). Von Balthasar explains that "in John the act of continual contemplation of the Beloved is inextricably an 'aesthetic' and an 'ethical' act: to see him as he *is* not only presupposes the readiness to renounce everything of one's own, but actually requires such readiness at every instant."[171] The form of Christ is self-surrendering love; truly "seeing" this form in faith means that we are configured to self-surrendering love, to the form of Christ (and indeed to the form of all divine and created reality, once we have the eyes to see it properly). From this perspective, "truth" is in fact identical with "love," since "truth" consists likewise "in the unconditional abandonment of what is one's own for the sake of the Beloved."[172]

Speaking about Christian experience, von Balthasar states that it is found where persons have been configured to the form of Christ's self-surrendering love: it is found in "sacrificial self-abandonment," since "the really beautiful shines from the place where the real has itself acquired form."[173] Christian experience is measured not by the world's standards but by Christ. We know that we have had Christian experience when we experience transformation. This transformation comes from God and configures us to the form of Christ, through "the believer's offering of himself to God and the impressing of the Christ-form by God upon the believer."[174]

Von Balthasar explains what is meant by being attuned to Christ, being a person in whom Christ lives, and being a "member" of Christ's body the church. It involves sharing, through the

171. Ibid.
172. Ibid., 237.
173. Ibid., 236, 239.
174. Ibid., 242.

Spirit, in the "form of the divine love" that is found "in the trans-figuring whirlpool of love of the mystery of the divine expression which lies between Father and Son, Ground and Image."[175] This means that we give ourselves up entirely in love, not in order to find ourselves approved in the church but in order simply to be at the disposal of our self-surrendering Lord. In this regard von Balthasar notes that, of course, the self-surrendering of the divine Persons "is wholly incomparable" to the analogous hu-man self-surrendering in faith and love.[176] On earth, the path of self-surrendering in love will be, as Christ exemplifies and promises, one of suffering, which forms the heart of Christian experience. At some length, he treats this path as described in scripture, in the Eastern patristic tradition culminating in Max-imus the Confessor, and in the medieval West culminating in Aquinas's theology of the gifts of the Holy Spirit and in Ignatius of Loyola's *Spiritual Exercises.*

Von Balthasar warns against the desire to see God more clear-ly than we see him in Christ. In Christ, God has made himself definitively perceivable; there is no beatific vision unmediated by the humanity of Christ. God's perceivable form in Christ ful-fills the entirety of God's revelation in history. Von Balthasar de-scribes the experience of the apostles as "archetypal."[177] Against all attempts to spiritualize God's perceivable form, perceiving this form in fact involves corporeal seeing, hearing, and touch-ing. And God freely makes this possible. As von Balthasar puts it (with the apostolic experience in view), "the truly beautiful is not magically 'conjured up' from man's emotive states, but, rather, surrenders itself on its own initiative with a graciousness that man cannot grasp."[178] In his sensory form (as presented in what von Balthasar calls "archetypal Biblical aesthetics"), God comes

175. Ibid., 255.
176. Ibid., 258.
177. Ibid., 309.
178. Ibid., 313.

to us in Christ in a surpassingly rich way, even as we yearn for more because we are presently too weak to take it all in.[179]

Von Balthasar also discusses Jesus' experience of God, which he argues "furnishes the form that conditions all other experiences, both before and after it."[180] It is not a feeling or an intuition of God; rather, it is ultimately a mission consciousness, the mission of the very expression (Word) of the Father. It is a self-emptying that is the human expression of the divine Son's glorious humility, and thus the human expression of the Father, since the Son images the Father. Jesus knows himself to be entirely one sent for this mission, indeed sent to *be* this mission. Von Balthasar reasons that Jesus "understands even his genuinely human experience of God as an expression and function of his divine person."[181] In his mission, his going forth from the Father to surrender himself in love for the sake of the world, he expresses both the Father's divine self-surrendering and his own personal distinction from the Father. Von Balthasar concludes that those who bear witness to Jesus and who share in his human experience of God can do so only by imitating and participating in his mission, in order to ascend with him to the Father.

Von Balthasar devotes attention to the Old Testament experience of God and to the Virgin Mary's distinctive experience, as well as to the apostles' experience (including Paul's). Especially with regard to Mary and the apostles, he sees things in terms of archetypal vocations or ways of being the church that function as "the very foundation of the life-form of believing man."[182] These vocations are embodied by Peter, Paul, Mary, and John (the beloved disciple). For my purposes, I can pass over this extensive discussion, which is focused on the way that life in Christ involves fleshly or incarnational experience of Christ's glory. Von

179. Ibid., 320.
180. Ibid., 322.
181. Ibid., 328.
182. Ibid., 364.

Balthasar also offers an extensive analysis here of the "spiritual senses."[183] His point is that everything spiritual in Christianity is always mediated by the physical and the historically concrete.

The section on Christian experience concludes with a discussion of the relationship of the senses and spirit in Christian anthropology, in which, with Barth, von Balthasar makes clear that "the split between the senses and the spirit rests on sin."[184] He does this also in dialogue with Romano Guardini, Gustav Siewerth, and Paul Claudel, each of whom underscores the intrinsic place of our senses in the spiritual life. This is important for von Balthasar because our seeing of the form of Christ is never, even after Christ's ascension, merely a matter of the spirit. Von Balthasar sums up by noting that when, in the incarnation, "flesh speaks to flesh," Christ's "flesh encounters man as God's *exinanitio* or 'self-emptying'"—the form of self-surrender in love.[185]

The revelation of the form of Christ brings about the "end" of divine revelation (with the death of the last apostle), but the activity of this revealed form—the Trinitarian form of divine self-surrendering love—continues with even greater intensity, since the Holy Spirit brings out the fullness of this revealed form through the church. Von Balthasar insists that the "Spirit is free to make use also of the Biblical modes of archetypal experience in order to demonstrate in the Church of all centuries the continual reality of revelation—not as something past, but as something present."[186] He argues that participation in the biblical modes of archetypal Christian experience—Peter, Paul, Mary, and John the beloved disciple—makes revelation present in the forms of the church across the generations, thanks to the working of the Holy Spirit. He explores the charisms and the

183. Ibid., 365.
184. Ibid., 388.
185. Ibid., 406.
186. Ibid., 408–9.

gifts, with an emphasis on the fact that the "sensory and imagi-
native" dimensions of Christian experience must not be given a
secondary place. The "form" of Christian experience is sensible
and incarnational. At the heart of Christian experience, again,
is "the surrender of one's own experience to the experience of
Christ, and Christ's experience is one of kenotic humiliation and
self-renunciation" in love, rooted in his mission as Son.[187] This
self-surrender, which fuels authentic mystical experience as well
as the experience of private prayer, is already an eschatological
foretaste of the "beauty of the New Age," since "the impotence of
the Cross, as an ecclesial participation, is objectively always the
expression of the superabundant might of Christ."[188]

Von Balthasar emphasizes that such experiences are not for
an elite but rather belong to the whole church. But they do so
always insofar as believers allow Christ to shine in them, rather
than being themselves the ones who want to shine. Christ must
bring us into his radiance of self-surrendering love, not simply
spiritually but in our "corporeal sense-experiences."[189] As von
Balthasar puts it, "if Christ is the image of all images, it is impossible that he should not affect all the world's images by his
presence, arranging them around himself."[190] The whole of creation is irradiated by the form of Christ. Von Balthasar observes
that, even now, "the reality of creation as a whole has become a
monstrance of God's real presence."[191]

This is most true for the church, participating in the biblical archetypal modes of Christian experience. Von Balthasar highlights
"the continuity between Mary's spiritual experiences in the body
and the Church's maternal experience," through which the church
teaches believers the meaning of the incarnate Word in "its whole

187. Ibid., 412.
188. Ibid., 415.
189. Ibid., 420.
190. Ibid., 419.
191. Ibid., 420.

incarnational concreteness."[192] Von Balthasar also describes the liturgical and sacramental ways in which we participate sensibly and spiritually in the form of Christ. He concludes this section on the experience of faith by noting that love—real love for neighbor—"bears within itself in sensory fashion the quintessence of dogmatics" because it contains the form of Christ as "the love and the glory of God, bleeding to death and forsaken."[193] The point of the whole section is that Christ has not abandoned us after his ascension; on the contrary, his manifestation of the form of divine self-surrendering love is, for those who desire to share in this *kenosis*, ever more present and accessible to us in ways that unite the sensible and spiritual as befits his incarnate form.

Objective Revelation

Von Balthasar devotes his next section to "The Objective Evidence," with subsections on "Need for an Objective Form of Revelation," "The Form of Revelation," "Christ the Centre of the Form of Revelation," "The Mediation of the Form," "The Attestation of the Form," and "Eschatological Reduction." The central point of his appropriation of transcendental apperception should already be evident: whereas for Kant the unchanging ground that unifies all phenomena in our concepts is our consciousness, for von Balthasar it is the divine Persons' self-surrender in love as manifested by the objective form of Christ. Likewise, indebted to Kant's understanding of aesthetics as a theory of vision, von Balthasar emphasizes a seeing of the form in which the aesthetic and the ethical (and the "useless") are united. But he completely explodes Kant's immanentism, Kant's separation of mind and body, and Kant's claim that we can know things only as they appear in the categories of our understanding.

In discussing the need for an objective form of revelation, von Balthasar focuses first on God's infinitely free subjectivity.

192. Ibid., 421.
193. Ibid., 424.

God can never be known comprehensively, even when he fully reveals himself. God's radical transcendence and radical immanence mean that our surrender to God must be utterly unconditional, in the sense that we must recognize that we do not stand on an ontological level with him. We are not dealing with a (big) being among beings. Since God is Creator, God has always been revealing himself, his Being and power and glory, in every creature. God's self-revelation in Christ does not merely intensify his revelation of himself through all creatures; neither does God's self-revelation in Christ contradict his revelation of himself through all creatures. The latter prepares for the former, which fulfills and goes radically beyond the latter. Since Christ is the Creator and the head who unites heaven and earth, the cosmos or "form of the world" is revealed to be a temple in and above which God's glory dwells.[194] Von Balthasar calls the revealed form of Christ "an infinitely determined super-form" that unites divine image (humankind) and divine archetype (the Son), and he argues that the form of Christ "is the crowning recapitulation of everything in heaven and on earth."[195]

It may still be unclear what this "form of Christ" or "form of revelation" is, given that Christ exists in diverse states (for example, as an infant or on the cross or in his body the church). Christ is the "radiant expression of God" because he is consubstantial with the Father and, at the same time, is fully human.[196] Christ is the expression of God not simply as self-surrendering love but precisely as self-surrendering love *for us*—which is why Christ's pouring out of himself for us in the Eucharist is what we should expect from Christ's pouring out of himself for us on the cross, and which is also why our future resurrection and our everlasting "marriage-feast" with the risen Christ make sense.[197]

Von Balthasar warns that "if, in the manner of Kant and his

194. Ibid., 431.
195. Ibid., 432.
196. Ibid., 436.
197. Ibid., 441.

followers, we construct a concept of knowledge and science by first bracketing out the unknowable," the result will be rationalistic impoverishment.[198] Against Kant, too, we cannot lose sight of the fact that beings manifest themselves objectively. In addition, the vanity of finite beings, the fact that they cannot sustain or explain themselves, ensures that the self-manifestation of beings always points to their creative ground. As is his wont, von Balthasar interprets this in terms of self-surrender: "The mystery of Being, which is manifest, invites the creaturely spirit to move away from and beyond itself and entrust and surrender itself to that mystery."[199] At the human level, of course, self-surrender in love is necessary. Von Balthasar observes that "man's right relationship to God has its measure in his right relationship to the world, to his neighbour."[200]

The incarnation of the Son constitutes the most perfect manifestation of God and, at the same time, the deepest hiddenness of God, since the Son takes the form of a servant. This point grounds the central claim that we would expect from von Balthasar: "Our task ... consists in coming, with John, to see his 'formlessness' ... as a mode of his glory because a mode of his 'love to the end', to discover in his deformity (*Ungestalt*) the mystery of transcendental form (*Übergestalt*)."[201] The "divine aesthetic" is the radiance, glory, and harmony of the absolute *kenosis* of self-surrendering love that, *for us*, bears and overcomes all sin and ugliness.[202]

Von Balthasar is aware that all this might sound like mere talk: Where is the "objective evidence" that Christ is what the church says he is? Von Balthasar sharply criticizes Kant's subjectivism, his refusal to allow beings any objective manifestation. Discussing the Kantian "subjective condition of the possibility

198. Ibid., 447.
199. Ibid., 450.
200. Ibid., 455.
201. Ibid., 460.
202. Ibid.

of seeing an object for what it is," von Balthasar praises it on the one hand, for it is not possible to see the form of Christ if one's total existence is not prepared for his claims upon oneself. But on the other hand, von Balthasar points out that "in theology, even the most existential form of Kantianism must distort and thus fail to see the phenomenon."[203] Christ, if he is the Word incarnate, must be able to make himself manifest; and no amount of human readiness can suffice for us truly to see Christ, without the aid of grace. Von Balthasar states that "the figure which Christ forms" must have "in itself an interior rightness and evidential power such as we find ... in a work of art or in a mathematical principle."[204] Christ's form must possess such "rightness" as to illumine and transform us. Each detail of Christ in the Gospels depends upon the other details and forms an integrated whole with the others. Every element of Christ's existence and mission fits together. Christ's sayings and sufferings do not distort the whole portrait of his intimacy with his Father but perfect it.

Against Schweitzerian attempts to dismiss Jesus as a failed eschatological prophet whose followers reinterpreted and rehabilitated him, von Balthasar points out that Jesus' ethical teachings are not presented as merely given for a short period of a few years. Nor does Jesus see his coming death as contradicting his claim to divine power or his insistence that he himself can measure things as only God can measure them. We encounter his divine power in reading the words of the Gospels, and we observe that the cross expresses his divine power by measuring and reconciling us. We find that "the Word which in the beginning rang out prophetically to its hearers in the Old Testament ... henceforth becomes a Word which speaks and is expressed through Christ's flesh, and which, becoming muted by the density of flesh, resounds all the louder."[205] In Christ's ultimate si-

203. Ibid., 465.
204. Ibid., 465–66.
205. Ibid., 474–75.

lence on the cross, we perceive love and, equally, obedience and absolute attunement to God. As von Balthasar says, "everything said and done is wholly proportioned: it fits like a glove."[206] This could not have been done by means of the invention of the community or the evangelists. The resurrection bears witness to the truth found in the crucifixion, namely, the truth that the incarnate Son has glorified the Father through the manifestation of supreme love.

In Christ, God acts to relieve human misery, and God does so by entering precisely into the depths of our misery, thus showing that Christ is indeed acting in perfect accord with divine love. Von Balthasar rightly proclaims the objectivity of "the interior attunement, proportion, and harmony between God and man in Christ-form," which thereby stands as the true revelation of radiant divine and human beauty, not an abstract ideal but a living human.[207] Obviously, a mere man could not say the things that Christ says about himself—or attempt to do the things that Christ does that only God can do—without arrogance. Christ can say and do them without arrogance, von Balthasar argues, not only because he is the divine Son but also because, as man, he says and does them explicitly out of obedience to the Father. Von Balthasar remarks that this means that there must be some analogous intra-Trinitarian obedience of the Son as Son. Insofar as obedience characterizes the form of Christ vis-à-vis the Father, that form must analogously express an intra-Trinitarian form. For von Balthasar, Christ's filial obedience is an expression of receptive, self-surrendering love.

Christ's form therefore supremely expresses God's love and shows itself to be the incomparable measure of all finite form or beauty. Von Balthasar notes that if Christ's form aimed to impose itself upon us in any way but by the beauty and attractiveness of love, we would know it was not divine. God conceals himself in

206. Ibid., 475.
207. Ibid., 477.

love, which humbles itself for our sake. When we test or "prove" the Christ-form, we see the necessary relationship of each element to the whole mystery. Again, this could not have been invented afterward, since the entire complex of elements had to line up seamlessly, in a supreme simplicity of love. Von Balthasar reflects upon Paul's combination of theological exuberance and sober instruction, a combination that succeeds in expressing Christ's power and Paul's own freedom in successfully following the (as yet unwritten) form of Christ. Von Balthasar attributes this to the Holy Spirit, who whets the Christ-centered enthusiasm of the saints and enables them to express Christ's form. Christ proves his truth anew in and through his saints. He likewise proves his truth through the inseparability of his form from the Old Testament (which he fulfills and goes beyond), as well as by his fulfillment of the partial truths contained in myths and in the "gods." Christ proves his truth not only by his relatedness to other religious founders but also by his crucial differences from them, most importantly the way that Jesus "draws the form of his teaching and the form of his life [his entire existence] together into a strict identity," which is possible both because of his cross and because of his resurrection (otherwise his wisdom would be foolishness).[208]

The problem of the one and the many—unity and difference— is transformed by Christ through his revelation of the Trinity. Von Balthasar states, "The otherness of creatures is essentially justified by the otherness that exists within the identity of God himself," and the cosmos is "justified in its existence because it is an expression of trinitarian love."[209] Divinization, then, is a sharing in the love of the Trinity that we receive in and through the incarnate Son, thus ensuring that our created humanity is not merely subsumed back into the One. The danger that eternal life could become boring disappears, because the believer knows

208. Ibid., 503.
209. Ibid., 506.

that God's "eternal incomprehensibility is for me a source of eternally overflowing insight and love."[210]

Von Balthasar addresses failure to see the objective form, most notably heresy. Because the form of Christ is a complex one, cutting off any of its aspects destroys the whole. Looking at the form of Christ can be impeded by one's dismay at the church's condition, but this does not excuse looking at Christ through secondhand distortions rather than "face to face."[211] Pascal, Kierkegaard, Newman, and Hamann are among those who have allowed themselves to be addressed by, and to stand under, "Christ's fiery glance."[212] In the Gospels, Christ conceals his identity so that his audience does not misunderstand the fulfillment and radical transformation that he brings to the office of Messiah; he must undergo, in suffering, "the contradiction of an infinite revealing love that immerses itself in a world of sin," and so the radiance of his form is present but in an unexpected way, and in the midst of spiritual darkness.[213]

It is in looking at Christ—through a conversion that turns us toward the Lord—that we become part of his church by acknowledging our sins, our need for redemption, and his supremely gracious love in his suffering for us. Christ then imprints his form upon us, so that we participate in his form. He selects "for himself a body of Scripture" that bears true witness to his form, and he gathers his church also in his Eucharistic form: "Wherever the community is gathered in its eucharistic memorial listening to the Word, there an event called 'church' occurs in virtue of the fact that the Lord becomes present in the assembly, testifying to himself and manifesting himself within it."[214]

Can we trust scripture and the church, both of which involve sinful humans mediating the Christ-form, to "communicate the

210. Ibid., 507.
211. Ibid., 514.
212. Ibid., 515.
213. Ibid., 519.
214. Ibid., 529–30.

Christ-form intact?"[215] Certainly the Bible, just as much as the church, is involved in the messiness of human history. But von Balthasar holds that the historical-critical method, in its classical form, takes on the limitations of Kant: "In Kantian fashion, Bultmann paves for faith a path whereby it criticises and limits itself and, thus, admits its inability to come to see the object of faith, namely, an 'historical Christ'."[216] Once faith is bracketed, faith's object cannot be seen. The same thing happens when Kant declares that we can know the appearances of things only in our mind's categories; the world as such disappears. Without doubt, "divine revelation has been received into the womb of human faith, a faith effected by the grace of revelation itself.... Nowhere does this become more impressively clear than in the textual history of the Old Testament, where the Word of God is carried in a millennial pregnancy by the believing meditation of the people."[217] Implanted within the people, God's Word "wants to include the form of man's answer to God."[218] Von Balthasar adds that, in scripture, we find both the glory of the Christ-form and its humiliation. We are not meant to cling to scripture or to mistake it for Christ, but scripture truly mediates Christ's glory, and scripture cannot be separated from the form of Christ. Von Balthasar praises historical criticism for exposing scripture's historical layers in a way that ensures that we appreciate scripture as testimony to a reality that transcends any human testimony. But von Balthasar warns that historical criticism cannot tell us the meaning of scripture, cannot answer the question of who Jesus is, and cannot tell us what is developing in the Old Testament.[219]

Turning to the relationship of scripture and the church, von Balthasar keeps the focus on Christ: scripture makes manifest

215. Ibid., 532.
216. Ibid., 534.
217. Ibid., 537.
218. Ibid., 538.
219. Ibid., 543.

the "canon," which is Christ's work of salvation and our new creation. Von Balthasar insists that, on the one hand, "the *conversio ad Scripturam* is the indispensable *conversio ad phantasma* ('turning to the objectively manifested image')," but on the other hand "as the Bride and Body of Christ, the Church cannot possibly have above herself any superior 'court' other than her Bridegroom and, in him, the triune God."[220] The key is that the form of scripture is none other than the form of Christ, and so scripture "serves the Spirit as a vehicle through which it constantly actualises, with grace and as grace, this total historical form of the revelation of salvation."[221] Scripture's "letter" therefore opens up to its Christological "spirit," insofar as it opens up to an ever greater participation in Christ's saving work. Here von Balthasar draws deeply upon Henri de Lubac's insights. Similarly, the church's dogmatic pronouncements "do not aim at constructing a system of utterances which eventually would come to replace Scripture either in whole or in part," but rather dogma serves to protect the form of Christ that scripture manifests.[222] The task of theology, then, is to interpret scripture in light of "the full sweep of the Church's thinking," through a contemplative act, "an act of adoration before Christ in the name of the Bride-Church."[223]

The church has no autonomous form, but rather always points (eschatologically) to the fullness of Christ in a manner that is "transparent to Christ."[224] Admittedly, the form of Christ is seen "more strongly in Scripture" than in the church, though the form of Christ governs and shines forth in both.[225] At every point in this discussion, von Balthasar has in view the Kantian project of turning Christianity into merely "a generally intelligible expression of the religious relationship between God and

220. Ibid., 545.
221. Ibid., 548.
222. Ibid., 555.
223. Ibid., 556.
224. Ibid., 559.
225. Ibid., 603.

man," no longer grounded in a historically specific form.[226] Von Balthasar employs aesthetic grounds to insist upon the necessity and centrality of the concrete form of Christ—and thus also upon the Marian form of the church in her conformity to Christ, her Christ-bearing, and her active obedience to Christ.

Trusting that the Holy Spirit ensures that the church mediates and manifests Christ's form so that holy people in the church will endure humiliation, von Balthasar feels no need to conceal the "deformations of the Church" caused, in every historical period, by sinners.[227] He looks to the Eucharist as the formative, ongoing encounter between the self-surrendering Christ and his church: "It is the Son who gives thanks in this self-surrender, and the Church gives thanks with him and through him."[228] In the visibility of their mediation of grace and in their communication of the salvific "gesture of Christ," the sacraments conform us to Christ's form, by the power of Christ and his Spirit.[229] Christ's form, again, is the image of the Father: thus for von Balthasar, the truth of faith (its fundamental dogma) is that "Jesus Christ is the only Son of the Father."[230] Inspired by the Spirit, scripture is normative for the church's faith, inasmuch as "the Church's pneumatic eye is able to read this form [the form of Christ] in Scripture."[231]

For von Balthasar, the Gospel of John especially shows how "Jesus is himself the Father's assumption of form, the Father's *eidos*."[232] This form is true, good, and beautiful, most importantly because the free "surrender of the Son becomes manifest as the love of the Father for the Son" and thereby as "the indivisible essential love of God himself."[233] Sent by the Father in the Spir-

---

226. Ibid., 561.
227. Ibid., 566.
228. Ibid., 575.
229. Ibid., 583.
230. Ibid., 591.
231. Ibid.
232. Ibid., 606.
233. Ibid., 616.

it, Christ invites us to "become interior" to the "radiant space" of the form of self-surrendering divine love, the love that is at the root of all nature and grace.[234] Examining the Old Testament testimony to Christ's form, von Balthasar argues that the Old Testament's forms do not come together, except in the sense that the Old Testament (as a covenant of grace) delivers God's judgment—always, however, the judgment of "a lover"[235]—and makes human failure apparent. Jesus' self-surrendering love shows that this divine judgment is, in fact, "the light of grace," since the Old Testament's divine "noes" attain "their purpose ultimately in his definitive yes."[236]

I have noted repeatedly that for von Balthasar, the unchanging ground that unites all appearances, all of nature, is divine triune self-surrendering love manifested in Christ. But does this insistence upon the all-encompassing Christological ground conflate the orders of nature and grace, with the result that there is no place for the natural created structure of things? In reply, von Balthasar argues that there is a natural structure of creatureliness that requires the world's surrender to its Creator. The world cannot possess itself autonomously. The world's surrender of its greatest creature (Christ) in self-sacrificial death, therefore, pertains on the one hand to the natural order of surrender, the natural creaturely "trace" of the Creator's triune self-surrendering love. But at the same time, Christ's self-surrender goes utterly beyond what is possible for the world as such. Von Balthasar puts it this way: "The world has to surrender its most sublime fruit in sacrifice so that God may at the same time consume and fulfil it.... This is a submission which lies in the world's essence as creature, but which is actually an overtaxing of its being (in a *potentia oboedientialis* that it has, not in itself, but in God)."[237] The

234. Ibid., 617.
235. Ibid., 656.
236. Ibid., 650–51.
237. Ibid., 674.

surrender of Christ both reveals the foundations of creation (by revealing what the creature owes) and explodes those foundations by going beyond them in supernatural love. Von Balthasar concludes that "this self-surrendering love of God is precisely the mystery 'into which the angels long to look' (1 Pet 1.12)."[238]

Conclusion

In his *Critique of Judgement*, Kant argues that the fine arts must, in order to be enduring and truly beautiful, be "brought into combination with moral ideas, which alone are attended with a self-sufficing delight."[239] Kant seeks to find a ground for the universality of aesthetic judgment. He finds that ground in our aesthetic ideas themselves, for which "an ideality of the ends [of things] and not their reality is fundamental."[240] Someone who has true aesthetic taste or judgment about what is beautiful will take pleasure, apart from any self-interest, in the beautiful thing. In perceiving the beautiful—which will always symbolize "the morally good"—we become "conscious of a certain ennoblement and elevation above mere sensibility to pleasure from impressions of the senses."[241] Thus, we recognize beauty in a universally valid way when we possess well-formed moral judgment.[242] In the enjoyment of artistic and natural beauty, our minds experience not only delight but also the elevation associated with true moral ideas, an elevation that suggests that the perception of beauty is a key to a good life.

Von Balthasar agrees with *some* of this, while warning strongly against an "aesthetic theology." Christianity hardly seems beautiful, and the cross stands as a mark of human sin and ugliness. But we can perceive the form of Christ's love, whose good-

238. Ibid., 677.
239. Kant, *Critique of Judgement*, 154.
240. Ibid., 178.
241. Ibid., 180.
242. See ibid., 183.

ness manifests the harmony and radiance of beauty. This beauty is the self-surrendering love of the Father, imaged for the sake of the fallen world by the incarnate Son. This beauty reveals the unchanging ground, Trinitarian love, which accounts for and gives unity to the vast outpouring of finite beings over space and time, as well as to the various forms of the Old Testament and of the religions. Kant's quest for the ground of the unity of all forms (transcendental apperception), a quest that for Kant has its terminus in one's own consciousness, is here transformed: the ground for the unity of all forms, and the truly beautiful form (not least because of its supreme moral goodness), is the divine consciousness, the self-surrendering love of the Father and the Son, incarnate in Christ on the cross.

The beauty of Christ does not deny destruction or death, nor does it glamorize them as good. Instead, it simply reveals that the ground of all created being is infinite, unfathomable Trinitarian love for us sinners, and it reveals that the beauty of all created being is self-surrender—for rational creatures, self-surrender in love—in imitation of the triune God's own life. As von Balthasar puts it, "in the face of the Cross, love is sobered to its very marrow before God's *agape*, which clothes itself in the language of the body; and, in the face of this intoxicating language of flesh and blood that gives itself by being poured out, love is lifted above itself and elevated into the eternal, in order there, as creaturely *eros*, to be the tent and dwelling place of the divine love!"[243] Nothing could be more beautiful.

This is the central message of von Balthasar's *Theological Aesthetics*, which deploys Kant's notion of transcendental apperception and his aesthetic theory of vision to mount a "Kantian" critique of Kant. For von Balthasar, the beauty of all beings shines forth with the impress of Christ's self-surrendering love, a form that we perceive through the light of faith in Jesus Christ and that marks the entire cosmos and reveals its Trinitarian

---

243. Von Balthasar, *Seeing the Form*, 673.

source. Von Balthasar thereby retrieves the revelatory beauty of Christ, and of all reality, in a way that speaks to moderns while overcoming, through a powerful critique of Kant and through a creative retrieval of the Christian tradition, the Kantian limitations of modernity's vision.

2 ◈ *Theo-Drama*

A HEGELIAN CRITIQUE OF HEGEL

More than anyone else, Cyril O'Regan has shed light on what he calls "the comprehensive, deep, and complex relationship between the theology of Hans Urs von Balthasar and the philosophical and religious thought of Hegel, which I take to be one of the major cruxes of modern theology, and one that theology must pass through to gain the possibility of a future."[1] There is no doubt that von Balthasar himself considered that any contemporary theology that does not pass through Hegel has cut itself off from critical and constructive resources that the church today needs. In part, the contemporary importance of Hegel for theology is due to the fact that Hegelian views of progress and of history are still very much with us, as are Hegelian views of Christianity as being essentially about the progressive unfolding of spirit. As von Balthasar describes the key claim of Hegel's

---

1. Cyril O'Regan, *The Anatomy of Misremembering: Von Balthasar's Response to Philosophical Modernity*, vol. 1, *Hegel* (New York: Crossroad, 2014), xiii. For discussion, see Aaron Riches and Sebastián Montiel, "On Re-membering *Geist*: Hegelian Hauntotheology and O'Regan's *Anatomy of Misremembering*," *Modern Theology* 32, no. 2 (2016): 268–78; as well as the "Book Symposium on Cyril O'Regan's *The Anatomy of Misremembering*," *Nova et Vetera* 14, no. 3 (2016): 983–1025, with essays by Rodney Howsare, Guy Mansini, OSB, and Anthony C. Sciglitano Jr., and with a response by O'Regan. See also Michael Schulz, "Die Logik der Liebe und die List der Vernunft: Hans Urs von Balthasar und Georg Wilhelm Friedrich Hegel," in *Logik der Liebe und Herrlichkeit Gottes: Hans Urs von Balthasar im Gespräch. Festgabe für Karl Kardinal Lehmann zum 70. Geburtstag*, ed. Walter Kasper, 111–33 (Ostfildern: Matthias-Grünewald-Verlag, 2006).

philosophy, "when absolute thought occurs in man, the axis of Being runs through him, and his concept comprehends absolute totality within itself."[2] Modern intellectual and cultural debates are often framed by Hegel's anthropocentric sense of absolute spirit's historical unfolding. In response, von Balthasar observes critically, "Christology in the Christian sense never has a chance to breathe within the circle of the Hegelian Spirit's gigantic monologue with itself. It makes no difference whether this monologue attains to the all-comprehensive totality of truth of the self-reflecting spirit with or without the historical Jesus."[3]

At the same time, von Balthasar refuses simply to dismiss Hegel as an enemy; he is also one from whom theology can learn. As Ben Quash puts it, "Hegel is both mentor and foe."[4] For von Balthasar, Hegel can help Catholic theology to be dogmatically richer and more persuasive, both in itself and in evangelizing the modern world. Quash rightly notes that von Balthasar's *Theo-Drama* proceeds "by taking the baton which Hegel proffered at the close of his grand aesthetic project and running with it."[5] Quash focuses on the distinctions made by Hegel between epic, lyric, and dramatic, which von Balthasar engages in the second volume of his *Theo-Drama*.[6] Von Balthasar also makes

2. Hans Urs von Balthasar, *The Glory of the Lord: A Theological Aesthetics*, vol. 5, *The Realm of Metaphysics in the Modern Age*, trans. Oliver Davies, Andrew Louth, Brian McNeil, CRV, John Saward, and Rowan Williams, ed. Brian McNeil, CRV, and John Riches (San Francisco: Ignatius Press, 1991), 587.

3. Hans Urs von Balthasar, *Theo-Logic: Theological Logical Theory*, vol. 2, *Truth of God*, trans. Adrian J. Walker (San Francisco: Ignatius Press, 2004), 49fn47.

4. Ben Quash, "Drama and the Ends of Modernity," in Lucy Gardner, David Moss, Ben Quash, and Graham Ward, *Balthasar at the End of Modernity*, 139–72 (Edinburgh: T&T Clark, 1999), at 145. See also Quash, *Theology and the Drama of History* (Cambridge: Cambridge University Press, 2005).

5. Quash, "Drama and the Ends of Modernity," 146; see also O'Regan, *The Anatomy of Misremembering*, 520.

6. I note, however, that Quash's conclusions about von Balthasar's engagement with Hegel are debatable: see for example O'Regan's review of Quash's *Theology and the Drama of History* in *Modern Theology* 23 (2007): 293–96. For Quash, von Balthasar is ultimately an "epic" theologian who flattens out dramatic tension and whose work, with its emphasis on obedience, revolves around a distorted ecclesiology. I do

use of Hegel's insights into identity and role and into the relationship of the individual characters to the ends of the action as a whole. Furthermore, von Balthasar's approaches to the collision of (fallen) finite freedom and infinite freedom, and to the immanent and economic Trinity, exhibit the influence of Hegel's insights into spirit's interior encounter with its opposite (finitude and mortality), a contradiction that involves a self-surrendering sacrifice and that ends in a definitive resolution.

Yet, even if von Balthasar's project in the *Theo-Drama* draws upon Hegel in certain positive ways, his project is a strong critique of Hegel. This can be seen again when von Balthasar, precisely in praising Hegel's *Aesthetics*, also gives it a subtle but devastating critique: "the *Aesthetics*—one of the richest and most successful of Hegel's works—is virtually no more than the portrayal of an awareness of the radiant blessedness of absolute knowledge itself, which can comprehend all things (even the most difficult and the most painful), justify all things and approve all things."[7] Obviously, some things must not be justified or approved, and so Hegel is deeply in the wrong. As O'Regan observes, von Balthasar powerfully resists Hegel's project as "the most blatant form of the misfiring of memory or misremembering in the post-Enlightenment era."[8] In his *Theo-Drama*, von Balthasar often finds himself in "proximity" to Hegel, but it is a critical proximity.[9] After all, Hegel offers no room for a truly personal, or truly transcendent, infinite spirit. Nor does he give real value to human bodiliness or individuality, or (correspondingly) to Christ's real humanity in its historical context. For von Balthasar, as O'Regan comments, "neither Hegel's philosophy nor his schematization of Christianity admits of being called dra-

---

not share Quash's views on these matters. But as O'Regan says in his review, "Quash makes a persuasive case that Balthasar's prime interlocutor throughout *Theo-Drama* is Hegel" (ibid., 293).

7. Von Balthasar, *The Realm of Metaphysics in the Modern Age*, 586.

8. O'Regan, *The Anatomy of Misremembering*, 521.

9. Ibid., 523.

matic since they lack the essential conditions that make drama possible: dialogue between two personal centers of freedom."[10]

O'Regan's massive book ranges far more widely than I can do in this chapter, and notably sets forth von Balthasar's "apocalyptic" theological answer to Hegel. My chapter has a much simpler scope, but develops the same basic claim that von Balthasar offers a Hegelian critique of Hegel. As with chapter 1, the present chapter has two parts. The first part surveys some of Hegel's philosophical contributions, found in his *Lectures on the Philosophy of Religion*, *Aesthetics*, *Philosophy of History*, and *Elements of the Philosophy of Right*. In this way, I introduce readers to Hegelian ideas that have bearing upon von Balthasar's *Theo-Drama*. The second section introduces the first volume of von Balthasar's *Theo-Drama*, with these Hegelian ideas in view. This first volume (*Prolegomena*) sets forth the essential components of the critique of Hegel that von Balthasar will advance in the remaining volumes of his *Theo-Drama*—although in my survey of the *Prolegomena*, attentive to the rich unfolding of his wide-ranging conversation, I take care not to impose my framework upon von Balthasar's book. I am not suggesting that Hegel is by any means the only significant interlocutor in the *Theo-Drama* or that Hegel's influence is not felt (or responded to) in the other parts of von Balthasar's trilogy. But I hope to show, without distorting or limiting the conversation found in von Balthasar's *Prolegomena*, that in his *Theo-Drama* he intends to offer a Hegelian critique of Hegel for the advancement of Catholic theology today.

Contributions of Georg W. F. Hegel

Philosophy of Religion

I will begin with Hegel's 1827 lectures on "The Revealed Religion," or "The Christian Religion." He describes Christianity

10. Ibid., 522–23.

as "the *consummate religion*."[11] Briefly, he defines "religion" as "the consciousness of God as such, consciousness of absolute essence."[12] Empirical consciousness can know absolute essence only in a finite way, and so, at this stage, religion has not yet come into its own. The religion that comes into its own is a religion whose object is self-differentiating consciousness, spirit as self-knowing. Spiritual things cannot be verified by sensible things; rather spiritual things can be verified only interiorly, in the self-consciousness or spirit. Our spirit resonates with what is noble, and ideas and insights affect our spirit, form our moral character, and develop our reasoning powers. Most importantly, spirit comes into its own through "philosophy, according to which the concept develops the truth purely as such from itself without presuppositions."[13] Spirit here attains to necessary truths. Since not all humans have philosophical abilities, spirit can also receive these truths on the basis of faith or authority, when the spirit recognizes sympathetically or connaturally that what it hears is indeed a necessary truth.

Spirit seeks in this development "to become the true and proper Spirit, the Holy Spirit, which comprehends the divine and knows its content to be divine."[14] Hegel holds that today, philosophy (not theology) carries forward real orthodox truth, the true propositions that constitute Christianity. In philosophical thinking, finite spirit knows infinite spirit "as its own essence," beyond the distinction of one spirit from another.[15] Spirit contains finitude within it; but finitude, in this sense, is transitional within the broader movement of spirit. Ultimately, spirit "determines itself infinitely," as "absolute subjectivity."[16] Hegel warns

11. Georg W. F. Hegel, *Lectures on the Philosophy of Religion*, vol. 3, *The Consummate Religion*, ed. Peter C. Hodgson, trans. R. F. Brown, P. C. Hodgson, and J. M. Stewart, with H. S. Harris (Oxford: Clarendon Press, 2007), 249.
12. Ibid., 250.
13. Ibid., 256.
14. Ibid., 261.
15. Ibid., 263.
16. Ibid., 268.

against defining God by predicating attributes of him, since this does not yet arrive at the living God who is pure subject, standing above all contradictory attributes as the one who resolves them. For Hegel, God "is absolute activity, creative energy [*Aktuosität*], and his activity is to posit himself in contradiction, but eternally to resolve and reconcile this contradiction: God himself is the resolving of these contradictions."[17] It is not that God *does* the reconciling of all things opposed to him; rather, God, as absolute spirit, *is* the reconciling. God is Trinity because the self-determination of God is God's entire idea, identical to God. This distinction of two who are nonetheless one is love, the Holy Spirit. Hegel describes the Trinity in another way: "God's determining of himself to distinguish himself from himself while [remaining] at the same time the eternal sublation of the distinction."[18]

From the category of "person," Hegel derives much assistance. He notes that "one" is abstract and exclusive. Persons, however, are free subjects, and furthermore "it is the character of the person, the subject, to surrender its isolation and separateness" in love.[19] Hegel notes that in Hindu philosophy, it was recognized that the one is lacking if it remains one; and, somewhat similarly, middle-Platonic philosophy conceived of an abstract triad. The Christian doctrine of the Trinity, too, has its ground in reason, even if it is revealed. Hegel appeals to Jacob Boehme's Trinitarian mysticism and to triadic patterns of thought set forth by Kant.[20] He observes with regard to the divine determining (the distinction of the "Son") that this distinction grounds all finite distinctions and that this distinction is sublated by the Spirit.

17. Ibid., 271.
18. Ibid., 278.
19. Ibid., 285.
20. See, for example, Kant's triadic presentation of the categories of quantity, quality, relation, and modality: Immanuel Kant, *Critique of Pure Reason*, trans. and ed. Paul Guyer and Allen W. Wood (Cambridge: Cambridge University Press, 1998), 212. For the triad "thesis—antithesis—synthesis," see Johann Gottlieb Fichte, *Fichte: Early Philosophical Writings*, ed. and trans. Daniel Breazeale (Ithaca, N.Y.: Cornell University Press, 1988), 63.

From the biblical story of original sin, Hegel obtains the idea
that in the totality of spirit, humans are "immortal," free, and
good. As "natural" beings (animals), however, we are in a state
of antithesis in relation to "God" and are mortal and "evil."[21]
This contradiction causes us anguish and unhappiness. We find
ourselves locked in an antithesis of "humiliation" and inwardness. The Spirit is the synthesis that reconciles and sublates the
antithesis. Here Hegel seeks to draw out the meaning of the incarnation. We must rise to certitude that God and man are one,
something that God has revealed, and something that is also a
necessary conclusion of reason. This is because human spirit, in
its totality, is able to contain "the absolute idea," even if humans
are mortal.[22] Hegel argues that "consciousness can achieve this
content, this substantial unity."[23] Rejecting the phrase "God-
man" as "monstrous," Hegel thinks that its meaning can nonetheless be appreciated: what is animal and mortal in human
nature does not impede the unity of the divine and human in
absolute idea or absolute spirit, humanity's highest consciousness.[24] What Christ reveals is "the consciousness of absolute reconciliation" of the antithesis of humanity in relation to "God."[25]
Humans can now be conscious that they are one with God; this is
what the "kingdom of God" means. We have received "an infinite
relationship to God," with a certitude of God's presence as the
satisfaction of the needs of spirit, now that Christ has overcome
finitude and evil.[26]

In overcoming finitude, Christ reveals finitude to be a moment within God, within absolute spirit. Hegel emphasizes that
"finitude, negativity, otherness are not outside of God and do not,
as otherness, hinder unity with God. Otherness, the negative, is

21. Hegel, *Lectures on the Philosophy of Religion*, 304–5.
22. Ibid., 312.
23. Ibid., 314.
24. Ibid., 315.
25. Ibid., 317.
26. Ibid., 322.

known to be a moment of the divine nature itself."[27] Death itself is part of this "moment." God overcomes all otherness—all
finite distinction that he himself determines—in the movement
of Spirit. Finitude and death do not remain in God once they have
been overcome. This reconciliation is possible only because God
is Trinity: "God *is*, but also is as the other, as self-distinguishing,
so that this other is God himself, having implicitly the divine
nature in it, and ... the sublation of this difference, this otherness, and the return of love, are the Spirit."[28] In the Trinitarian
process, spirit differentiates itself and overcomes this differentiation. The community recognizes a "divine history" in which
we see the working out of "a moment in God himself" that has
now passed.[29] Hegel defines "sacrifice" as sublating what is other
and finite. In God, such a sacrifice has taken place as part of the
unfolding of "the nature of God himself."[30]

Lastly, we arrive at the unification brought by the outpouring of the Spirit. Hegel associates this with the community of all
people "who are in the Spirit of God."[31] To be "in the Spirit,"
each person needs to undertake the process of consciousness by
which he or she comes to recognize the truth of the synthesis
or reconciliation (the overcoming of finitude through the attainment of infinite spirit), as has been manifested symbolically in
Christ's reversal of the "fall." The divine spirit and human spirit
are now seen as identical, since the Spirit exists in human spirit, which brings forth divine Spirit. The otherness and finitude
and weakness of humans do not destroy this unity because the
antithesis of finitude has been overcome. Hegel states, "For in
the idea, the otherness of the Son is a transitory, disappearing
moment, not a true, essentially enduring, absolute moment."[32]

27. Ibid., 326.
28. Ibid., 327.
29. Ibid.
30. Ibid., 328.
31. Ibid., 329.
32. Ibid., 332.

What endures is the reconciliation of the community of finite spirit in infinite Spirit.

The human person attains to this self-conscious unity of the finite and the infinite when, through a "process of the subject within and upon itself," the human person recognizes that "the pure self-consciousness that knows and wills the truth is precisely the divine Spirit within it."[33] The human person thereby becomes "actual as spirit," which is the truth of humanity, the vocation for freedom that is shared by all humans but must be appropriated.[34] The goal is "universal spirituality," the recognition of "the eternity of spirit."[35] In this condition, the eternal truth of the world becomes clear as rational freedom. Thus, Hegel concludes that philosophy exhibits "the reconciliation of God with himself and with nature, showing that nature, otherness, is implicitly divine, and that the raising of itself to reconciliation is on the one hand what finite spirit implicitly is, while on the other hand it arrives at this reconciliation, or brings it forth, in world history."[36]

For the purposes of von Balthasar's *Theo-Drama*, what is especially notable in this part of Hegel's *Lectures on the Philosophy of Religion* consists in his account of God's self-differentiation (which produces the "Son") encompassing finitude, negativity (including death), and otherness. These elements, in their contrast with immortal and free spirit, cause humiliation and anguish. All these elements, however, belong to God himself in a moment of his history because they belong to the dialectic emergence of universal spirit. In a "moment" in God's history, which Hegel depicts as a moment of "sacrifice," these differences are sublated. Reconciliation in the "Spirit" then draws all things into the perfect freedom and pure self-consciousness of knowing

33. Ibid., 333.
34. Ibid., 335.
35. Ibid., 340.
36. Ibid., 347.

the truth, that is to say, into the actualization of universal spirit. Now that finitude, otherness, and death have been overcome, the identity of the finite and the infinite has appeared in history as absolute spirit. Thus, through the unfolding of the history of God, free human persons find their fulfillment in the unity of spirit. The key is to recognize the intradivine place of contradiction (including our own finitude, otherness, and death). God's— or absolute spirit's—"activity is to posit himself in contradiction, but eternally to resolve and reconcile this contradiction: God himself is the resolving of these contradictions."[37]

Aesthetics

Let me now add a bit from the first volume of Hegel's *Aesthetics*— insofar as Hegel's positions here bear upon themes addressed in von Balthasar's *Theo-Drama*. Hegel emphasizes that "romantic art" explores "absolute inwardness" or "spiritual subjectivity with its grasp of its independence and freedom."[38] According to this view, romantic "art knows now only *one* God, one spirit, one absolute independence which, as the absolute knowing and willing of itself, remains in free unity with itself."[39] Hegel notes that within absolute spirit, there is the moment in which absolute spirit (God) enters into external existence and shapes it, elevating it "to spiritual subjectivity" and embodying in an external form its present "certainty of itself as the Absolute."[40] As Hegel observes, absolute spirit "puts himself into the very heart of the finitude and external contingency of existence, and yet knows himself there as a divine subject who remains infinite in himself and makes this infinity explicit to himself."[41] Absolute spirit actualizes itself by entering into otherness and making infinite

37. Ibid., 271.
38. G. W. F. Hegel, *Aesthetics: Lectures on Fine Art*, vol. 1, trans. T. M. Knox (Oxford: Oxford University Press, 1975), 519.
39. Ibid.
40. Ibid., 520.
41. Ibid.

spirit explicit within finitude, thereby showing that finitude is overcome within God himself. The finite and the infinite are revealed to be identical: "the actual individual man is the appearance of God," and "the actual individual person in his inner life ... acquires infinite worth," because in the free person "alone do the eternal moments of absolute truth, which is actual only as spirit, unfold into existence and collect together again."[42]

This emphasis on absolute spirit manifesting itself through finite spirit—indeed on the necessity of absolute spirit doing so (because finitude is a moment within absolute spirit)—makes clear that the fruit is the realization of absolute spirit. From this standpoint, then, Hegel addresses the figure of Jesus. He argues that in the events of Jesus' life, we perceive precisely what absolute spirit is. The historical events of incarnation, crucifixion, and resurrection show us the true character of absolute spirit, or God. Jesus' life reveals the eternal and infinite spirit. For Hegel, so also do the lives of all persons whose finite consciousnesses or finite spirits express infinite spirit, since "God" (or absolute spirit) appears in all who enjoy true "spiritual consciousness" as expressive of "eternal moments of absolute truth."[43] The unity or reconciliation here found in the "diffusion of this self-contemplation of spirit" constitutes "peace" or the "Kingdom of God."[44]

Hegel emphasizes that absolute spirit cannot be revealed without otherness and death as a moment within the unfolding of absolute spirit. He remarks that "the spirit, in order to win its totality and freedom, detaches itself from itself and opposes itself, as the finite of nature and spirit, to itself as the inherently infinite."[45] In the actualizing of spirit, there is an opposition, an anguish, a presence of "evil" that must be overcome through a form of death, or what Hegel describes as "a process in the

42. Ibid.
43. Ibid., 520.
44. Ibid., 522.
45. Ibid.

course of which a struggle and a battle arises, and grief, death, the mournful sense of nullity, the torment of spirit and body enter as an essential feature."[46] Only in this way can finite spirit be elevated to infinite spirit. The unfolding of spirit, the history of spirit, requires as a moment within itself "the infinite grief of this sacrifice of subjectivity's very heart, as well as suffering and death."[47] Christ therefore reveals the history of "God," absolute spirit; death or crucifixion itself belongs within this history. Yet, death does not have the last word because it "is only a perishing of the *natural* soul and *finite* subjectivity."[48] Positively speaking, death accomplishes the liberation of the finite spirit and the spiritual reconciliation of "the individual person with the Absolute."[49] Spirit lives only by undergoing this death.

Still speaking of "romantic art," Hegel notes that for such art the many persons and events of the world can be "gathered up into *one* ray of the Absolute and its eternal history of redemption."[50] The concrete history of redemption here reveals what characterizes God in the "eternal history" of absolute spirit. The heroes of this history display "a heroism of submission," or self-surrender to the law of the life, death, and resurrection that marks the unfolding of absolute spirit.[51] In this self-surrender, we find "the inner battle of man in himself and his reconciliation with God," the union of finite and infinite spirit.[52] Hegel notes, however, that while this submission is a constant, the diversity of human characteristics and local surroundings makes the self-surrender ever unique and distinctive. As Hegel puts it, "the spirit therefore unfolds itself in the course of its development into an infinitely enhanced wealth of inner and outer collisions,

46. Ibid.
47. Ibid.
48. Ibid., 523.
49. Ibid.
50. Ibid., 525.
51. Ibid.
52. Ibid.

distractions, gradations of passion, and into the most manifold degrees of satisfaction."[53]

Hegel addresses the question of whether the content that he ascribes to romantic art arises from romantic art itself. He answers that the content it seeks, in fact, belongs to "religion" rather than arising from romantic art itself. By "religion," he means what is found in his *Lectures on the Philosophy of Religion*: namely, he means his own account of the true meaning of Christianity. Romantic art, however, cannot achieve the full reconciliation that "religion" attains. Instead, romantic art inevitably leaves us with two unreconciled worlds: "a spiritual realm, complete in itself, the heart which reconciles itself within and now bends back the otherwise rectilineal repetition of birth, death, and rebirth ... into the genuine phoenix-life of the spirit"; and "the realm of the external as such," now completely disconnected from the spirit.[54] This inability truly to integrate external or empirical reality shows that art cannot be the highest form of the human spirit. Only "religion" or philosophy can accomplish the unity ardently sought by art. While lauding the fact that "romantic art has for its substantial content the reconciliation of God with the world and therefore with himself," Hegel argues that art cannot be its own endpoint.[55] The reconciliation that art seeks can be found only objectively in "religion" as philosophically understood.

I should also observe that Hegel draws upon the tragedies of Shakespeare in order to reflect on the connection between action and character in romantic art. In Shakespeare, a person's fate does not solely develop out of his or her external action or out of the progress of events; it also expresses a development of his or her internal character or "subjective inner life."[56] Indeed, some of Shakespeare's greatest figures are defined solely in terms of

53. Ibid., 525–26.
54. Ibid., 527.
55. Ibid., 530; cf. 574.
56. Ibid., 579.

their inner lives or spirits. According to Hegel, in Shakespeare "everything has a place" and "every sphere of life, all phenomena" can and do appear. Hegel suggests that artists should seek a deeper unity of the artist's subjectivity and the world's objectivity—a goal that has been achieved, he thinks, especially by some of Goethe's best poems.

The concluding section of the second volume of Hegel's *Aesthetics* treats drama, which Hegel deems to be "the highest stage of poetry and of art generally."[57] Speech has a unique capacity to express spirit, and drama unites the subjectivity of lyric poetry with the objectivity of epic poetry. In a drama, we see a "complete action" that arises from the interior spirit of the protagonists and that takes the form of a real event, with its complex pattern of actions and reactions, leading to a resolution.[58] Hegel focuses upon the way in which drama goes beyond lyric and epic poetry, namely, by grounding the action in "the self-conscious and active individual" and without separating the person's inner life from the external realization.[59] Unlike in lyric poetry, in drama the events are not in a passive relation to the main character; rather, "the action is the achievement of his will and is known as such as regards both its origin and beginning in himself and also its final result."[60] The main character's inner dynamism of spirit drives the action, which expresses his or her interior spirit and which also takes an objective form in the external world, prompting reactions and further actions leading up to the dramatic resolution. Hegel is particularly interested in drama because it unites action as expressing interior spirit with "*its* external realization."[61] The unity of inner life and external realization stands at the center of what dramatic poetry can achieve.

57. G. W. F. Hegel, *Aesthetics: Lectures on Fine Art*, vol. 2, trans. T. M. Knox (Oxford: Oxford University Press, 1975), 1158.
58. Ibid.
59. Ibid., 1160.
60. Ibid., 1161.
61. Ibid., 1160.

In an epic, it is the events of world history (whether real or invented) that govern the development of the play. In drama, by contrast, the inner life of the hero governs the unfolding of events. Hegel emphasizes that in drama "the action rests on the self-determination of the individual's character and must follow from this original inner source."[62] Drama therefore has a special ability to portray the expression of the human spirit in concrete external events. Drama shows how the human spirit molds and informs events, and how events display the power of the inner life.

Hegel adds the point that "drama has to fix our eye steadily on *one* aim and its accomplishment."[63] The agent's spirit seeks, in the clash of events, one goal that will express his or her spirit. Of course, others will oppose the main character, and their reactions (rooted in their diverse goals) will influence the outcome. At stake is truth and goodness (the "Divine")—but not the "divine" in the form of gods. Rather, humans, in their inner spirit, generate truth and goodness, and so the "divine" is "brought into existence as something concrete, summoned into action and put in movement."[64] Drama is absolute truth, generated by the inner life of spirit, in action in the external world, in relation to the goals of other agents. Hegel, however, does not think that the ultimate outcome lies in the hands of humans. On the contrary, "the Divine itself, as a totality in itself," works necessarily to accomplish resolution and reconciliation, overcoming all finitude and otherness.[65] Thus, the dramatist cannot simply set up various passions and ideas working in relation to each other. The dramatist must know and appreciate the underlying movement of spirit, that is to say, "the inner and universal element lying at the root of the aims, struggles, and fates of human beings," leading to "the actual accomplishment of what is absolutely rational and true."[66]

62. Ibid., 1161.
63. Ibid., 1162.
64. Ibid.
65. Ibid., 1163.
66. Ibid.

Another element that Hegel values in drama—again by contrast to epic and lyric poetry—is its "tighter consistency" due to the "individual interconnection which is the basis of their [the characters'] existence in the drama."[67] He thinks that this interconnection requires focusing on one locality and on a short space of time, but he grants that there are dramatists who do not follow these rules. He observes, however, that "the truly inviolable law is the unity of the action."[68] This rule becomes difficult because, in a drama, the various characters each have different ends or goals that they are pursuing, and they conflict with each other. The "true unity" of the dramatic action, then, consists in "the total movement" in which "the collision is displayed as conforming with the characters and their ends, and finally their contradiction is annulled and unity is restored."[69] How can a unity be attained that truly fulfills the inner goals of the conflicting agents? Hegel argues in answer that "a genuine end is ... only attained when the aim and interest of the action, on which the whole drama turns, is identical with the individuals and absolutely bound up with them."[70]

He admits that this identity between the aim of the action and the individual actors is difficult to attain when one is dealing with a multifaceted plot. As an example, he notes the way that Shakespeare, in his tragedies, manages to wrap up subplots at the end of the play. The key is that "the *one* collision which is at issue [in a given play] must find its settlement in that one independently finished work."[71] The whole of the drama turns on this "collision" between conflicting aims, and the drama's power consists in its complete resolution of this collision. Just as in his philosophy of Christianity, Hegel suggests with regard to drama that it properly has three acts: the emergence of the difference,

67. Ibid., 1164.
68. Ibid., 1166.
69. Ibid.
70. Ibid., 1167.
71. Ibid.

the resulting collision, and finally the resolution. He notes, however, that in most drama, the collision is itself subdivided into
three acts, so that the result is five acts in all. What he looks for in
a good drama consists in "the exposition of the inner spirit of the
action in respect of not only the general nature of the action and
the conflict and fate involved, but also the dramatis personae
and their passion, 'pathos', decision, mutual involvement and
working on one another."[72] The "inner spirit of the action" has
its power in light of the collision of the "dramatis personae,"
who, in a great drama, will appear in the end to be *intrinsically*
bound up with the aim of the action as a whole.

Hegel also points out that in a "perfect drama," the author—
while certainly not playing a role among the characters—does not
recede in importance; on the contrary, a perfect drama exhibits
"self-conscious and original creative activity and therefore also
the art and virtuosity of an individual author."[73] The action of a
great drama cannot amount to something insignificant or minor;
it must connect with the quest of the human spirit and bring real
resolution. The individual spirit of the dramatist must therefore
possess "the most profound insight into the essence of human
action and Divine Providence."[74] Furthermore, the dramatist
must be able to describe accurately the "eternal substance" or
truth "of all human characters, passions, and fates."[75]

In Hegel's view, action has two components. First, given his
understanding of spirit, it is not surprising that he considers every action to include an element that pertains to absolute spirit,
insofar as the agent has any truth or genuineness. In the "individual's character and aim," we must look for "the Divine actualized in the world, as the foundation of everything genuine and
absolutely eternal" in the individual agent and in the action.[76]

72. Ibid., 1170.
73. Ibid., 1179.
74. Ibid.
75. Ibid.
76. Ibid., 1194.

In addition to this "divine" component—indicating the presence of absolute spirit—there is the subjectivity and freedom of the individual in his finite spirit. These two elements define the worth of action.

On this basis, Hegel defines tragedy as involving "the Divine … as it enters the world and individual action," in which a collision occurs that involves a substantial truth on both sides, but which destroys the deeper "unity of ethical life" through a one-sided focus.[77] This destruction places the person in the wrong since the "ethical order" is in fact "eternal and inviolable."[78] Always, tragedy bears reference to divine reconciliation, which will not allow the imbalance and disharmony to stand. In Hegel's understanding, comedy arises when individual subjectivity acts in a manner that stands in some way above or athwart eternal truths and values. This means unwittingly and cheerfully exposing the depth of one's "own inner contradiction," either by lightly employing one's full power of spirit to embrace unsubstantial aims (such as riches) or by lightly proposing to undertake truly substantial aims (such as governance) via insufficient instruments.[79] Hegel argues that comedy, too, must end with a resolution. This is so because we see in comedy "the contradiction between what is absolutely true and its realization in individuals," and this contradiction begs for dramatic resolution.[80]

A central difference between tragic and comedic drama, in Hegel's view, consists in tragedy's emphasis on the substantial truth present in its characters and aims, by contrast with comedy's emphasis on the characters' individual subjectivity. For dramatic poetry to exist, one must have a notion of free individuality, something that Hegel thinks began first among the Greeks, even though they focused on "the universal and essen-

77. Ibid., 1195, 1197.
78. Ibid., 1198.
79. Ibid., 1200.
80. Ibid., 1201.

tial element in the aim which the characters are realizing."[81] Hegel argues that Muslim art has no real place for drama because the individual is not free; God determines everything. In modern Western drama, the individual subjectivity has central place, as the human spirit seeks to fulfill the aim of his inner life in collision with others, a collision that must lead in the end to resolution. Hegel underscores that tragic drama requires that the dramatist make manifest "the authority of a higher world-governor, whether Providence or fate."[82]

The Philosophy of History

In *The Philosophy of History*, Hegel gives a special dramatic role to the German people. Hegel states, "The German Spirit is the Spirit of the new World. Its aim is the realization of absolute Truth as the unlimited self-determination of Freedom—*that* Freedom which has its own absolute form itself as its purport."[83] The realization of freedom occurs for Hegel through human spirit knowing its identity with infinite spirit, while at the same time knowing its own finitude and otherness, and perceiving that these latter are included within the history of infinite spirit moving, through sacrifice, toward the reconciliation of the objective and the subjective in the unity of absolute spirit. For Hegel, this is the true meaning of the doctrines of the Trinity, Christ, the outpouring of the Spirit, and the kingdom of God. Given this view, he holds that "the destiny of the German peoples is, to be the bearers of the Christian principle."[84] Specifically, the Reformation inaugurates "the period of Spirit conscious that it is free, inasmuch as it wills the True, the Eternal—that which is in and for itself Universal."[85] The key to attaining such freedom is not

81. Ibid., 1206.
82. Ibid., 1208.
83. Georg W. F. Hegel, *The Philosophy of History*, trans. J. Sibree (Buffalo, N.Y.: Prometheus Books, 1991), 341.
84. Ibid.
85. Ibid., 412.

grasping autonomy but rather surrendering oneself to absolute truth.

Hegel's position revolves around the discovery that infinite spirit is found in finite spirit, which belongs to every human. Each of us, therefore, must interiorly discover infinite spirit, absolute truth and freedom, to which we must devote ourselves (because absolute truth is both subjective and objective). Hegel emphasizes that we can do this only when we surrender ourselves, our finite particularity. He states that "the subject himself must be imbued with Truth, surrendering his particular being in exchange for the substantial Truth, and making that Truth his own."[86] We find ourselves in surrendering ourselves, and in recognizing that infinite truth dwells in us and marks our spirit. Hegel concludes, "Thus subjective Spirit gains emancipation in the Truth, abnegates its particularity and comes to itself in realizing the truth of its being. Thus Christian Freedom is actualized."[87] Real freedom consists in surrendering our particularity and in actively enabling infinite truth to reconcile us to ourselves and to all things. As Hegel concludes the *Philosophy of History*, "the History of the World is nothing but the development of the Idea of Freedom. But Objective Freedom—the laws of *real* Freedom—demand the subjugation of the mere contingent will."[88] This subjugation, allowing infinite spirit to reign in the person, brings about the true freedom of the subjective spirit.

Lastly, let me add a brief note from Hegel's *Elements of the Philosophy of Right*. Hegel argues that the lover realizes the following: "I am not isolated on my own [*für mich*], but gain my self-consciousness only through the renunciation of my independent existence [*meines Fürsichseins*]."[89] Such self-surrender

86. Ibid., 416.
87. Ibid.
88. Ibid., 456.
89. G. W. F. Hegel, *Elements of the Philosophy of Right*, ed. Allen W. Wood, trans. H. B. Nisbet (Cambridge: Cambridge University Press, 1991), §158, p. 199. Von Balthasar cites this passage in his *Truth of God*, 44–47. In the end, von Balthasar

enables the lover to find himself (or herself). Describing two "moments" in love, Hegel states that in the first moment the lover recognizes that he (or she) does not want to live for himself (or herself) alone; and in the second moment, the lover finds himself (or herself) in the beloved and vice versa. The lover realizes, "I gain recognition in this person, who in turn gains recognition in me."[90] For Hegel, however, the mutual self-surrender of persons leads to a higher unity, namely the unity of the two persons who are now one in marriage. I mention this text from Hegel's *Elements of the Philosophy of Right* in order to indicate the presence of the crucial theme of discovering oneself through self-surrender (which Hegel describes as "the most immense contradiction").[91]

More could be said, especially by recourse to Hegel's *Phenomenology of Spirit*. But for my purposes, the essential contours of Hegel's thought have been set forth. The following seven elements are crucial. First, for Hegel, God's self-differentiation encompasses all possible otherness or contradiction. Absolute spirit has its opposite as a moment within its unfolding. God's "activity is to posit himself in contradiction, but eternally to resolve and reconcile this contradiction: God himself is the resolving of these contradictions."[92] Second, the world's history reflects absolute spirit's eternal history. Third, the key to the world's history (and thus to absolute spirit's history) consists in submission or surrender to the law of life, death, and resurrection. Fourth, persons realize or actualize themselves by experiencing the anguish of

concludes that Hegel's logic requires that "Hegel understands the passage over to the other as alienation and not as love (or loving self-emptying), that is, because he logicizes and, ultimately, absorbs love in absolute knowledge.... In order to respond to Hegel, we would need to appeal to Blondel's observation that logical 'contradiction' (*antíphasis*) enjoys at best a 'subalternate legitimacy' in the dialectic of life and that it emerges as a real contradiction only in the opposition of evil to good" (ibid., 48).

90. Hegel, *Elements of the Philosophy of Right*, §158, p. 199.
91. Ibid.
92. Hegel, *Lectures on the Philosophy of Religion*, 271.

finitude and surrendering this particularity in sacrifice. Fifth, dramatic action is a unity, a totality involving many actors, that involves a "collision" between finite and infinite freedom that ends in a resolution and reconciliation. Sixth, dramatic action that displays the virtuosity of its author must show the identity between the individual subjectivities and the aim of the whole action. Seventh, drama is about the divine as actualized in the world and therefore requires a notion of providence leading the whole action to resolution. All of these points have bearing upon von Balthasar's *Theo-Drama*, although the content of his *Theo-Drama* differs critically from Hegel.

Hans Urs von Balthasar's *Prolegomena* to His *Theo-Drama*: A Hegelian Critique of Hegel

The first volume of von Balthasar's *Theo-Drama* bears the title *Prolegomena*. Von Balthasar suggests that in this volume we find the necessary material, which, when rightly assembled, will take shape as "a Christology, a doctrine of the Trinity, an ecclesial and Christian doctrine of how to live."[93] In the world of theatrical drama, he aims to find resources that, when modified, can be deployed theologically.

He begins the book by recalling his *Theological Aesthetics*. There, he argued that the form of revelation—Christ's self-surrendering love—is the form in which all reality participates, since the ground of all reality, both natural and supernatural, is found in self-surrender in love. Since this is so, the perception of the form always involves participation in the dramatic action, since we are called to reciprocate God's self-surrendering love. God's action calls forth the action of his free creatures. Von Balthasar states that in Christ "the divine ground actually approaches us totally unexpectedly, of its own accord, paradoxi-

---

93. Hans Urs von Balthasar, *Theo-Drama: Theological Dramatic Theory*, vol. 1, *Prolegomena*, trans. Graham Harrison (San Francisco: Ignatius Press, 1988), 9.

cally, and challenges us to face it."[94] We therefore cannot interpret or contemplate revelation as observers. Rather, once we see
the form of revelation, we can rightly respond only existentially;
we must adhere to "the absolute commitment found in that drama into which the one and only God sets each of us to play our
unique part."[95]

Theologians, therefore, cannot do theology correctly if by
"theology" they mean an objective, neutral study of facts. This
is so because theology actually has to do with divine action and
human action, including the action of the theologian. By developing a "theodramatic theory," von Balthasar hopes to find a
mode of theologizing that retains the vibrancy of action.[96] He is
concerned that theological concepts about God, Christ, and life
in Christ have made these realities seem boring or static, when
in fact nothing could be more dynamic. He fears that by contrast
to the work of historians or dramatists—whose work makes clear
that they are dealing with active agents involved in exciting and
important matters—the work of theologians makes even the living God seem dull.

Von Balthasar notes that on the stage, the "drama of existence" becomes "explicit so that we may view it"; theatrical drama reveals to us "the character of existence" with its "interplay
of relationships."[97] Spectators of a play become immersed in it
as though they were the actual characters. In "theo-drama," revealed by Christ, we actually are immersed in it, even though
God is always the primary actor and even though (here the dramatic analogy somewhat breaks down, as von Balthasar admits)
"the involvement of man in the divine action is part of God's *action*, not a precondition of it."[98] The key to what God does, and
thus the key to the dramatic action as a whole, is that it is *good*.

94. Ibid., 16.
95. Ibid.
96. Ibid., 17.
97. Ibid.
98. Ibid., 18.

Not only has God created us, but in Christ God has reconciled the world to himself by "a real giving," by his "totally free love" in treading "the stage of the world."[99] God's action in the world reveals God's own inner life: "The analogy between God's action and the world drama is no mere metaphor but has an ontological ground: the two dramas are not utterly unconnected; there is an inner link between them."[100] One question that this point raises, von Balthasar notes, is whether the death of the Son of God has an analogous relation to the inner-Trinitarian life (as Hegel thinks it does). He postpones his answer to this question, however.

Von Balthasar makes clear that the outcome of the divine action does not remain concealed. The victory of God stands assured, though precisely what this victory will look like remains something of a mystery. God has won the victory, but since it is a victory "for us," we must appropriate it by sharing in the dramatic performance of self-surrendering love. It may seem that the drama of human action cannot be brought to "a singleness of meaning that can come only from God," a singleness of meaning necessary for dramatic coherence.[101] But von Balthasar affirms that God will accomplish this resolution because God has chosen to insert our drama into his own infinite drama of self-surrendering love.

One of the valuable things about theatrical drama, according to von Balthasar (and here he is in implicit dialogue with Hegel), is that it conditions us to understand human life as a "role" within a larger and coherent totality, a role whose meaning comes from above rather than being given by the self. Theatrical drama assures us that the higher (authorial) level from which we can perceive the full meaning of the action is not "a static level where nothing happens and which relativizes all events beneath and

99. Ibid., 18–19.
100. Ibid., 19.
101. Ibid., 20.

external to it."[102] The dramatic question of human life comes to a head in Christ's cry from the cross, when Jesus asks why God has abandoned him. The divine action culminates in the resurrection of Jesus. This dramatic action, von Balthasar suggests, reflects the inner-divine drama itself.

Nine Inadequate Proposals for Replacing Neo-Scholastic Theology

Von Balthasar associates his approach with other efforts to re-new theology in the decades prior to the original publication of his book in 1983. All such efforts, he says, involve a similar diag-nosis of "the shortcomings of the theology that has come down to us through the centuries."[103] The problem with the received theology is that it has become "stuck fast on the sandbank of rationalist abstraction."[104] Neo-scholastic theological portraits of the triune God, Christ, and life in Christ strike von Balthasar as rationalistic, in the sense of overly systematized and lifeless. He examines nine solutions that contemporary theology has put forward.

The first organizes theology in light of "event." God is event, the event of Christ seizes us, and everything is located in the "now" of God's saving event. In this context, von Balthasar also addresses Schweitzerian apocalyptic readings of Christiani-ty that deny that the promised "event" ever materialized. The problem with the focus on "event," however, is that "there is something timeless and context-less in this concentration on the pure event, which does not do justice to the genuinely historical nature of biblical revelation."[105] Without deprecating "event," it is more accurate to think in dramatic terms, with God acting throughout horizontal time.

The second proposed solution organizes theology in terms of

102. Ibid.
103. Ibid., 25.
104. Ibid.
105. Ibid., 27.

"history." From this standpoint, it is the present historical moment that governs everything; each historical moment has its own criteria for authentic proclamation and life, and so Christian doctrine must be reinterpreted and even reversed to meet the needs of the present (even if there is a guarantee that God is acting salvifically at each period). This standpoint, however, fails to do justice to what Christ definitively brings, to the distinctiveness of Christ's historical life, death, and resurrection. It fails to do justice to the time of the church as distinctively marked by what Jesus has brought. Without this definitive teaching, there would be no criteria for interpreting the "authenticity" of any historical moment. Von Balthasar adds the category of "history" becomes strikingly anthropocentric, to the point of not being able to render account of the living God's action.

A third proposed solution consists in raising "orthopraxy" above "orthodoxy." On this view, what is needed is Christian practice, actual love of God and neighbor, rather than worrying so much about the subtleties of doctrine. Von Balthasar warns that this solution, "while it drags Christianity out of the scholar's study and sets it on the world stage where it is to act and prove itself, abbreviates it to an ethics or a guide to human endeavor."[106] God's transcendent action in Christ goes missing. Christian action, too, becomes deracinated, because it is faith in God and his action in Christ (ultimately, self-surrender) that must govern Christian action. After all, human action is not on the same level as divine action: the latter accomplishes everything, even while inviting and requiring the participation of humans.

Von Balthasar names the fourth proposed solution "dialogue." He grants the importance of dialogue between people (including within the church), as well as covenantally between God and God's people. But he adds the cautionary point that much dialogue is not genuine, since for genuine dialogue to arise, both parties have to be seeking the true and the good. Further-

106. Ibid., 33.

more, Christ acts on the cross at the point where all dialogue has failed. Christianity, therefore, must not be reduced to dialogue. The Christian engaged in dialogue will have a different hope than his or her non-Christian dialogue partner.

The fifth proposed solution is "political theology." Von Balthasar recognizes that Christianity is political in the sense of "public" and also in the sense of relativizing the state. Christianity requires bringing faith in Christ (active through charity) into public and political life, on the side of justice and peace. Yet, the consummation of the kingdom of God will be God's gift, not a human achievement. Furthermore, Christ did not come as a political ruler in any normal sense of that term. Von Balthasar notes, therefore, that in fact "what is decisive is not the idea of a this-worldly approximation to the Kingdom but that separation of aeons which is made clear by Christ in his death and Resurrection."[107]

The sixth proposed solution has to do with the future. Christianity, of course, looks always to the coming eschatological future. Von Balthasar cautions, however, that it does not do so in the manner in which Israel looked forward to the coming of the Messiah. For future-focused theology, utopian and revolutionary schemes inevitably find a significant place. A better approach, says von Balthasar, is to be found in retrieval of "apocalyptic" thinking, which recognizes that history is the locus of "a drama between heaven and earth."[108]

The seventh and eighth proposed solutions highlight "function" and "role." By functionalism, von Balthasar means French structuralist theories, according to which the contingencies of history can be understood once we grasp their underlying structures. He judges much structuralist theory critically, since he thinks it can all too often rest in "an extreme form of Neo-Kantianism in which the world of the senses (which can never

107. Ibid., 39.
108. Ibid., 42.

be expressed in words) is now constructed by historical persons who resist being absorbed into the structure."[109] But he nonetheless values the way that functional or structural analysis exhibits "the matrix of suprasubjective social relationships," the matrix that forms the totality in which individuals play a part or function.[110] Structural analysis also helps to desacralize social phenomena such as sports or celebrity culture. With regard to theology, structural analysis cannot appreciate the governing presence of the incarnate Word in the church or validate the truly sacral character of roles in the church. Even so, structural analysis can help in appreciating the tension found in missions given to individuals (on the one hand) on behalf of the whole church (on the other hand).

With regard to "role," the question consists in whether we can find our identity in social roles. Without social roles, we would be at a loss, but at the same time social roles cannot fit all that we are. We are more than interchangeable parts filling certain roles for society. Religiously, the question of "role" finds expression in theories of reincarnation. Von Balthasar notes that Christian theo-drama alone, through the figure of Christ, can resolve this problem of uniting role and identity.

The ninth and last proposed solution—recall that the problem was an allegedly rationalistic or conceptualistic theology that turned Christian realities into abstractions rather than doing justice to a living dynamism—has to do with the problem of evil. In earlier Christian theology, the problem of evil was construed in terms of angelic and human sin, since God was assumed to be infinitely good and just. Now, however, the problem of evil often appears to modern thinkers as intrinsic to the world, which is therefore either absurd or invented by a god who is not only good but also evil, or at least profoundly incompetent. History seems to be spiraling toward human extinction; sin seems to be thriv-

109. Ibid., 44.
110. Ibid., 45.

ing, no matter what the cross might have done. Von Balthasar argues that the result serves theo-dramatic theology, since at present "the confrontation between divine and human freedom has reached a unique intensity; the contest between the two has moved into the center—the really dramatic center stage—of the problem of existence."[111] For von Balthasar, this collision raises the question of whether God has limited his freedom or power, or at least the question of what we should learn from the incarnate Son's "Godforsakenness" on the cross. I note that reference to divine "Godforsakenness" should remind us of Hegel's insistence that God contains within himself his own contradiction and that in some sense God is the resolving of that contradiction.

Hegel and the Solution: Theo-Drama

Von Balthasar engages Hegel directly as an *opponent* of the employment of drama in theology, given the limitations of drama—limitations that Christianity overcomes. As von Balthasar states, "Hegel's view of drama touches the nerve of our endeavor" and it is necessary "to feel the weight of Hegel's critique."[112] Von Balthasar recognizes that for Hegel the highest point of art consists in drama. He focuses first on Hegel's treatment of Greek (epic) drama, in which the focus is on God (or absolute truth) entering the world, rather than on individual inner subjectivity. He describes Hegel's account of Greek tragedy and comedy, noting that Hegel thinks that Greek comedy, when followed to its limit, dissolves art. Von Balthasar remarks that, in Hegel's view, the dissolution of Greek epic serves the rise of Christianity. In Christianity, the drama of Christ—the drama of God—affirms "the element of subjectivity in God; God himself is portrayed as having appeared and died and as being now seated at the Father's right hand, in the man Christ."[113] The key idea that Hegel draws from

111. Ibid., 50.
112. Ibid., 54.
113. Ibid., 60.

this is that God has died and therefore God has identified himself, in love, with his own contradiction or negation, a situation that attains resolution through the outpouring of Spirit, which reveals the unity of finite and infinite spirit. Von Balthasar concludes that, for Hegel, "Christianity itself is now the absolute drama, the truth of both tragedy and comedy."[114]

Yet, Hegel thinks that religion alone can arrive at this resolution; art or drama in itself cannot reach it. As von Balthasar points out, Hegel does not think that the striving of romantic art toward resolution can attain its goal. Von Balthasar notes that since Hegel considers "the entire Christian phenomenon as the 'image' of the absolute process," romantic art can strive to display this absolute process only until it is recognized that the solution lies in "religion," by which Hegel means in "the universal history of Spirit."[115] Romantic art endures until it is realized that "Christianity replaces art."[116] At the final stage, once Christianity itself is known to be simply "the *image* of the absolute history of Spirit," it becomes apparent that "Christianity is not only coextensive but identical with the human (which in turn is the manifestation of the divine)."[117]

Von Balthasar is quite right to observe critically that Hegel "fits the Christian approach into an all-inclusive history of the human spirit: Christianity had to make its appearance at this *particular* point in the development."[118] Von Balthasar critiques Hegel for treating Christianity in a reductive way, as though Christianity merely imaged the greater process by which absolute spirit realizes itself in and through the world. If Christianity were merely an image of the necessary process of absolute spirit, then Christ could not actually accomplish anything that absolute spirit was not necessarily accomplishing on its own. Von

114. Ibid.
115. Ibid.
116. Ibid., 61.
117. Ibid.
118. Ibid., 65.

Balthasar notes that Hegel's view of Christianity lacks "the real, active power of the life, suffering, and Resurrection of Jesus on behalf of all men, which in turn grounds the active, real power of the exalted Christ to give men an inner participation in his universal mission."[119] Christ is free and living, and his life, death, and resurrection are acts of free and personal divine power that enable humans to attain personal union with his "universal mission" of self-surrender.

Thus, von Balthasar emphasizes against Hegel that "the Lord who works is a person and remains this particular person after his Resurrection."[120] The process of absolute spirit realizing itself does not subsume or sublate the sacrificial moment of Christ. Christ is personally alive and active in a manner that Hegel, with his denial of personal immortality and bodily resurrection, cannot perceive. I note that von Balthasar's notion of our participation in the universal mission of Christ nonetheless has points of contact with Hegel's insistence upon the goal of identity between the accomplishment of the aim of the whole action and the resolution of the inner subjectivities of the characters. Ultimately, this could be the case only if the aim of the whole action was revealed to be self-surrender (in love) and if self-surrender was in fact the fulfillment of the inner subjectivity of human beings, as von Balthasar thinks it is.

Having criticized Hegel, von Balthasar gives him some praise as well. He says of Hegel that "no thinker before him [whether theologian or philosopher] more profoundly experienced and pondered Christian revelation in dramatic categories."[121] Evidently, therefore, von Balthasar sees his own work as one of building upon Hegel while critiquing Hegel's limitations. Von Balthasar grants that Hegel's dialectic of spirit's unfolding comes, in its essential pattern, from the dramatic flow of the

119. Ibid.
120. Ibid.
121. Ibid., 66.

Old and New Testaments. He states, "it was precisely from the utterances and counter-utterances of the Old Testament and the synthesis of the New that Hegel read off his fundamental dialectical rhythms."[122] Since this is so, we can expect von Balthasar to exploit the same "dialectical rhythms," even while he strongly rejects Hegel's reductive rendering of Christ's personal work and of the triune God. He points out that, for Hegel, existence means absolute spirit's giving birth to itself in the objective world, submitting to its opposite (suffering and death), and rising in a glorious reconciliation.

Von Balthasar resonates with Hegel's view that tragedy shows "the Absolute at play with itself: in the Christ-event it will be seen to be a play in all earnest"; he agrees with Hegel that "both tragedy and the Passion have the same basic nature: they are act. Reality is action, not theory."[123] At the same time, von Balthasar does not share Hegel's understanding of the nature of "the Absolute" or "the Christ-event." Therefore, he sharply differs from Hegel's position, on the grounds that Hegel has profoundly distorted both Christ and the Trinity. He notes that, for Hegel, "absolute Spirit simply contemplates its own being, namely, that of the self-alienated God who returns to his identity"; it follows that in Hegel "Christology has been superseded by philosophy (in a way that is both Nestorian and Monophysite, since the *purely* human is also the pure representation of God)."[124] Von Balthasar also critiques Hegel's understanding of the Trinity as both "Patripassian and Sabellian," given that, for Hegel, that God must have (or even be) internalized suffering.[125] He repudiates Hegel's implication that God's or Christ's actions are *merely* dramatic, like the events of a play; rather, Christ's Passion is

122. Ibid.
123. Ibid.
124. Ibid., 66–67.
125. Ibid., 67. Patripassianism is the heresy that the Father suffered on the cross; Sabellianism is the heresy that the Persons of the Trinity are not really distinct but rather the Father acts in history as "Son" and as "Spirit."

analogously dramatic. Whereas Greek tragedy is impersonal, Christ's Passion and resurrection are profoundly personal. Von Balthasar also rejects Hegel's notion of "the total World Spirit" that integrates all spirit. He points out that "the Christian *person* has risen above all these powers," even above the pure spirits that are the "angelic powers."[126]

Attending more closely to what Hegel means by "romantic" drama, von Balthasar critiques Hegel's view that romantic drama (as Hegel understands it) could in part mirror real Christian existence. The key to von Balthasar's critique is that Hegel has no notion of a living Lord, Jesus Christ, who personally and freely "can give the Christian a genuine mission by enabling him to share charismatically in his saving act."[127] Absent the free Christ who gives each Christian a real participation in his (Christ's) mission, there can be no Christian existence, no Christian drama. Hegel's emphasis on the centrality of inner subjectivity for romantic drama, therefore, signals to von Balthasar that Hegel's use of romantic drama will not work for anything but a spiritualized or privatized Christianity.

In Hegel's view, the period of romantic drama has come to an end. Von Balthasar agrees with this insofar as he thinks that drama itself is in decline. Extending his critique of Hegel, however, he implicates Hegel in this decline—although he also implicates neo-scholasticism. Along the latter lines, he suggests that the decline may well have roots in the fact that "personalist Christology, with its notion of a real acting and being on behalf of others and of a real participatory mission, has dwindled to nothing (as a result of orthodoxy and liberalism) and is no longer a lived reality."[128] He criticizes Hegel's view of the kind of plays that Hegel thinks would be characteristic of Christian drama, since Hegel describes a period of "chivalry" that is of little worth (though

126. Ibid.
127. Ibid.
128. Ibid.

I note that, for Hegel, "romantic" drama expresses Christianity insofar as art is able to do so). Von Balthasar argues that a living, personalist Christology would have preserved us from the Hegelian dialectic, that is to say from "the universal, impersonal, dialectical law of 'die and become.'"[129]

Via this critical dialogue with Hegel, von Balthasar identifies five issues that will be central for the project of his *Theo-Drama*. For each of these issues, although von Balthasar makes it explicit only with respect to the fourth and fifth issues, Hegel's impact is evident even when von Balthasar critically differs from Hegel.

The first issue identified by von Balthasar consists in the meaning of "mission." The Christian must enter into and become one with the mission that Christ gives him or her. Because Christian subjectivity has its center in mission, Christianity is oriented to the whole world. Here I think of Hegel's insistence that divine spirit must be actualized in the world and that finite spirit comes into its own in sacrifice. Second, von Balthasar describes the issue of the distinction between the "'substantial' nature" of the whole Church and the individual's vocation.[130] Throughout his account of drama, as we saw, Hegel underscores the distinction between individual subjectivity and the "substantial" truth that is reflected in the totality. Von Balthasar's third issue involves the universality and particularity of each Christian mission, which results in "conflicts and collisions" between Christians, as well as between Christians and non-Christians.[131] Von Balthasar adds that the mission of a particular Christian "may embody the objective spirit of an epoch ... or even the spirit of a continent," which means that Christian concerns will interact with the wider spirit of the time.[132] Hegel influences this discussion of "collisions" and "objective spirit."

129. Ibid., 68.
130. Ibid.
131. Ibid.
132. Ibid.

The fourth issue that von Balthasar names draws explicitly—though still critically—upon Hegel. Von Balthasar remarks that "if every mission … is a participation in the whole mission of Christ (which Hegel admits in his way), the drama of each particular Christian life can, in its own way, be a kind of reflection of the mission of Christ (which, with regard to the romantic drama, Hegel failed to see)."[133] As noted above, in romantic drama Hegel thinks that only the ultimate resolution or reconciliation of infinite and finite spirit is lacking. But the important point here is that von Balthasar recognizes that Hegel, in his own distinctive way, sees individual subjectivity as reflecting Christ's mission, namely his sacrifice or self-surrender, which is crowned by his rising in the Spirit. Each individual mission must be linked with the aim of the whole dramatic action, and this aim is revealed in Christ's self-surrender.

The fifth and final issue named by von Balthasar consists in whether the drama in the world reflects an intradivine drama and also whether God's involvement with the world risks making God into an impersonal "all-embracing dimension."[134] The key question here has to do with the relationship of the economic Trinity and the immanent Trinity. Von Balthasar recognizes that the two "coincide" for Hegel.[135] Von Balthasar also raises the question of divine *kenosis*. What is at stake is whether Hegel is correct that God, in himself (in his own "eternal history"), contains even what contradicts God, even while also containing the Holy Spirit as the resolution and reconciliation of all things.

Having articulated these five programmatic issues for his *Theo-Drama*, von Balthasar is not yet done with Hegel. He again takes up Hegel's suggestion that drama has reached an end beyond which it cannot go, given the limitations of art vis-à-vis "religion." Specifically, von Balthasar returns to Hegel's definition

133. Ibid., 68–69.
134. Ibid., 69.
135. Ibid.

of tragedy, this time by quoting Hegel's description of tragedy as divine essence (i.e., truth or ethics) differentiating itself into the conflict of infinite and finite, ending in a resolution or reconciliation that reveals the unity of infinite and finite. Appreciatively, von Balthasar notes that Hegel here assumes the existence of an "absolute (divine) idea of ethics," something that can no longer be assumed today in a Europe in which Christian convictions have vanished.[136] Von Balthasar also gives general approval to Hegel's view that in tragic drama, "identity" has to "reconstitute itself ... through the (loving) self-sacrifice of its distinctiveness."[137] Von Balthasar suggests that Hegel's dialectic reflects the Jewish "duality" between mortal humanity and divine communion, a duality overcome in Christ. Even more approvingly, von Balthasar observes that "for Hegel, both pre- and post-Christian drama is measured against the phenomenon of Christ: he is this distinctive individual who appears on the stage to take into himself, by dying on the Cross, the destiny of the world's guilt (which is not his) so that, transfigured, he can bring both back to the unity of the ethical."[138]

As noted above, von Balthasar rejects the impersonal character that Hegel gives to "the phenomenon of Christ" and to "the unity of the ethical." But von Balthasar still bemoans the fact that the Christian framework that sustained Hegel's insights has been largely lost in German intellectual culture. Hegel's understanding of tragedy is much richer and suppler, in von Balthasar's view, than that of later thinkers who deny any relation "between the tragic and anything that might bring about 'reconciliation'" and who therefore equate the tragic with the absurd or, at best, with a sacrifice made for the benefit of later human society (as in Marxism).[139]

136. Ibid., 71.
137. Ibid.
138. Ibid., 72.
139. Ibid.

As von Balthasar makes clear, Hegel deserves credit for perceiving that no dramatic action is possible without a framework
of absolute meaning. Dramatic action requires a political framework rather than a simply private or individual one. Absurdity,
freedom, and revolt cannot by themselves ground truly dramatic
action since they become simply boring or self-contradictory if
held up as an absolute meaning. Von Balthasar argues, therefore, that positing an absolute meaning is still quite possible.
He also surveys the effects produced upon drama by Marxist
optimism on the one hand and Holocaust-generated despair on
the other. In both cases, "the individual and his question are
mowed down" because there is no real future for the individual person.[140] He sees Thornton Wilder and Bertolt Brecht as the
contemporary dramatists who fight for the dramatic place of the
individual, without which the real significance of the community
of persons cannot be upheld. The framework of absolute meaning that von Balthasar defends is the Christian one in which humans exist in a tragic or paradoxical condition, fallen and mortal
but desirous of everlasting communion with God—a desire that
art can point to, but that no art can fulfill.

Christianity and Drama

In the pagan world, the theater contained great drama but also
lewd and cruel entertainment. Plato condemned the actions and
nature of the gods as depicted in drama. Von Balthasar gives
many examples of the conflict between the church and the theater, including the refusal of two priests to come to the bedside
of the dying dramatist Molière. Even when theologians such as
Thomas Aquinas or popes such as Clement XII argued that actors and actresses did not commit a sin by taking the stage and
should be admitted to the communion table, these views were
generally not taken up and implemented. Without excusing the
harshness of the church's condemnations, von Balthasar admits

140. Ibid., 82.

that "perhaps the actor actually does embody a dangerous temptation for all of us—that is, the possibility of not being ourselves,
the temptation of having more than one 'I'"; and von Balthasar is
also aware that the profession was at times connected, for actresses at least, with prostitution.[141] He gives attention to the medieval Christian development of church-sanctioned mystery plays,
which branched into sharp parody and bore fruit also in the inter-
mingled religious and secular drama of sixteenth-century Spain.

Von Balthasar concludes that "Hegel is right: the depth at
which, in Christianity, the theological-dramatic plot thickens
cannot be shown on the stage, nor can the decisive consequences of this event, that is, the transformation of the world's whole
condition, the hidden advent of the New Aeon."[142] At the same
time, however, he deems that since God's action for us is indeed
a theo-drama, there are valid (even if seriously limited) dramatic
ways of exhibiting this action. He discusses four points that tell
in favor of Christian drama.

First, when we see Christian theatrical drama, we become
more deeply aware that what Christ does is "for us." This is true,
for instance, with regard to the harrowing of hell as depicted in
Easter plays, or with regard to plays about the Last Judgment. We
gain a sense of Christ's dramatic contact with and presence to his
people, and a sense of the eschatological character of our actions
even now. Second, Christian theatrical drama underscores that
the history of salvation and the whole history of the world have
their center in the Eucharist: when we learn to perceive things
properly, we find that everything revolves around the wedding
banquet of the Lamb, and we discover that the things of this
world have been created for this banquet. Third, Christian theatrical drama highlights believers' sharing in the mission of the
Lord, often in situations of intense suffering; in this respect von
Balthasar considers that Hegel is blind to Hamlet's stance as a

141. Ibid., 105.
142. Ibid., 112.

Christ figure. Fourth, the absolute truth and goodness of God, upheld by the church, is needed for drama to proceed. This explains why even atheists set up their plays against the shadow of the church. As noted above, revolt or absurdity has no traction without absolute truth as its underlying ground; and the tragic drama of Christianity, in which Truth is crucified and exhibits its power in powerlessness, provides the deepest ground of all.

In sum, explicitly in opposition to Hegel, but clearly drawing on him, von Balthasar argues that "revelation is the ultimate precondition on the basis of which existence (and its reflected image, drama) can experience genuine tragedy—and not a tragedy which dissolves in meaninglessness."[143] Ultimately the difference between Hegel and von Balthasar does not consist in this claim about the necessity of revelation for drama. Rather, the critical difference, whose importance cannot be exaggerated, consists in whether revelation flows from the personal freedom of God.

Von Balthasar asks, however, whether a "theo-drama" would find itself cut off from the Christian tradition. His response is that drama is by no means alien to theology. Not only does divine revelation have a dramatic form, but the theological tradition of answering objections also has dramatic form, as does the existential contemplation that one finds in monastic and mystical theology. The alienation from drama happens, in his view, "when exegesis begins to go its own way and becomes 'scientific'" so that as a result "dogmatics increasingly becomes a 'textbook'," a monologue of answers without real searching or questioning.[144] Rather than a "prefabricated answer," what is needed is an answer with real dramatic roots in contemporary questions and in the scriptures, since these roots allow the Holy Spirit to work with freshness in theological pondering.

Von Balthasar explores the relationship between the natural and supernatural dramas of reality. The natural drama is ground-

143. Ibid., 123.
144. Ibid., 127.

ed in creation and made visible in myth; it is the tension between finite and infinite freedom. Von Balthasar warns against rationalistic reduction of God's freedom, since God's salvific initiative and inner life can be known only on the basis of revelation. On the basis of creation, we can conclude neither that "God's existence is identical with his initiative on the world's behalf, as idealism maintains," nor that "the absolute source of all dramatic interplay between God and the world is the mystery of that life in God which is shared by the divine life-centers ('Persons')."[145] The latter claim cannot be justified by reasoning upward from the exigencies of spirit, as Hegel does. In fact, however, it has been revealed to be true—though not in the impersonal way that Hegel understands it.

Preparing for the second and third sections of his *Prolegomena*, von Balthasar suggests that a central task of the remainder of the book (and, indeed, of the whole *Theo-Drama* itself) will be to sort out the distinction between the natural and supernatural—a distinction essentially rejected by Hegel—without denying the power of Hegel's insights. The meaning of finite existence and action, in relation to the existence and action of the Absolute or infinite, will be a central question, both in the light of creation and in light of Christ. This question bears upon the meaning and fulfillment of the human "I." A second question presents itself as equally or perhaps even more important: Does God, who transcends the finite action, risk himself by entering into the action? More specifically—and in a clearly Hegelian mode—von Balthasar phrases this crucial question as follows: "What is meant by 'God's history', by his kenosis, by the death of the Son of God? What is the relation between the economic and the immanent Trinity in all this?"[146]

These questions will not be fully comprehensible unless one grasps the concerns that motivate them. Fundamentally, as noted above, von Balthasar is concerned by portraits of the triune

145. Ibid., 129.
146. Ibid., 130.

God that seem to render God less interesting than human history, as though God were static and boring. Von Balthasar bemoans the impotence of "a systematics in which God, absolute Being, is only the Unmoved before whom the moving world plays out its drama."[147] He associates such systematic presentations of God with neo-scholastic textbooks. However, he also recognizes the danger of striving to make God interesting in a manner that produces "a mythology which absorbs God into the world and makes him to be one of the warring parties of world process."[148] Although von Balthasar is well aware that his questions about God's inner life or "God's history" vis-à-vis the work of salvation echo Hegel in certain respects, he recognizes that in Hegel "the two extremes meet," since Hegel presents *both* an impersonal absolute spirit and an absolute spirit who is subsumed ultimately into the world process.[149] Appreciatively, von Balthasar thinks that Hegel shows that God cannot be less interesting than human history; critically, von Balthasar thinks that Hegel is himself an exemplar of reductive gnosticism.[150] In his Hegelian critique of Hegel, therefore, von Balthasar aims to produce a theo-dramatic theory that avoids the pitfalls of Hegel while doing justice to Hegel's insistence that we cannot reasonably worship a God who is too abstract or static to be the God of history.

Dramatic Resources: From the Greeks to Modern Drama

The second section of the *Prolegomena* bears the title "Dramatic Resources." This lengthy section is filled with information about the history and development of theater. For my purposes of showing that the *Theo-Drama* offers a Hegelian critique of He-

147. Ibid., 131.
148. Ibid.
149. Ibid.
150. For discussion, see Cyril O'Regan, *Gnostic Return in Modernity* (Albany, N.Y.: SUNY Press, 2001), 1–22; O'Regan, "Balthasar and Gnostic Genealogy," *Modern Theology* 22, no. 4 (2006): 609–50.

gel—at whose dramatic center is divine self-surrender in love—
this section can be surveyed relatively quickly.

Von Balthasar points out that in Homer's epics, the gods
appear as spectators and participants in the human drama. In
Stoic philosophy, too, noble actions appear as a "play" worthy
of divine spectators. St. Paul understands himself as a dramatic
spectacle to the world for the sake of the world (1 Cor 4:9). For
Plato, the true God is good, not like the morally offensive gods.
In the *Laws*, Plato presents human beings as puppets of God, engaged in a morally serious dramatic imitation of God. In Helle-
nistic thinkers, von Balthasar finds reflection on the connection
between our "I" and the roles that we have been given to play in
life, roles that are a divine gift of participation in the marvelous
works of the universe. He pays particular attention to Marcus
Aurelius's deployment of the imagery of the stage to describe
human life. For Marcus Aurelius, death is simply the departing
from the stage, the just and non-deplorable permanent ending of
a role that one has been graciously given to play.

In the *Republic*, Plato sets forth the myth of souls choosing
what states of life into which they wish to be born. In this myth,
one has chosen one's own role on earth, and it is suited to one's
state of soul. At the same time, however, one may play one's role
well or badly, depending upon one's moral choices. Plotinus understands the world's diversity in terms of the goodness of having diverse characters in a play. Life's trials and triumphs, when
apprehended by means of the stage analogy, take on a pleasing
aspect that one cannot easily perceive when one is in the midst of
them. The soul has freedom to act out his or her role well or badly, to rise toward spirit or decline toward mere matter. Yet the role
is given by God, and Plotinus denies that God allows the actors to
take over the play, whose whole course God knows.

The themes of God watching his people and of an instance
of divine punishment constituting a spectacle whose purpose is
to warn the world can be found frequently in scripture. In es-

chatological literature, the victorious righteous, who suffered in the world, rejoice over the justice accomplished in the damnation of the wicked. The Fathers and medieval scholastics sound this same note. The basic point is role reversal: the victims, who were a spectacle in the world, will now triumphantly look upon their oppressors. The early Christians were often a spectacle, jeered by their persecutors and by their cultured despisers.

Maximus the Confessor describes scripture as a "play" by which to educate people toward knowledge of God and his plan. Clement of Alexandria describes life as playing the role that God has given us. Augustine describes a dramatic tension between allegiance to the city of God and allegiance to the city of man; some persons act the part of the former city while in fact belonging to the latter. Luther presents the world as filled with dramatic disguise. God conceals himself so as to give humans freedom, and God conceals himself in taking on the damnation due to sinners. Erasmus sees the world as filled with human folly, in which God willingly participates (and which God thereby redeems) by undergoing the folly of the cross.

The theme of the world stage, with God as the author, finds expression in dramatists and poets such as Shakespeare, Pierre de Ronsard, Francisco de Quevedo, and especially Pedro Calderón de la Barca. Von Balthasar describes Calderón's *Great Theatre of the World* at some length. Calderón gives a central place to a God-given mission of service to God. In all of these dramatists, von Balthasar finds scenes where a king lays aside his royal power. Throughout their work, at stake is the fulfillment of the "I," the identification and attainment of the person's true identity. While generally praising Baroque theater, von Balthasar comments: "Two questions are never solved: How is the transitory role related to the eternal God …? And what is God's relation to the role-play? Is he merely its inventor, spectator and final judge?"[151]

151. Von Balthasar, *Prolegomena*, 178. See also O'Regan's extensive discussion of baroque theater in *The Anatomy of Misremembering*.

The Enlightenment, however, turns away from God and attempts to ground the "I" autonomously. In Schelling, inspired by Hegel, we find the tension that all the actors must be filled with absolute Spirit, even while absolute Spirit arises only through the sum of the freedom and action of finite spirits. As von Balthasar puts it, idealist philosophy eliminates "the distinction between the 'I' and God and thus becomes an intoxicated or progressive deification of the 'I' or replaces God with the 'I' or subordinates the empirical 'I' to an egoless (and possibly demonic or nihilistic) Absolute."[152] We are back to the problems found in Hegel and thus to von Balthasar's critique of Hegel.

For von Balthasar, the answer appears in the Christian understanding of "mission," a God-given role or vocation that reconciles finite freedom and destiny with infinite freedom through service and thus through self-surrendering love.[153] But von Balthasar points out that this answer does not seem possible to the most prominent late nineteenth-century dramatists, namely, Franz Grillparzer, Friedrich Hebbel, and Henrik Ibsen. They are caught up in a problem epitomized by Goethe's *Faust*, and which is ultimately Hegel's problem as well: namely, the "I" has to imagine itself "to be a mirroring of the Whole or identical with it," with the end result of endangering individual freedom and subjectivity.[154] Ibsen shows that absolute egoism, in its upward thrust toward the glory of the infinite, leads to isolation, guilt, madness, and suicide. But Ibsen sees no way out of this dilemma, since, for him, God and Christ are not an option—although Ibsen retains utopian dreams.

In the early twentieth-century Austrian dramatist Hugo von Hofmannsthal, von Balthasar finds the reemergence of the Christian principle. Although in early plays he sought "the infinity of life on the foundation of the 'I'," Hofmannsthal's later work ex-

---

152. Von Balthasar, *Prolegomena*, 183–84.
153. Ibid., 190.
154. Ibid., 191.

hibits "the christological principle—God's death on the gallows for our sake—as underpinning the unutterable brokenness of the here-and-now."[155] Hofmannsthal's twentieth-century opposites, in von Balthasar's presentation, are George Bernard Shaw (whose sources are Ibsen and Nietzsche) and Luigi Pirandello (who shows that, absent the Creator, the world is a farce and the "I" a fleeting illusion). The point that von Balthasar makes in this survey of modern drama is that the path taken by Hegel leads, because of his impossible conflation of finite and infinite spirit, to dramatic disaster.

Von Balthasar concludes this survey with four themes that characterize the "theater of the world," whose exemplars are Calderón and Hofmannsthal, for whom theater can truly illuminate human creaturely existence. The first theme is that such theater emphasizes the finitude of the characters, despite their freedom, while also making clear that the meaning of the play goes beyond what the characters can know and indeed constitutes an eternal meaning. Second, the role and the "I" of the character are related but not identical. The character can freely shape the role, and the character can play an inferior role well. At the same time, the role (with its particular social context) shapes the character's "I." Third, the theater of the world gives a voice to "the divine Director," who possesses "the absolute reason of global responsibility" for the play, while also recognizing that the actors are not puppets but have the freedom to play their role well or poorly.[156] This theme raises the question of whether the actors, by rebelling, can thwart the purposes of the director—since it would seem that if they cannot, then they are still essentially puppets. Fourth and last, the content of the theater of the world focuses on human persons who, in the non-identity of their "I" and their role in the world, bear responsibility for their actions but cannot perceive the unified meaning toward which all the actions

155. Ibid., 225.
156. Ibid., 255.

in the play tend, under the director's guidance. A key question, then, consists in how to recognize the will of the director. Von Balthasar notes that in the theater of the world, a clue to the director's will consistently comes from a character in a lowly role. This is because what is at issue concerns the difference between self-seeking power and self-surrendering love.

Author, Director, Actor, Spectator

The second section of von Balthasar's examination of "Dramatic Resources" has the title "Elements of the Dramatic." His idea is to show "how the theatre springs from existence and is characterized by it."[157] Commenting on theater's origins in primitive cult, von Balthasar suggests that "existence itself must give rise to a 'faith' that its tentative projects will somewhere meet with a 'seeing', a 'solution' that will satisfy."[158] He comments on the relationships between the author, director, actor, and spectator. He observes that good theater reminds us that not only do we wish for a goal or solution in the light of which our whole life has meaning, but also we experience a difference between our "I" (insofar as we can know ourselves) and the roles that we play in society and in our own mind. In a good play, we can see how meaning and unity can be given and attained. When theater becomes practical in the sense of trying to impose a worldview, as though the dramatist were indeed the embodiment of providence, then theater overreaches. Instead, what drama can best do is remind us of our freedom and challenge us to live it in a way that fulfills us.

With regard to the author, von Balthasar is again interested in the issue of the relationship of infinite freedom and finite freedom: how the unity of the action is achieved through the conflicts and collisions of the various "often antinomian" characters, without making the characters mere puppets and therefore

157. Ibid., 259.
158. Ibid., 260.

lifeless.[159] He quotes Hegel on this topic, since Hegel insisted that the author or dramatist must have a profound breadth of spirit. The one dramatist must bring forth many characters, most of them differing significantly from the dramatist; and these characters must, in and through the unified action of the play, express the dramatist's word about reality. Von Balthasar focuses on the creative tension between "allowing the characters to develop in their own way and guiding their interplay from a position of ultimate superiority."[160] Of course, he has in view the question of "a free God, who makes room for created beings endowed with freedom" and who is both in and above his creatures.[161] In allowing for the freedom of the characters, the dramatist must not overlook the total movement of the play and the need for a just and fitting resolution.

Without actors, the dramatist's vision could not come to fruition. The actor has been given a role (a character), but he or she must breathe life into it. The actor has a mediating role, in the sense that he or she mediates or represents the dramatist's character to the audience. Here the key is what von Balthasar calls "*disponibilité*" for the role—pouring oneself into it completely.[162] When this happens, the actor can lose himself or herself in the role, a danger that concerned the church. The actor's sense of self can become fluid. This danger, however, can also be found in the various roles that characterize every person's life and that easily (even unconsciously) conceal the real person. Indebted to Gabriel Marcel, von Balthasar finds in the actor's *disponibilité* a clue to the life of Christ, which is fully expressive of the mission given him by the Father and thereby constitutes "a humble, facilitating representation of the divine."[163]

The director takes "responsibility for the play's performance,

159. Ibid., 271.
160. Ibid., 276.
161. Ibid., 277.
162. Ibid., 289.
163. Ibid., 294.

for making it present here and now" by guiding the oft-fractious ensemble of actors.[164] Here von Balthasar analogously has in view the work of the Holy Spirit. He explains that the director is entirely at the service of the actors, but in a manner that often involves conflict and collision with them. The success of the director comes about invisibly to the spectators; he or she seeks to implement the dramatist's vision and to draw out the potential of the actors.

Von Balthasar also describes the presentation of a play, the audience, and the horizon of meaning in which plays function. Citing Hegel, von Balthasar remarks upon the audience's "twofold need to see and to surrender ourselves to something that transcends and gives meaning to the limited horizon of everyday life."[165] He notes the link to cultic participation, since in viewing a great play "even the unpurified spectator, moved and carried along by the 'purificatory' action, is drawn into a process of catharsis whereby ... he is placed before the same horizon as that to which the cult refers," namely that of the very depths of human existence.[166] This is only so, however, when we are dealing with a play that falls within the context of the theater of the world. Absent God, a play can score political or emotional points but cannot introduce anything that exhibits true human fulfillment, since it must assume that human persons are headed into the abyss of impersonal extinction. Von Balthasar distinguishes between the horizon of fate and the horizon of providence, and he notes how each appears in Christian drama. Here he makes fully explicit the Trinitarian connection that he is working toward: "God the Father, who sends him, remains in the background as the real 'spectator' before whom 'the great theatre of the world' is performed; but since Father and Son are one, this role of spectator on God's part cannot be separated from his entering into the

164. Ibid., 298.
165. Ibid., 308.
166. Ibid., 312.

action on the stage."[167] But he adds that God's "entering into the action" is so explosive and rich that theatrical drama cannot adequately display it, since human theater has a tendency to reduce the mystery. He notes that this happens fully in Hegel, for whom "the whole horizon is incorporated into the subject, that is, into the total subject of the World Spirit," resulting in the conflation of presentation, audience, and horizon.[168]

Time, Death, Happiness, Tragedy, Judgment

Von Balthasar reflects on the particular way that theological drama can express our experience of time. He speaks of "the thrill of a play, in which the eternal destiny of man is set forth within a finite time-span."[169] Each moment of a drama is "pregnant with the future, facilitating various forms of dramatic intensity."[170] As he notes, this works only when the dramatist includes a "vertical" or transcendent dimension, allowing the events to be viewed from the divine perspective (even if this is only implied). Thus, he remarks that "deprived of that vertical dimension that takes human beings at their word, the horizontal dimension robs temporal life of all meaning."[171] He also observes that a dramatic situation can exist only where one finds two dimensions: the social dimension of a variety of humans involved in constantly changing dynamics due to collisions and conflicts, and the dimension of the totality of human life and thus the question of whether either individual action, or the totality of human life, has any enduring meaning whatsoever. Given these two dimensions, the mission or vocation of individual characters can have real dramatic tension.

This mission or vocation, furthermore, finds itself pressed by the threat of death. As von Balthasar says, "The final moment

167. Ibid., 319.
168. Ibid., 321.
169. Ibid., 349.
170. Ibid., 348.
171. Ibid., 353.

of time ... presents two sides: it is man's ultimate humiliation, striking him down and changing his organism into corruption, and at the same time it is something most precious and noble if he accepts it as the total offering and final form of his existence."[172] The key, in von Balthasar's view, is "the act of self-surrender," in which death can positively illuminate the life one has lived; if this cannot be done, then alienation takes over.[173] He also treats the dramatic sense of the immanence of death, the borderline between life and the eternal realm of death, atoning death, the relationship of death and love, the meaning of death on behalf of someone else, the unmaking and death of kings, and the relation of death to the ongoing sequence of the generations. In this section, while treating Shakespeare extensively, he gives ample evidence of the lively state of theatrical drama up through the mid-twentieth century.

Von Balthasar explores the way in which theatrical drama treats the elusiveness of the absolute Good. In comedy, the characters achieve a relative happiness, though we know that it will be a tenuous one. In tragedy, the striving of the person toward the good can lead to a "total witness of life" in which the person freely dies for the sake of the good.[174] Von Balthasar suggests that theatrical drama helps us to see that "man finds himself in a thicket of relative goods and values and tries, with the aid of an internal compass, to find his way to the Absolute."[175] As von Balthasar points out, humans have conflicting motivations: we may be filled with desire to serve (whether God or a good cause), but at the same time we may also possess a desire for self-promotion and self-advancement, which we think that we can attain through service. In modern plays, too, the divine realm (when not portrayed as existing simply within the hero)

172. Ibid., 370.
173. Ibid., 374.
174. Ibid., 414.
175. Ibid.

often "is an obscured, distorted, ultimately powerless, annihi-lated heaven, misinterpreted as man's demonic antagonist" or at least as a realm of futility that testifies finally to the futility of all existence.[176]

Examining various definitions of tragedy, von Balthasar notes that some allow for an ultimate reconciliation, while oth-ers insist that nothing is a tragedy unless the conflict remains unresolved—whether in itself or (in a manner that ultimately abolishes tragedy) in terms of the totality of the world's meaning-lessness. The question then is whether Christianity can contain real tragedy. In this regard, von Balthasar proposes that the Fa-ther's abandonment of Jesus on the cross "underpins everything in the world that can be termed 'tragic'."[177] He observes that "this overarching Christian reality (God on the Cross abandoned by God) goes way beyond the problems of the mere opposition of human and divine freedoms."[178] Here I recall Hegel's view that within God's own eternal history there is found every contradic-tion to God, a claim that involves the collision between infinite and finite freedom—but that, when understood in a truly person-al manner (as Hegel does not do), goes well beyond it.

Could it be, however, that what is "tragic" consists simply in a doomed person's noble and self-transcending action, even if the action occurs within a Godless and therefore ultimate-ly meaningless frame? Von Balthasar admires and approves of such an action, but he can see that the very possibility of a self-transcending action requires the real existence of "transcen-dence." He notes, too, that such an action cannot be solely the expiation of personal guilt. It must involve fighting against some-thing that, from the "transcendent" perspective, should not be.

The reason that Christianity does not obliterate tragedy is that God, in entering into the world's contradiction, does this

176. Ibid., 422–23.
177. Ibid., 429.
178. Ibid.

freely and lovingly as an utter gift rather than undertaking an impersonal resolution or reconciliation that would, at a higher level, subsume all tragedy. Von Balthasar emphasizes that it is precisely "*in* his [man's] humiliation" that "[man] needs once again to encounter the mystery of the mighty God whose love was not able to answer his Son when, on the Cross, he cried out for him," due to "an incomprehensible but ever-present guilt in the relationship between heaven and earth."[179] Thus, God does not subsume tragedy, but rather God enters into it personally and with love.

Von Balthasar adds that among the German idealists and those influenced by them, we find the claim that both tragedy and comedy "rest on the contradiction within the subject between the finite and the infinite."[180] They therefore argue that existence is a "tragi-comedy," a claim denied by Søren Kierkegaard, who points out that the tragic is ultimately not comical. Others such as Eugène Ionesco, however, find the world so utterly tragic as to be comical, a farce. Von Balthasar remarks, "By affirming the ethical ... but rejecting the metaphysical, tragi-comedy hovers between despising and accusing God and accepting that the world has a hidden meaning."[181] The hidden meaning would be found either in God (if he exists) or somehow in the structure of the world. Von Balthasar grants, of course, that the distinction between tragedy and comedy need not be a sharp one, since tragic elements can occur in comedies and vice versa.

In addition to the problem of the absolute Good (i.e., God) no longer seeming credible or real—which leads to the supposition that all is a tragic farce rather than being either "tragedy" or "comedy" in a traditional sense—there is also the problem of how theatrical drama can contain a truthful judgment about the goodness or badness of actions. In a tragedy, some aspect of

179. Ibid., 435.
180. Ibid., 442.
181. Ibid., 449.

justice must be at stake; and the same often holds, in a different way, in comedy. But how can fallible human judgment make a decision in the name of absolute justice, in the name of the Good? As an example of errors in this regard, von Balthasar aptly gives the treatment given to Shylock in *The Merchant of Venice*. But to Shakespeare's credit, von Balthasar also finds in his plays profound themes of "pardon, mercy, indulgence, grace."[182] After showing the presence of these themes in a variety of Shakespeare's plays, he highlights *Measure for Measure* as "a Christian mystery play, no matter whether or not the poet intended it as such."[183] In *Measure for Measure*, where the guilty and the innocent are judged together so that all might receive mercy, we perceive the coming together of tragedy and comedy along fully Christian lines. Indeed, for von Balthasar, Shakespeare exemplifies the fact that Christianity cannot be satisfied with either tragedy or comedy, but must allow for a world of both tragedy and comedy that ends by attaining to the "highest good" through (costly) forgiveness.[184]

Psychology and Sociology

The third and final section of von Balthasar's *Prolegomena* is titled "Transition: From Role to Mission." It begins with the relationship of the "I" and the roles we play, with how our willing of our self can arrive at our true self, given that we are never satisfied or quenched in our yearnings. Each of us must seek our true "I." Are we merely a chance production of our ancestors' fortuitous sexual encounters? Even if so, what is the ground of this biological ground? For Plato and (even more) Plotinus, we are souls; we can know our selves by knowing our souls' dynamic structure and origin. Von Balthasar turns to the Stoics, in particular Epictetus, for reflection upon our God-given freedom and

182. Ibid., 466.
183. Ibid., 470.
184. Ibid., 478.

our limiting roles. Epictetus considers that the good that perfects human beings coincides with the ethical good. We must obey God from within our roles, praising God with gratitude for the gift of existence. But von Balthasar rejects Epictetus's sharp dualism between body and soul, his pantheistic cosmology, and his denial of personal life after death—a denial that colors individual life with a lack of ultimate meaning.

With respect to the importance of accepting the self's limits, von Balthasar notes contributions made by modern psychology: Sigmund Freud, Carl Jung, and Alfred Adler. He comments upon Freud's existential despair due to his atheism, and he rejects Freud's reduction of everything to sexual drives, along with nearly all of Freud's claims. Yet von Balthasar takes seriously Freud's portrait of the human plight, in which everything "has the seed of death in it" and "there are only 'objects', there is no 'thou' that could form a bridge leading out of the lonely isolation."[185] In Jung, von Balthasar finds everything focused upon the relationship between "the tiny ego-consciousness" and "the gigantic world of the unconscious (primarily the collective unconscious), the stream of life on which individuals are carried along."[186] Jung seeks to recover for the "I" the mythic symbols that express the unconscious realm on which the "I" rests, symbols that metaphysics and church dogma once mediated but now seemingly cannot. Jung sets the "self" against the "ego," and the "persona" against the "role." Von Balthasar notes that Jung's focus on the "self" leads him essentially to bypass "the whole dialogical plane, the realm of becoming-a-self in the context of one's fellow human beings."[187]

Jung also argues that the archetypal divine, the horizon of the "self," must include both masculine and feminine, and both light and darkness. Furthermore, the realization of "self" rad-

185. Ibid., 513.
186. Ibid., 514.
187. Ibid., 518.

ically individualizes the unique person (in a profound loneli-
ness, exemplified archetypally by Christ) while at the same time
making him or her "an incarnation of that totality into which
he has transcended himself and to which he has surrendered
himself."[188] Here Jung, like Freud (though along different lines),
emphasizes limitation: we must not imagine ourselves to be the
totality, we must avoid arrogance and recognize the severe limits
of our knowledge and of our self-determination.

Adler, for his part, contrasts the poles of personality and
community, and emphasizes the integrative role of the mother's
love as well as the significance of purposeful action. The risk of
Adler's position, for von Balthasar, consists in the possibility that
the individual person simply dissolves into his or her roles: "In
Adler's context the idea that the individual's authentic uniqueness might be guaranteed by God cannot occur.... Adler's man
must *accept his limits* and become one with his social role."[189]
This is a reduction of the human person, who, due to the desire
for transcendence, is always more than his or her social roles.

Von Balthasar explicitly mentions Hegel for the first time in
this final section when he credits Hegel with recognizing the alienation of our "I" from our social roles. According to von Balthasar,
this insight of Hegel's (shared by others as well) influenced the
path of twentieth-century sociology. After briefly mentioning
Émile Durkheim and William James, von Balthasar turns to the
German role-psychologist Ralf Dahrendorf and his opponents. In
this debate, von Balthasar considers Kantian and Hegelian an-
thropologies to be at odds. As a Kantian, Dahrendorf holds that
autonomous, self-determining "man, entering into the role offered him by society, becomes alienated, a scientific statistic."[190]

188. Ibid., 521.
189. Ibid., 530. I have removed the italics from the name "Adler." For the texts
that von Balthasar has in view, see his references in his book. Here and elsewhere
in my book, it would be too distracting for me to list all the texts that von Balthasar
engages.
190. Ibid., 533.

Dahrendorf's Hegelian opponents insist that role is not alienation, because the human being "both *is* and *has* a social role";
infinite freedom can express itself in and through finite freedom
in a manner that reveals the identity of absolute spirit, reconciling all things.[191] Von Balthasar also treats George Mead, the early
Jürgen Habermas, T. W. Adorno, and others. At issue is the observed "dichotomy between the 'I' and its changing social roles," a
dichotomy that, in Adorno, leads to a denial of the stable identity
of the "I."[192]

Von Balthasar gives extensive attention to the early thought
of the sociologist Peter Berger. Berger shows that in cultures
governed by "myth," it is necessarily the god who gives the stable name—the stable identity—to the person. But when society
itself is recognized as the highest reality, then we can see both
that individuals produce society and that society produces individuals. Berger and others suggest that primary socialization
occurs through one's mother, and "after this primary discovery
of self comes the secondary socialization" in which roles are
involved.[193] Social roles seem to imprison a person, and yet our
voluntary acceptance of these roles give us a sense of freedom;
we are like puppets (of society) who freely accept our roles. We
can also lay aside our social roles and transform their meanings
or create new roles. Von Balthasar's conclusion is that Berger
and the other sociologists are not really able to anchor "the personal uniqueness" and self-transcending dignity of individual
humans.[194]

Role as Alienation and Attempts at Mediation

The next part of this section bears the title "Role as Alienation."
Here von Balthasar begins not with the Stoics, as he did in the

---

191. Ibid., 534.
192. Ibid., 536.
193. Ibid., 540.
194. Ibid., 544.

above discussion of "role" and human limits, but with the Neoplatonists. The Stoics see human beings as anchored solidly in a divine order, even though each individual human life will be extinguished permanently and even though God is impersonal. The Neoplatonists see humans as striving urgently toward reunion with an impersonal God. For Plotinus, "Everyone will discover, in the uniquely One, his own inalienable uniqueness, a discovery that can only coincide with the loss of individual selfhood."[195] At stake here is whether the creature, eternally known by the Creator, is less in itself than in the Creator—and therefore stands in an alienated condition until it is once more subsumed into the Creator. Von Balthasar reviews the "divine ideas" tradition through such figures as Augustine, Anselm, Bonaventure, and Aquinas. He also reviews the debate about whether the "agent intellect" is solely one, emanating from God. Although Aquinas rightly insists upon the integrity of the creature's being in itself and upon the fact that rational creatures possess their own distinct agent intellects, von Balthasar suggests that Aquinas was not, philosophically speaking, yet "in a position to lead the battle for the Christian dignity of the individual to a triumphant conclusion."[196]

After Aquinas's death, Meister Eckhart moves in the opposite direction by insisting that we must empty ourselves of everything that might belong to us as distinct creatures, so as to be fully united to the divine Son and to share in his divine knowing and willing. According to von Balthasar, Eckhart urges moving "beyond" the divine Persons to their wondrous "ground," the unfathomable divine essence. The "I"—even the "I" of the divine Persons—is thus an alienation at its core, even if Eckhart attempts to temper this conclusion. Von Balthasar considers Eckhart to be advancing along a path toward German idealism. He states, "In varying degrees and forms, from Fichte, via Schelling,

195. Ibid., 545.
196. Ibid., 550–51.

to Hegel, we encounter the same tendency to dissolve the empirical, personal 'I' in the 'essential', the 'ideal'."[197] Even though German idealism seeks to promote the highest realization of the self through thinking and moral action, it in fact alienates the personal "I."

Von Balthasar treats Fichte and Schelling as predecessors to Hegel, but I will focus simply on what he says about Hegel. This lengthy discussion concentrates on Hegel's *Philosophy of Spirit* (from his *Encyclopedia*) and his *Phenomenology of Spirit*, which I did not summarize at the outset of this chapter, but whose theses will nonetheless be recognizable. For Hegel, the absolute law of our human spirit is divine. In Hegel's view, this becomes apparent through Christianity, which shows how "God" becomes man in order to overcome all possible contradiction to "God" (or absolute spirit), resulting in the outpouring of the Spirit and the reconciliation of all things through the identity of finite and infinite spirit. The key consists in stripping oneself of everything particular (including hope for individual life after death) and thereby transcending particularity by embracing absolute spirit. Von Balthasar remarks that for Hegel "the normative is the 'generalized individual', in whose substantial ethical world particular individuals have their true freedom (provided each of them is integrated into it)."[198] To be integrated into the "generalized individual" means to achieve the surrender of one's individual "I" and to become a part of the "We." Indeed, this is what "spirit" consists in: the interpenetration and identity of the "I" and the "We," finite spirit and infinite spirit.

Von Balthasar summarizes Hegel's steps in *Phenomenology of Spirit* from sense perception to the awareness that to know consciousness we must go behind its finite modes (e.g., finite thinking, reasoning). Von Balthasar comments that when we have done this, we discover that "consciousness is life and de-

197. Ibid., 558.
198. Ibid., 581.

sire" and that "it experiences the self-subsistence of its object [i.e., consciousness], which is another 'self'."[199] Here takes place a "conflict"; we must see in "God" (infinite consciousness) all that contradicts "God," above all, death and non-being. Individuality is what must be willing to die, in order to allow absolute spirit, absolute freedom to stand forth. In *Phenomenology of Spirit*, Hegel depicts this conflict as the "master/slave" dialectic. The slave comes into his own by surrendering to and serving the master; finite consciousness comes into its own by surrendering to and serving infinite consciousness.[200] The infinite is present in the finite rather than being (as in orthodox Christianity) transcendent to the finite. The source of the reconciling action is always infinite spirit, not finite spirit.

As von Balthasar notes, Hegel explains this whole dynamic in Christian terms: "The death of God that is represented (in the death of Christ) as the form of reconciliation and the self-revelation of the infinite spirit is, in its truth, the form of inner self-reconciliation, not for the 'unhappy' consciousness, but for the consciousness that has realized itself as spirit."[201] The individual point of view, one of finitude, is completely surrendered and overcome. Even one's conscience cannot be taken to be ultimate, since it remains on the side of particularity. What is necessary, instead, is to focus on the reconciliation of the finite and infinite that has been achieved by absolute spirit. Our knowledge of our spirit as universal occurs in our knowledge of our spirit as pure individuality; for the reconciliation to take place, both perspectives (both "I's") must be relinquished.

Von Balthasar emphasizes that the individual person is completely obliterated in Hegel's thought. The death of the individual constitutes the noble sacrifice for the sake of absolute spirit, and,

199. Ibid., 583.
200. See G. W. F. Hegel, *Phenomenology of Spirit*, trans. A. V. Miller (Oxford: Oxford University Press, 1977), 115–19.
201. Von Balthasar, *Prolegomena*, 586.

unlike in Christianity, "no personalizing vocation is imparted to the individual."[202] The "sacrifice" that is symbolized by Christ's death and that pertains to the history of absolute spirit consists in a shattering of all individuality. Von Balthasar comments simply that "in its sacrifice for the sake of the whole, the 'I' as such is not sustained."[203] The "I," therefore, belongs to the realm of alienation for Hegel. His vision of absolute spirit lacks real interpersonal communion. Von Balthasar's critique of Hegel's negation of personality (divine and human) leads him to reject "all attempts to reinterpret Hegel in a personalist sense."[204]

How then to understand the "I" in relation to God? As we have seen, von Balthasar accepts that roles are needed given human creaturely limitations, but he complains that such limitations are often taken as ruling out the possibility of transcendence. He likewise accepts the human desire for the infinite but complains that many hold that a particular role (or individual identity) alienates humans from the infinite. In a comparatively brief final part of this section, he explores what he terms "Attempts at Mediation." Again he focuses on pre-Christian and post-Christian (modern) thought. For ancient near-Eastern pre- Christian peoples, the king possessed the role fitting to the "I," a role of mediation that unites the king with the god whom he serves and represents. Representing the god, the king struggles against the forces of chaos. Indeed, the king often is understood to be not solely human but in some real way the son and image of god. The king therefore is the true "I," and his subjects reflect him to various degrees. One can see a Christological application.

Among ancient and modern peoples, the "genius" also represents god. In its ancient origin, related to the Greek *daimōn* that Socrates understood himself to possess, the "genius" was a god who functioned like a guardian angel. The German ro-

202. Ibid., 588.
203. Ibid.
204. Ibid., 589.

mantics associated "genius" with the spirit possessed by great creative artists that enables them to advance the development of the human spirit. This role can be seen potentially to represent the Holy Spirit.

Von Balthasar commends the late nineteenth- and early twentieth-century thinker Georg Simmel's defense of personal individuality against German idealism and modern technological civilization. Simmel anticipated von Balthasar's *Theo-Logic* by conceiving of "the subject-object relationship" as "an intimate reciprocal influence, a mutual 'fitting-in', based on their continual coming-forth, together, from life's ground."[205] Simmel undertook a wide range of inquiries, including reflecting upon the connection between "life" (individual) and "form" (social) and highlighting the significance of Goethe. Von Balthasar, however, ends by critiquing Simmel quite strongly, despite valuing Simmel's intentions. For example, according to von Balthasar, Simmel understands God as the "absolute reciprocity (in terms of 'reflection') of the things in the world."[206] Von Balthasar warns against this view, as also against Simmel's specific view of the soul's immortality, on the grounds that Simmel has rejected all duality and has rejected "the creaturely distance separating man from God."[207] In his rejection of orthodox Christianity, Simmel takes a position that seems strongly influenced by Hegel's (and others') notion of God's history played out in the world, so that what happens in the world reflects God's personal life and the result after death is undifferentiated, absolute spirit rather than interpersonal communion.

The final attempt at "mediation," at uniting but not conflating God and the individual "I" who seeks God (within his or her limited creaturely roles), is the "I-Thou" philosophical theology of Ferdinand Ebner, Martin Buber, Gabriel Marcel, and Franz

205. Ibid., 615.
206. Ibid., 622.
207. Ibid., 623.

Rosenzweig. Even when they are solely doing philosophy, these thinkers show that the link between God and the personal "I"—and thus the ground of the "I" in its many limited roles—can come only from divine revelation, from the divine "Thou." As von Balthasar puts it, "only through the 'name' that God uses to address the individual human being is he validly and definitively distinct from every other human being."[208] Only the divine "Thou" can raise up and sustain, rather than limiting or conflicting with, the personal human "I." Furthermore, the divine "Thou" must come to us freely; we cannot generate it out of our intrahuman "I-thou" relationships, even though in truth "every 'I' has a direct relationship with this Thou."[209]

Even more than Buber, the hero of this part is Rosenzweig, who argues that we find our "I" in response to God's summoning and that our "I" is entirely receptive to God's commandment, which gives us the mission of love. Ebner, the only Christian among these thinkers, has the final word, because he perceives that everything depends upon faith in the crucified Christ, who cannot be idealized as spirit or known solely as the Thou who commands or even solely as Spirit-filled Word, but rather is suffering, incarnate love. Here, in the crucified Christ's absolute self-surrender in love, we find the divine "Thou" who bestows upon us our "I," our mission of self-surrender in him for the sake of the world.

Von Balthasar ends his *Prolegomena* to his *Theo-Drama* with some "Concluding Remarks." In response to the question "Who am I?" von Balthasar has attempted to move from "role" to "mission." The key is recognizing that only God can give this mission, this name that truly personalizes the individual by giving the individual life an enduring place in relation to God. Called by God, the individual becomes a "partner" with God; this is why "theo-drama"—as a history that truly relates to God—is possible.

208. Ibid., 628.
209. Ibid., 635.

From Theodor Haecker, von Balthasar draws the insight that only Christ perfectly embodies his mission, so that his identity is the same as his role. From Aquinas, von Balthasar adds that Christ's mission is identical with the intradivine procession of the Son. His mission is one of obedience to the Father, and it is one of suffering out of love. Through the same Spirit who unites him to his Father, Christ can enable those who share in him by faith and love to embody a mission, to "close the tragic breach between person and role."[210] The Spirit ensures that the individual and the social are perfectly reconciled, since mission involves both the intensely individual relationship (through self-surrender) of the "I" to the triune God, on the one hand, and the absolute self-surrender of the "I" to the world in the context of the whole church, on the other.

Von Balthasar concludes, "It follows quite naturally that if, obedient to his mission, a person goes out into a world that is not only ungodly but hostile to God, he will be led to the experience of Godforsakenness."[211] The concluding question of the *Prolegomena* consists in how this "highest reality of earthly existence" can "point to an existence in God"[212]—that is to say, how the tragic and Godforsaken death of the Crucified (and the tragic and Godforsaken deaths of those who are united to him) can have meaning in relation to a God for whom peaceful reconciliation eternally reigns.

Conclusion

Von Balthasar's *Prolegomena* does not place us in direct contact with all that we find in the additional four volumes of his *Theo-Drama*. Von Balthasar takes seriously the task of setting forth the "dramatic resources" that, when understood analogously, provide a basis for theo-dramatic theology. He also devotes a

210. Ibid., 646.
211. Ibid., 647.
212. Ibid., 648.

good deal of space to showing the way in which theo-dramatic theology can fulfill the goals of other forms of theology that today are seeking to supersede the neo-scholastic model. He explores the meaning of tragedy and comedy, and their unification in Shakespeare's plays of mercy. He explores the ways that German idealism, modern psychology, and modern sociology have construed the identity of the "I," the "self," given the multiple roles that we play and given the possibility that our identity is constructed solely on the basis of our social roles. He examines the existential despair that we find in Freud or Ionesco, a result of the modern dissolution of the frame of the "world stage" (despite the counterexample of Hofmannsthal) for lack of a divine Author. The *Prolegomena*, clearly, provides an education that can be taken on its own terms, without reference to the other volumes of the *Theo-Drama*.

Yet, von Balthasar certainly intends for the *Prolegomena* to be intimately related to the rest of the *Theo-Drama*. It sets up the ground of human identity, of the human "I." This ground is given by the triune God. It comes to us in Christ's revelation of the Father through Christ's absolute self-surrender in love for us on the cross. In self-surrender, Christ is abandoned by God, by the Father (Mt 27:46). Christ, the innocent Son, takes our sin upon himself, in dying for our sin. He thereby manifests the "highest reality of earthly existence," which is self-surrender in love—and yet this reality is an experience of Godforsakenness.[213] How can this be?

In answering this question, von Balthasar has in view a Hegelian critique of Hegel. The critique is a profound one: Hegel depersonalizes what is in fact personal all the way down. Hegel turns Christianity into a story of the dialectical emergence of absolute spirit, and Christianity must never be reduced in this way. Von Balthasar makes clear in his *Prolegomena* that he stands against, not with, Hegel.

213. Ibid., 648.

In this critique, von Balthasar nonetheless draws crucially upon Hegel: his critique is, in a positive sense, Hegelian. First, Hegel describes the need for the identity, in a good play, between the individual subjectivities of the characters and the aim of the whole action. For von Balthasar, only if the aim of the whole action is unity with the triune God, whom Christ has revealed to be self-surrendering love, can the individual subjectivities in their diverse desires be brought together fully: their self-surrender will fit with the goal of the whole dramatic action, a goal grounded in the divine Persons themselves. Second, von Balthasar devotes a whole volume of his *Theo-Drama* (namely, the second volume) to the collision between infinite and finite freedom. In the final two volumes of the *Theo-Drama*, he makes clear that the triune God contains in himself all otherness, all contradictions and alienations, all distances. God is caught up in the earthshaking events of human history, at whose heart is the most earthshaking event of all: the Godforsakenness of the incarnate Son in his utter self-surrender in love. The Son is the expression of the whole Trinity, and he is this expression because the Father pours himself out. Rather than remaining enclosed in himself, the Father pours himself out so as to beget a divine Person who is radically other even while being radically the same. As the bond of love, the bond of unity that the Father and Son breathe forth, the Holy Spirit is the resolution of this otherness. If the Cross is the pinnacle of the human drama, we can be sure that the generative and spirative Trinitarian life, expressive of humble self-surrendering that allows the other to be and to be other, has no rival for dramatic goodness.

If we go back to the first part of the *Prolegomena*, where von Balthasar sketches the varieties of ways in which post-Vatican II theologians are trying to move beyond neo-scholasticism, we can see von Balthasar's goals more clearly. He recognizes that historicist and political-liberationist theologies took center stage after the Council. Dogma was relativized; the purpose of the church was now seen as orthopraxy, and the relationship between doctrinal orthodoxy and pastoral orthopraxy was put in question. Dialogue came to be seen as the path by which orthodoxy could lay down its weapons, humble itself, and discover the true orthopraxy of love and tolerance of others. In all this, God's Word, as known and handed on dogmatically, looked more and more like a highly fallible human word.

Von Balthasar presents his theo-dramatic theology as the corrective to this anthropocentric and historicist theology. It is a corrective, however, that incorporates the dramatic action for which praxis-centered theologies call. It deepens this dramatic action theologically by rooting it in the self-surrendering love of Christ, which reveals the depths of the Father's self-surrendering love. Dogma and praxis are reunited in the mission of self-surrendering love, expressive of the intra-divine processions. History is reclaimed not as the place solely of human action, but as the place of the collision between infinite freedom and (fallen) finite freedom, where the triune God "risks" everything in self-surrendering love, in allowing otherness to be. Because the theo-drama, both in God and in the world, involves radical self-surrender in love, the dogmatic basis of distinctive Christian praxis and of distinctive Christian identity becomes apparent once more, as does the power and intensity of the collision, since radical self-surrender in love is not at all what we sinners want to do.

Recall that Hegel urges that we submit and surrender to the dialectical law of life, death, and resurrection, by which finite and infinite spirit are reconciled in the unity of absolute spirit. Such a notion, von Balthasar makes clear, is far too impersonal, far too immanentist (since absolute spirit is not transcendent), and far too predictable for actual drama. Working with Hegelian themes of God's self-differentiation encompassing all otherness through sacrifice, God's history sublating all otherness, infinite freedom and finite freedom colliding, individual subjectivities being reconciled in the fulfillment of the whole of history, and so forth, von Balthasar offers a Hegelian critique of Hegel that retrieves the fundamental dogma and praxis of Christianity.

The main point is that God the Trinity is extraordinarily good. God is triune self-surrendering love, encompassing and allowing otherness, willing to surrender himself freely out of love for us, his creatures who are sinners. This radical self-surrendering, encompassing and overcoming otherness, not only is something that God deigns to do in his goodness but is the free Trinitarian goodness that God in fact *is*. Likewise, in freely surrendering ourselves, configured to Christ, we become who we are meant to be, through an intimate and deifying participation in the divine goodness.

3 ⚭ Theo-Logic

A NIETZSCHEAN CRITIQUE
OF NIETZSCHE

A number of scholars have commented upon Hans Urs von Balthasar's engagement with Friedrich Nietzsche. Edward Oakes observes that "what most characterizes Balthasar's attitude toward Nietzsche may perhaps be summed up in one word: fascination."[1] Oakes suggests that, in Nietzsche, von Balthasar finds the "link between the idealism of Kant and Hegel, and the existentialism and vitalistic philosophies of the 20th century."[2] Peter Henrici shows that von Balthasar finds in Nietzsche an instance of "dialogic" that in the end "expressly closes itself against love."[3]

1. Edward T. Oakes, SJ, *Pattern of Redemption: The Theology of Hans Urs von Balthasar* (New York: Continuum, 1994), 99. See also Peter Henrici, SJ, "The Philosophy of Hans Urs von Balthasar," in *Hans Urs von Balthasar: His Life and Work*, ed. David L. Schindler, 149–67 (San Francisco: Ignatius Press, 1991), at 158–63; Alois M. Haas, "Hans Urs von Balthasars Nietzschebild: Eine Problemskizze," in *Logik der Liebe und Herrlichkeit Gottes: Hans Urs von Balthasar im Gespräch. Festgabe für Karl Kardinal Lehmann zum 70. Geburtstag*, ed. Walter Kasper, 146–62 (Ostfildern: Matthias-Grünewald-Verlag, 2006); J. Gesthuisen, *Das Nietzsche-Bild Hans Urs von Balthasars. Ein Zugang zur* Apokalypse der deutschen Seele (Rome: Gregorian University Press, 1986). Henrici states of Nietzsche that "it is clear that he [von Balthasar] is again and again fascinated by him, although it was clear from the outset (even clearer than in the case of Hegel) that no Christian can follow his thought" ("The Philosophy of Hans Urs von Balthasar," 159).

2. Oakes, *Pattern of Redemption*, 100.

3. Henrici, "The Philosophy of Hans Urs von Balthasar," 160. Henrici adds that in *The Apocalypse of the German Soul*, "the issue is the true form (*Gestalt*) of love: Nietzsche's titanic 'power-love' encounters in Kierkegaard 'the descending power and love' of the Crucified" (ibid.).

Specifically with regard to the *Theo-Logic*, Alois Haas has point-ed out, "As early as the first volume of the *Theo-Logic*, he has re-course to Nietzsche as a means of privileging" the "form of knowl-edge" that "oscillates from essential to existential-historical knowledge."[4] In agreement with these insights, this chapter will introduce the final part of von Balthasar's trilogy, the *Theo-Log-ic*, by arguing that it should be read as a Nietzschean critique of Nietzsche. The point of the chapter is that von Balthasar's *Theo-Logic* turns around Nietzsche's understanding of truth. Whereas for Nietzsche truth is the will to power, for von Balthasar truth is the will to self-surrendering love.

Von Balthasar does not explicitly announce such an inten-tion, no more than he claims the *Theo-Drama* to be a "Hege-lian" critique of Hegel. Yet I think that there are sufficient clues throughout the first volume of the *Theo-Logic* to indicate why the *Theo-Logic* as a whole can and should be read as a Nietzschean critique of Nietzsche. As with the preceding two chapters, the emphasis here must be on "critique." Obviously, von Balthasar is no Nietzschean. But von Balthasar is appreciative of Nietzsche's position that truth involves the will to life and of Nietzsche's ac-centuation of the volitional or "existential-historical" dimension of truth. In this regard, von Balthasar's perspective displays the influence of Maurice Blondel and Martin Heidegger.[5] It was not for nothing that von Balthasar edited three small volumes of ex-cerpts from Nietzsche's writings in addition to treating him at length in *The Apocalypse of the German Soul*.[6]

---

4. Haas, "Hans Urs von Balthasars Nietzschebild," 160.

5. See Peter Reifenberg, "Blondel and Balthasar—eine Skizze," in *Logik der Liebe und Herrlichkeit Gottes*, ed. Walter Kasper, 176–203 (Ostfildern: Matthias-Grünewald, 2006); Cyril O'Regan, "Hans Urs von Balthasar and the Unwelcoming of Heidegger," in *Grandeur of Reason: Religion, Tradition, and Universalism*, ed. Conor Cunningham and Peter Candler (London: SCM, 2010), 264–98; O'Regan, "Heidegger and Christian Wisdom," in *Christian Wisdom Meets Modernity*, ed. Kenneth Oakes, 37–57 (London: Bloomsbury, 2016). I agree with O'Regan regarding the importance of Heidegger—who himself was deeply influenced by Nietzsche—in von Balthasar's *Theo-Logic*.

6. See Hans Urs von Balthasar, *Apokalypse der deutschen Seele: Studien zu einer*

In this chapter, I first set forth Nietzsche's position on truth, as found in a variety of his works. I summarize certain important portions of these works so as to ensure that the reader appreciates the scope of Nietzsche's position. The works I have chosen generally come from Nietzsche's late period: *The Will to Power*, *Thus Spoke Zarathustra*, *Twilight of the Idols*, *The Anti-Christ*, *On the Genealogy of Morals*, and *Ecce Homo*. Second, I survey the first volume of the *Theo-Logic* both as a way of introducing readers to the key themes that drive von Balthasar's approach to truth and in order to show why I understand the *Theo-Logic* to be a Nietzschean critique of Nietzsche. As in the previous two chapters, my survey, with its sometimes verbatim presentation of the unfolding of von Balthasar's book, may leave readers wondering why so much detail is being given. My purpose once again is to give readers a full sense of the extraordinary range of von Balthasar's reflections, rather than imposing my limited lens. Yet, I hope to show that, drawing upon Nietzsche and critically reversing Nietzsche, von Balthasar's fundamental aim in the *Theo-Logic* is to demonstrate that self-surrendering love, which is the form of all reality (beauty) and the drama of all reality (goodness), is also the *truth* of all reality.

Nietzsche's Perspective on Truth

The Will to Power

Friedrich Nietzsche did not write a book titled *The Will to Power*, although he contemplated doing so. After his death, however, his sister, Elizabeth Förster-Nietzsche, published topically arranged excerpts from his notebooks under the title *The Will to Power*. The material contained in this book encapsulates Nietzsche's essential thought, even if his sister's anti-Semitism influenced

---

Lehre von letzten Haltungen, vol. 1, *Der deutsche Idealismus* (Salzburg: A. Pustet, 1937); vol. 2, *Im Zeichen Nietzsches* (Salzburg: A. Pustet, 1939); vol. 3, *Die Vergöttlichung des Todes* (Salzburg: A. Pustet, 1940).

the book negatively in certain ways. Included in this published edition of *The Will to Power* is a preface that Nietzsche wrote for a projected book of the same name, in which he explains that his purpose is to seek "new values" that can sustain humanity after the period of utter nihilism that he sees on the horizon.[7]

I will here examine a brief set of texts from his notebooks that his sister arranged under the rubric "The Will to Power as Knowledge." In note 480, Nietzsche comments that such things as spirit, reason, will, consciousness, and truth are fictions. What "knowledge" is, instead, is "a tool of power."[8] When we increase in power, we increase in knowledge. "Power" ultimately means the ability to preserve the self and the species. When we desire increased "knowledge," this means that we desire increased ability to preserve ourselves and our species by mastering the things around us. There are no facts, only interpretations; and these interpretations have behind them not an "interpreter" but a biological drive for power (self-preservation). Our biological drives conflict with the biological drives of others. Nietzsche states, "Every drive is a kind of lust to rule; each one has its perspective that it would like to compel all the other drives to accept as a norm."[9] There is no "interpreter," no substantial subject, but rather there is "something that in itself strives after greater strength."[10]

Nietzsche recognizes that bodies exist, and what bodies want is life. Whatever produces more life therefore counts as "truth." He holds that it is "improbable that our 'knowledge' should extend further than is strictly necessary for the preservation of life. Morphology shows us how the senses and the nerves, as well as the brain, develop in proportion to the difficulty of finding nour-

7. Friedrich Nietzsche, *The Will to Power*, trans. Walter Kaufmann and R. J. Hollingdale, ed. Walter Kaufmann (New York: Random House, 1967), 4. For Elizabeth Förster-Nietzsche's unfortunate editing, see Christian Niemeyer, *Nietzsche verstehen. Eine Gebrauchsanweisung* (Darmstadt: Lambert-Schneider-Verlag, 2011), chap. 2.

8. Nietzsche, *The Will to Power*, 266.

9. Ibid., 267.

10. Ibid., 270, note 488.

ishment."[11] If "knowledge" or "truth" therefore correlates with whatever assists the bodily drive toward self-preservation, and if "power" is the ability to preserve the self and (correspondingly) to master others and "shape things according to our wish," then the dynamism toward truth stands unveiled simply "as a means of the preservation of man, as *will to power*."[12] Our brain seeks to maximize our power and self-preservation, not to know things as they are. What we count as "knowledge" consists in what our brains, through "abstraction and simplification," arrive at for the purpose of "taking possession of things."[13] We "impose upon chaos as much regularity and form as our practical needs require."[14]

Thus Spoke Zarathustra

Nietzsche's poetic rhapsody *Thus Spoke Zarathustra* begins with the arrival of Zarathustra, coming down from the mountain where he has filled himself with wisdom. He seeks to bring his fellow humans a gift, beginning with the point that "God is dead" and culminating in the "Superman," the overcoming of mere man.[15] He urges those who are able to hear him that they should "Become hard!"[16] Rather than being soft and yielding, humans need to be "inexorable," to be willing to "cut to pieces," so as to be true creators.[17] He offers a heartfelt prayer to his own will.[18] He seeks and longs for "higher men," "higher, stronger, more victorious, more joyful men" who recognize that each person is a law for himself.[19]

11. Ibid., 272, note 494.
12. Ibid., 272, note 495.
13. Ibid., 274, note 503.
14. Ibid., 278, note 515.
15. Friedrich Nietzsche, *Thus Spoke Zarathustra*, trans. R. J. Hollingdale (New York: Penguin, 1969), 41.
16. Ibid., 231. I have removed the italics from the quoted phrase.
17. Ibid.
18. See ibid., 235.
19. Ibid., 294; cf. 296.

According to Nietzsche, the death of the meek Christ opens the way for the "Superman" who exercises his will with absolute freedom.[20] He is the one who has found "Life," which stands "beyond good and evil"—the power of self-will, not impeded by anything.[21] The Superman rejects the small things that the "mob" wills, and instead wills with greatness and abandon, freed from any prudential or petty calculus.[22] He rejoices in "Eternity" or "the Ring of Recurrence," filled with the "creative breath" of his will, "the thunder of the deed," playing "dice with the gods at their table" and flinging himself freely "about, out, back," no longer weighed down by extrinsic law or piety.[23] He triumphs by being truly a self-creator. True wisdom, true "love of truth," consists in daring to will what the self *now* wants, doing nothing for any purpose other than sheer exercise of will to power, filled with the "eagle's wings and serpent's wisdom" of "the wildest, most courageous animals."[24]

The Twilight of the Idols

Nietzsche puts things in a less rhapsodic way in *The Twilight of the Idols*, written in 1888 (the last year of his sanity). Here Nietzsche promotes "an overflowing feeling of life and energy within which even pain acts as a stimulus."[25] This "will to life," which in his view Christianity seeks to subdue and suppress, is what he considers to be the only truth, the only wisdom. Opposing Greek tragedy to Christianity, he approves of what he calls the Diony-

20. Ibid., 297.

21. Ibid., 242.

22. See ibid., 298.

23. Ibid., 245, 247. Along these lines, see also Nietzsche, *The Gay Science: With a Prelude in German Rhymes and an Appendix of Songs*, ed. Bernard Williams, trans. Josefine Nauckhoff and Adrian Del Caro (Cambridge: Cambridge University Press, 2001).

24. Nietzsche, *Thus Spoke Zarathustra*, 313. See also Nietzsche, *The Gay Science*.

25. Friedrich Nietzsche, *The Twilight of the Idols, or How to Philosophize with a Hammer*, in Nietzsche, *Twilight of the Idols and the Anti-Christ*, trans. R. J. Hollingdale (New York: Penguin, 2003), 121.

sian "affirmation of life even in its strangest and sternest problems, the will to life rejoicing in its own inexhaustibility through
the *sacrifice* of its highest types."[26]

What Nietzsche is looking for is the "exuberant and even
overflowing" instinct that is "an *excess* of energy."[27] In his view,
philosophers such as Socrates, Plato, and Aristotle, with their
emphasis on virtue, proved that they had lost the essential Dionysian impulse and fallen into decadence. While he abhors Immanuel Kant, he praises Johann Wolfgang von Goethe's real contact with life and Goethe's understanding of the nobility of utter
freedom, the nobility of "a man to whom nothing is forbidden,
except it be *weakness*."[28] Nietzsche appreciates the genius, the
great man, who masters his time period and who is "explosive
material in whom tremendous energy has been accumulated."[29]
With respect to philosophical reasoning, he concludes that "all
that philosophers have handled for millennia has been conceptual mummies; nothing actual has escaped from their hands
alive," because they seek to follow reason rather than the impulse of the instinct for life.[30]

The Anti-Christ

Nietzsche's foreword to another book that he wrote in 1888, *The
Anti-Christ*, insists upon "unconditional freedom with respect
to oneself" as the path of wisdom.[31] At the outset of the book,
he defines "good" and "bad." The latter is weakness; the former
is the "will to power" and "power itself in man."[32] Lest this be
misunderstood, in the foreword he comments that power does
not consist in "the wretched ephemeral chatter of politics and

26. Ibid.
27. Ibid., 119.
28. Ibid., 114.
29. Ibid., 108.
30. Ibid., 45.
31. Friedrich Nietzsche, *The Anti-Christ*, in Nietzsche, *Twilight of the Idols and
The Anti-Christ*, 125.
32. Ibid., 127.

national egoism."[33] What the bulk of humanity conceives of as power is not power at all. It is merely pettiness, a common effort to attain progress and equality. By contrast, the will to power lifts one up uniquely and constitutes an achievement of real daring and real courage, the courage truly to follow one's own instincts, "the preservative instincts of strong life."[34] Nietzsche notes that Christianity attributed this courage to the devil, and instead elevated the weak and crucified. Pity replaced courage. This distorted valuation makes Christianity depraved, and it also has infected German philosophy, since Kant and others simply brought theological ideals into philosophy. Hidden theologians such as Kant have warped the meaning of "true" and "untrue"; the measure of these terms is the growth of life, not a priori reason.[35] What is "true" corresponds to the will to power, the life instinct. Nietzsche argues that "*we ourselves*, we free spirits, are already a 'revaluation of all values', an *incarnate* declaration of war and victory over all ancient conceptions of 'true' and 'untrue'."[36]

Nietzsche holds that humans simply are animals, and therefore we find truth when we follow our will to power or instinct for life, self-preservation, and growth. Descartes defined animals as machines; Nietzsche supposes that humans too are machines, lacking the faculty of "free will" or "pure spirit."[37] He considers that this lack is not a cause for alarm. Rather, it should lead humans to embrace their animal instinct for life (or thirst for "power") and to allow this instinct to unfold boldly, strongly, and passionately. Intellectually, after all, strength consists not in belief—which is a dependence upon others and therefore weak—but in thoroughgoing skepticism. Truth is not a matter of ideas, but rather the truth consists in "the instinct for *realities*,"

33. Ibid., 125.
34. Ibid., 129.
35. Ibid., 135.
36. Ibid.
37. Ibid., 136–37.

for "health, beauty, well-constitutedness, bravery, intellect," and "*life itself.*"[38]

Nietzsche makes clear that he would rather have a powerful, masterful pagan "god," incarnating "natural values," than the pitiful Christian God of the weak.[39] But Nietzsche suggests that Christ may well have lived the very opposite kind of life from what the church proclaims. After all, Christ acted politically and mutinously, Christ rejected the "Jewish Church" with superiority and contempt, Christ insisted upon practices rather than dogmatic beliefs or mere ideas, and Christ lacked any petty obedience to the herd that could impede his freedom for action.[40] If so, then it was Paul, "the genius of hatred," who perverted Christianity once and for all, by turning Christ's defiant life into a system of dogmatic faith, personal immortality, sin and guilt, and equality rather than the natural instinct of dominance, which is the true "rationality."[41] The New Testament stands against nature and against the natural instinct for life, the will to power; therefore in the New Testament "everything is self-deception and closing one's eyes to oneself."[42] For Nietzsche, truth, the opposite of self-deception, consists solely in the will to the preservation and extension of self. Christianity lifts up weakness, morbidity, and bodily and spiritual asceticism, whereas in fact what is true in life consists in what is healthy in body, "well-constituted, proud, high-spirited."[43]

On the Genealogy of Morals

In *On the Genealogy of Morals* (1887), Nietzsche argues that nature does not prove God's providence or the existence of a "divine reason" that seeks our salvation.[44] Rather, nature seeks what na-

38. Ibid., 193, 199.
39. Ibid., 147.
40. Ibid., 151; cf. 163–65.
41. Ibid., 166, 168.
42. Ibid., 173.
43. Ibid., 180.
44. Friedrich Nietzsche, *On the Genealogy of Morals*, trans. Walter Kaufmann

ture seeks: the human animal seeks the flourishing of animal life, to be "happy, well-constituted, powerful in soul and body."[45] Nietzsche praises the Old Testament because it contains "great human beings" and "the incomparable naïveté of the *strong heart*"; it contains real "impassioned vehemence."[46] This contrasts with the New Testament's (especially Paul's) promotion of "feelings of guilt, fear, and punishment; . . . the scourge, the hair shirt, the starving body, contrition."[47] In everything, Christianity fights and undermines "the curative instinct of life," the instinct possessed by those who possess "health and might," against whom the priest, the epitome of the envious and vengeful "*delicate* animal," works.[48] Influenced by Christian falsehood, we suppose that virtue is sickness, weakness, and asceticism, "as if health, well-constitutedness, strength, pride, and the sense of power were in themselves necessarily vicious things for which one must pay some day."[49] It is this animal nature—human nature in its full animal power—that is inevitably recognized and appreciated by the "will to truth."[50] Truth is our flourishing in health, strength, pride, and power; truth is the will to seize these things and to express them fearlessly. Nietzsche bemoans the intentional squelching and envious flattening of "man, the human *animal*," so that strong humans cannot or do not boldly express their strength (thereby becoming weak or sick themselves).[51]

Nietzsche holds that the fruit of human evolution "is the *sovereign individual*, like only to himself, liberated again from morality of custom, autonomous and supramoral . . . in short, the man who has his own independent, protracted will."[52] He ex-

---

and R. J. Hollingdale, in Nietzsche, *On the Genealogy of Morals* and *Ecce Homo*, ed. Walter Kaufmann, 15–163 (New York: Vintage Books, 1989), at 161.

45. Ibid., 124.
46. Ibid., 144.
47. Ibid., 141.
48. Ibid., 126, 128.
49. Ibid., 123.
50. Ibid., 161.
51. Ibid., 162.
52. Ibid., 59.

plains further what this liberated will involves. Such a person has "a proud consciousness . . . of his own power and freedom, a sensation of mankind come to completion."[53] In such a person, human will is no longer cowed. Therefore, a person with truly free and unbreakable will inspires trust, fear, and reverence. Such a person possesses "mastery over circumstances, over nature, and over all more short-willed and unreliable creatures," because his will, in its freedom, truly has "become instinct, the dominating instinct."[54] Such a person affirms himself, in all his desire for health, strength, power, and the like; and such a person's will to power cannot be sickened by envy, weakness, or pity, because such a person knows that the will to power is truth, the truth of what the human should be.

Ecce Homo

In his final work, *Ecce Homo* (1888), Nietzsche suggests that falsehood is the will to meekness, the will to chastising oneself and weakening oneself for whatever cause. All "ideals" that go against the reality of human nature have in fact poisoned human health. Truth, by contrast, is the will to power, the will to dare, the will to reject false ideals and to affirm the truth about human health and strength. This freedom of truth, this will to dare, Nietzsche finds that he himself has penetrated to "the innermost wealth of truth."[55] He warns that he does not wish to engender more ideals or more faith. Instead, those who strive to follow him must attend to the truth about human health and strength. Having been among the sick (both physically and in academic life), Nietzsche knows how to look "from the perspective of the sick toward *healthier* concepts and values and, conversely, looking again from the fullness and self-assurance of a *rich* life down

53. Ibid.
54. Ibid., 60.
55. Friedrich Nietzsche, *Ecce Homo*, trans. Walter Kaufmann, in Nietzsche, *On the Genealogy of Morals* and *Ecce Homo*, 217–335, at 219.

into the secret work of the instinct of decadence."[56] He identifies himself as one who is fundamentally healthy, for whom, therefore, "being sick can even become an energetic *stimulus* for life, for living *more*."[57] He personally took himself in hand, when he could have collapsed into sickness, and exercised his will to life and health.[58]

Nietzsche describes the profound inspiration that he has felt while writing. It comes to him as a "rapture whose tremendous tension occasionally discharges itself in a flood of tears," an experience of a "depth of happiness" that colors everything, an experience of "a gale of a feeling of freedom, of absoluteness, of power, of divinity."[59] When he is thus inspired, writing becomes fundamentally involuntary; it simply flows. He describes his creative work as taking place commonly while walking, given the connection between truth and health. He points out that his "will to power" is most certainly not power to the German nation, the *Reich*.[60] Neither "buffoons of politics" nor buffoons of "the church" can understand the meaning of his work, which involves knocking down all ideals in order to be free for what is truly strong and real, truly life.[61] He blames "the Germans" for an "innermost *cowardice* before reality, which is also cowardice before the truth," rooted preeminently in idealist thought (which he considers to be Christianity in a different, equally false form).[62] He describes "nationalism" as the "most *anti-cultural* sickness and unreason there is."[63]

Nietzsche concludes *Ecce Homo* by commenting that he is the first person to stand openly against the lies that have lasted

56. Ibid., 223.

57. Ibid., 224.

58. A few weeks after finishing *Ecce Homo*, he collapsed into a permanent insanity, likely caused by the progressive impact of his syphilis.

59. Ibid., 300–1.

60. Ibid., 318.

61. Ibid., 319.

62. Ibid., 320.

63. Ibid., 321.

many millennia: the lies about God, soul, and truth. The only real truth is the will to power, the will to life—not "free will" but rather trust in healthy instinct, against "all that is weak, sick, failure, suffering of itself."[64] All other values and moralities are false, decadent, and must be destroyed. Nietzsche recognizes that the completion of this destructive task will involve calamities, but this destructive task will also be deeply creative because it will unleash the truth, namely, the will to healthy and powerful life (as found in the "Superman"), rather than the craven calculus, envious and vengeful *ressentiment*, and the idealist lies of "good" and "evil" that now govern society insofar as society stands as the redoubt of "herd animals."[65]

Hans Urs von Balthasar's Nietzschean Critique of Nietzsche

The first volume of the *Theo-Logic* is titled *Truth of the World*. In this volume, directly addressing Nietzsche on truth, von Balthasar argues that "the well-formed subject's contribution to the truth is never arbitrary, never merely a function of the interests and aims of a narrow subjectivity. In other words, the raison d'être of knowledge has nothing to do with a will to power."[66] He grants that the subject makes a "contribution to the truth" and that, when this happens, the subject is able to be truly "creative" and to gain in "life."[67] But truth requires not the will to power but rather the will to love, the will to self-surrender, the will "to serve the truth."[68] Von Balthasar hammers this point home: "Not dominion, but service is primary in knowledge.... The first lesson that existence teaches the subject is the lesson

---

64. Ibid., 334–35.
65. Ibid., 330–31.
66. Hans Urs von Balthasar, *Theo-Logic: Theological Logical Theory*, vol. 1, *Truth of the World*, trans. Adrian J. Walker (San Francisco: Ignatius Press, 2000), 70.
67. Ibid.
68. Ibid.

of self-abandonment [*Hingabe*], not dominion in the pursuit of interest."[69] Self-surrender does not mean less life and therefore less truth; on the contrary, it means more life and more truth. Von Balthasar explains, "Self-abandonment opens up more of the world and reaps a richer harvest of truth than self-interest, because the self-interested hear only what they want to hear, not what in fact is and is true."[70]

This is a clear though implicit critique of Nietzsche's claim that it is only by following one's instinct for strength and life (the will to power) that one finds "truth." For von Balthasar, those who follow such a path veil the truth—a charge that Nietzsche, employing the German meaning of Friedrich Schleiermacher's name, applies to "Fichte, Schelling, Schopenhauer, Hegel, and Schleiermacher ... as well as Kant and Leibniz: they are all mere veil makers."[71] Von Balthasar holds that those who obey the will to power blind themselves to truth because they inevitably see only what their own will ordains. He points out that "the urge to know" must be awakened by "the other's truth," by the other manifesting itself to us.[72] Therefore, the will to have more life requires being more open to the other; and this requires self-surrender to what is not ourselves, to "the world's initial on-rush."[73] It is through the not-"I" that we awaken to our "I." Von Balthasar states that "the most marked index of the finite subject's creaturehood is the fact that it is already serving before it awakens to itself as subject. It awakens in the act of service."[74] The living subject finds health, strength, and life—and therefore truth—in free, self-surrendering love.

Von Balthasar makes the same point, again implicitly but clearly against Nietzsche, somewhat further on in *Truth of the*

69. Ibid., 70–71.
70. Ibid., 71.
71. Nietzsche, *Ecce Homo*, 321.
72. Von Balthasar, *Truth of the World*, 71.
73. Ibid.
74. Ibid.

World. Speaking of the process by which we attain truth, von Balthasar remarks: "An even more decisive counterpart to the will to unveiling is the will to *trust*."[75] When a lover seeks to unveil a beloved by means of power, the beloved turns away in anger and fright. In seeking the enhancement of our life, we find that the self-surrender that is trust gains us the unveiling of what we desire (the language here shows that in engaging Nietzsche, von Balthasar is often engaging Heidegger as well). The will to power is life-enhancing only when it is a will to self-surrender in trust and love; only then is it the truth of reality, the "truth of the world" and the logic of God.[76]

With this in view, let me now return to the beginning of von Balthasar's book for the purpose of surveying it in its entirety. The first volume of the *Theo-Logic* was published in 1947, well before any other volume of the trilogy. To the original volume, however, von Balthasar adds a fifteen-page "General Introduction." He explains that "our task in the present theological *Logic* will be to reflect upon the relationship between the structure of creaturely truth and the structure of divine truth. This reflection will set the stage for an inquiry into whether God's truth can exhibit and express itself (in various forms) within the structures of creaturely truth."[77] Von Balthasar affirms the distinction between nature and grace, and therefore between philosophical reflection and theological reflection. As he states, "By its very nature, theological insight into God's glory, goodness, and truth presupposes an *ontological*, and not merely formal or gnoseological, infrastructure of worldly being. Without philosophy, there can be no theology."[78]

Von Balthasar remarks that a central aspect of his study of the analogous truth of being will consist in showing how being

---

75. Ibid., 212.
76. To quote the title of von Balthasar's book.
77. Ibid., 7.
78. Ibid.

is one, which will enable him also to show how being, in its unity, is at the same time Trinitarian. He observes that the truth of being anchors the beauty and drama of God's self-revelation, for at issue is whether the "creaturely *logos*" has "the carrying capacity to harbor the divine Logos in itself."[79] Is the creaturely realm sufficiently "true" as to be able to support the creaturely incarnation of the divine Word? Furthermore, does the creaturely realm have sufficient truth to enable all other humans, those who are not the Word incarnate, to follow Christ "within the world and its logic"?[80]

Questions such as these, von Balthasar argues, require that the theologian first be a philosopher—a philosopher enlightened by divine revelation, but a philosopher nonetheless, attentive to "the mysterious structures of creaturely being."[81] Creaturely being is worthy of wonder and astonishment. It is so in part because of the polarities that comprise it: between essence and existence (known as the "real distinction"), individual and universal, form and light, obedience and freedom, and "finite and infinite freedom, where the former attains its realization precisely by surrendering itself to the latter."[82] These polarities reveal the intrinsic complexity and mystery of creaturely being as true. Von Balthasar observes that "the more deeply the knower delves into these structures, the more they unveil themselves to him and, at the same time, withdraw behind the veil of their mystery."[83] Here we find an unveiling of the truth of creaturely being that is at the same time a veiling. The same point holds for the unveiling of the analogous truth of divine being. Thus the truth of being involves the combination of unveiling and veiling, knowledge and faith, that we find in the mystery of persons, in the interpersonal experience of love.

79. Ibid., 8.
80. Ibid.
81. Ibid.
82. Ibid., 9.
83. Ibid. The influence of Heidegger is evident here.

Von Balthasar comments that he will inquire into whether "love might not be the hidden ground underlying the transcendentals and their circumincessive relation."[84] Already in the word "philosophy"—*philo-sophia*—we see the interior unity of love and wisdom. Moreover, to say that God is "love" and that God is "wisdom" is to make an analogous statement about the truth of the being of God. The truth of divine being is love. Truth, being, and love are identical in God.

At the same time, von Balthasar raises the question of whether the analogy between the truth of creaturely being and the truth of divine being really can work. After all, in creaturely being we see the polarities noted above; whereas in divine being, there is no polarity between essence and existence or between infinite and finite (since God is simply infinite). What, then, makes "finite being an 'image and likeness' of absolute being"?[85] Von Balthasar suggests that the answer may be found in the distinct relations that constitute the divine Persons. The answer requires a "horizon" that "is theological and trinitarian."[86] This thesis will be unfolded largely in the second and third volumes of the *Theo-Logic*.

In the first volume of the *Theo-Logic*, *Truth of the World*, his standpoint is philosophical and his goal is "to uncover the structures that characterize the truth of finite being."[87] He does not follow his usual procedure of dialoguing explicitly with numerous interlocutors, including biblical sources and exponents of the tradition as well as contemporary scholars. Implicitly, he engages with various schools of neo-scholastic thought (prominent at the time that he wrote this book, in the 1940s). He argues for an enhanced place of the will and specifically of love in the knowing of truth, he insists upon a fully realist account

84. Ibid.
85. Ibid., 10.
86. Ibid.
87. Ibid.

of truth, and he suggests that the ability of human natural reason to identify essential structures of the world—the truth of the world—requires the conclusion that there are "truths that genuinely belong to creaturely nature yet do not emerge into the light of consciousness until they are illumined by a ray of the supernatural," whether prior to or after the coming of Christ.[88]

Von Balthasar makes explicit in his "General Introduction" that he has Nietzsche's metaphysical proscriptions in mind in his *Theo-Logic*. He quotes Nietzsche as urging that any philosopher who appeals to the unity of the beautiful, good, and true be physically beaten. He traces Nietzsche's reductionary metaphysical assumptions to Kant, who holds that the transcendentals are logical categories rather than metaphysical properties. Nietzsche goes further by insisting that truth contradicts the other transcendentals: truth is ugly. Von Balthasar agrees that truth, once understood in Nietzschean terms, is indeed ugly, since for Nietzsche "existence is governed by the will to power, which uses the transcendentals to its best advantage: truth, *pravda*, is what serves the interests of power, and so forth."[89] As von Balthasar points out, the Nietzschean will to power capsizes because of the "self-contradiction" found in our desires: when we (fallen humans) get what we *think* will make us healthy and satisfied, it destroys us or, in due time, collapses from within. Von Balthasar comments in this regard that "the power of being and of its ineliminable qualities is stronger than any human nihilism," even if the Nietzschean perspective may seem for a while to be achieving its goal of "the annihilation of the depth dimension of being."[90]

In his "General Introduction," von Balthasar briefly summarizes the second and third volumes of *Theo-Logic*. Can the creaturely image be (in the incarnation) the archetype itself, so

88. Ibid., 13.
89. Ibid., 16.
90. Ibid.

that the Word becoming flesh is not simply an impossible and unintelligible contradiction? The second volume, which begins with an important section on "Logic and Love,"[91] provides von Balthasar's mature reflections on the analogy of being, the Trinitarian image and vestige, the Spirit-filled Christ as the revelation of the Father, the Trinitarian relations, the way in which Trinitarian difference grounds creaturely difference, the "flesh" as befitting the Word, the incarnation as illuminating all things, and (lastly) the incarnate Word as a sign of contradiction in the world. The third volume—explicitly a continuation of the second—focuses on the Holy Spirit in himself and in the church and world, concluding with "the return, not only of Son and Spirit to the Father, but of the whole creation together with them and in them."[92] Von Balthasar reflects on how Jesus, "translating the logic of his divinity into the logic of his humanity," is interpreted to the world by his Spirit, who in the church (through teachings and sacraments) guides "the human spirit into the rightness of the logic of the Logos," which turns out to be "the mystery of mutual substitution as a *sequela crucis*" in self-surrendering love, through which we truly die and rise with the self-surrendering Son by his Spirit.[93] At the center of all truth is the Trinity's "ever-greater love."[94]

Let me now turn back to the first volume of the *Theo-Logic*. At the outset of *Truth of the World*, von Balthasar posits that one might begin with the assumption that truth exists. But if truth exists, what is its nature? This question reintroduces, more strongly, the question of whether truth exists, because if we do not know *what* truth is, we can hardly be sure *that* truth is. At the same time, for those who know that truth exists and what it is,

91. See Hans Urs von Balthasar, *Theo-Logic: Theological Logical Theory*, vol. 2, *Truth of God*, trans. Adrian J. Walker (San Francisco: Ignatius Press, 2004), 27–33.
92. Hans Urs von Balthasar, *Theo-Logic: Theological Logical Theory*, vol. 3, *The Spirit of Truth*, trans. Graham Harrison (San Francisco: Ignatius Press, 2005), 433.
93. Von Balthasar, *Truth of the World*, 18–19.
94. Ibid., 21.

there is always an ever-deepening "astonishment" and "marveling" at the knowledge of truth.

Von Balthasar compares all this to the stages of love: at first one doubtfully and repeatedly poses the question of whether one is loved and, indeed, of what love is; and one discovers that "behind every reassuring certainty there is an expansive new horizon," namely, "the world of love itself, wherein it [one's ongoing questioning] forms a part of love's vitality and essence."[95] Even when we know that love exists, we can and do question it, ever more deeply. The same is the case for truth. By means of the analogy of the experience of love, von Balthasar makes the point that "the man who does not dare to jump into the truth will never attain the certainty that truth in fact exists."[96] We will be too timid, too unsure of ourselves, to claim that we actually know truth. We must begin with an act of natural faith, a "self-abandoning confidence" that is "the prior condition of any certainty about the existence of the rational."[97] To come to know that truth exists, we must begin with a faith that is a "self-abandoning" or, indeed, with a self-surrendering.

Von Balthasar describes "an intensification of the original question that, rather than developing *away* from the origin, develops *into* it."[98] The more one has familiarity with truth, the more truth "unfurl[s] its inexhaustible plenitude—which only goes on becoming more and more inexhaustible."[99] Since truth is a property of being, truth cannot be reduced to a few propositions; truth cannot be exhaustively defined or delimited. On the contrary, "the very act of defining" is encompassed within the (unbounded) sphere of truth and being.[100] Truth, like being, is always greater than what we have thus far apprehended. In the

95. Ibid., 24.
96. Ibid., 25.
97. Ibid.
98. Ibid.
99. Ibid., 26.
100. Ibid.

philosophy manuals or textbooks in use in 1947, von Balthasar complains, the theme of truth is addressed simply under the rubric of a few "meager propositions" that defensively seek to prove the certitude of the existence of truth.[101]

The key issue, then, is not whether truth exists (it does) but how to get to know it; and the answer is to entrust oneself "to the simple a priori quality of truth itself insofar as it inheres in being as such, where it confronts the thinker as an ever new marvel."[102] Truth, like being, confronts and surprises and amazes us, if we are attentive. Such truth goes beyond the "theoretical" and includes the "personal and ethical."[103] There is no "theory" or pure realm of truth cut off from the ethical, the realm of the good, and thus the realm of decision and action. Indebted to John Henry Newman, von Balthasar is here challenging "modern rationalism," with its attempt "to narrow the range of truth to a supposedly isolable core of pure theory."[104] We have seen how Nietzsche, too, strongly reacts against this reduction. "Truth" and "decision" are intimately connected and inseparable, because the transcendentals of truth, goodness, and beauty interrelate in being. Put simply, "irrationalism" cannot be defeated without defeating rationalism as well.[105]

Von Balthasar proceeds upon the assumption that there is, in the real world, no "pure reason"; rather, there is only reason that has responded negatively or positively to grace. Yet, far from holding that the depth dimension of philosophy is in fact its theological elements and coloration, von Balthasar insists that "the intrinsic fullness of philosophical truth—quite apart from the theological light that always falls upon it—is much richer than most accounts of it would lead us to suppose," and he insists that prior to giving an account of grace, we must seek to display phil-

101. Ibid., 28.
102. Ibid.
103. Ibid.
104. Ibid., 29.
105. Ibid., 30.

osophically "the whole breadth, depth, and manifold variety of nature in its proper domain."[106] In this sense, theology needs a robust philosophy in order to be able to describe theological realities with any adequacy.

Von Balthasar concludes his introduction to *Truth of the World* by noting that his method will be a largely phenomenological one, seeking to apprehend "the truth of the world in an original act of beholding."[107] He will not seek to produce a philosophy "for" theological topics, nor will he seek to provide an epistemology. Instead, he will focus on the transcendental property of being that is truth.

Consciousness, Subject, Object

Truth of the World's first constructive section bears the title "Truth as Nature." Von Balthasar begins by cutting through epistemological quagmires and reminding us that "truth is as evident as existence and essence, as unity, goodness, and beauty."[108] No matter how much we disbelieve in goodness, for example, when we see a selfless act of love, we know it is good. Likewise, those who disbelieve in truth must believe in their doubt, and this requires presupposing truth. Even when doubters seek to deny that they believe in their doubt—arguing instead that everything is mere opinion—they can hardly deny that they are expressing their opinion. It is true, then, that there is a relationship between their opinion and their expression of their opinion.

Von Balthasar argues that, at bottom, we either recognize that being discloses itself in our consciousness or simply refuse to admit the obvious. Once we admit that being discloses itself in our consciousness, we admit that the truth of being exists and that truth's nature, or "essence," is the "familiarity of being."[109]

106. Ibid., 32.
107. Ibid.
108. Ibid., 35.
109. Ibid., 37.

Our consciousness is not abstract; it is an inner "reality of *being* conscious."[110] It therefore has being. Von Balthasar comments, "It is this being ... that is immediately unveiled and present to consciousness. The thinking subject is always one that exists and recognizes that it does."[111] Even if it turns out that we cannot know the being of things—that we can know only appearances, not objects—the very fact that we experience the reality of being conscious means that already "the sphere of mere, insubstantial appearance has been breached" and "being itself has come into appearance and has become present, as being, to consciousness."[112]

Already, then, simply by knowing or experiencing the truth of being conscious, we can affirm that being discloses itself to us and discloses itself as true. Von Balthasar finds here (with Heidegger strongly in view) "an initial description of truth as the unveiledness, uncoveredness, disclosedness, and unconcealment (ά-λήθεια) of being."[113] Since being itself actually appears, it manifests itself as true. The point is that "being is not concealed in itself like some unknown 'thing-in-itself' that remains incommunicado behind an uncommunicative appearance."[114] Simply in the experience of being conscious, we can know that being truly can unveil itself. We can also know that consciousness does not impede the manifestation of being. Rather, consciousness gives us encounter with being; in consciousness, being "bear[s] witness to itself."[115]

The main point of this early section of the *Truth of the World* is that when we know being (as we do in being conscious), we know that we are touching core reality rather than something that conceals an even deeper substrate—even though what we

110. Ibid.
111. Ibid.
112. Ibid.
113. Ibid.
114. Ibid.
115. Ibid., 38.

know has inexhaustibly rich and complex truth. We know that being, having unveiled itself, is reliable in the sense that we can rightly surrender ourselves to it. We know that "once being has become evident, this evidence immediately harbors the promise of further truth," further discovery of "the rich coherence of being."[116] A being opens itself up to us and does so in a way that allows us to feel that it is reliable or credible. We thereby know the world partly and yearn to know more. When we know a being, we know that we do not yet know the totality of being or even the totality of the particular being, and thus we have "the experience of being flooded by something that overflows knowledge in the heart of knowledge itself, or, to put it another way, the awareness of participating in something that is infinitely greater in itself than what comes to light its disclosure."[117] This latter awareness is not "irrational" but rather belongs to rationality, since we cannot pin down the fullness of being but must allow mystery to persist even in knowledge.

Von Balthasar adds that although knowledge is the adequation of the mind to the thing, this requires the mind (the subject) freely allowing itself to "be determined and measured by the thing"—and therefore the thing or object also has something of an active role.[118] The interplay between active object and free subject involves the object measuring the subject (the mind), as well as the subject measuring the object in the act of the judgment of truth. Von Balthasar emphasizes that the subject does not simply receive the truth of the object, but positively "bring[s] it into being" through a "spontaneous, creative achievement."[119] He credits the subject with a "sovereign power freely and spontaneously to give form," and he emphasizes that "the subjectivity of the worldly subject means freedom and, with freedom, the

116. Ibid., 39.
117. Ibid., 40.
118. Ibid., 41.
119. Ibid.

right freely to shape the world around it."[120] This emphasis on the relationship of truth to free creativity fits with Nietzsche. Von Balthasar, however, emphasizes that the subject's creative freedom includes "receptivity" to what the object offers: the subject is both "contemplative" and "creative" vis-à-vis the object.[121] He keeps in view, as well, the point that the subject "is unveiled to itself," that is to say, knows itself in its self-consciousness.[122]

Returning to the being of consciousness, von Balthasar argues that the light of consciousness involves the fact that here being and consciousness coincide: the consciousness is what it knows, and therefore consciousness can "measure" or know any instance of being. At one and the same time, the consciousness knows itself as being and knows, through itself, any "outer dimension of being."[123] Von Balthasar also reflects further upon "receptivity," which is possible due to consciousness's interiority. We have the power to "be enriched with the gift of their [objects'] distinct truth."[124] Communication or sharing, without which life would be boring, requires that no one knows everything. Instead, our receptivity to others is grounded by a certain kind of "poverty." This receptivity is, von Balthasar points out, something that Nietzsche's Zarathustra, who fancies himself only a giver of knowledge (not a receiver, because he is not "poor" enough), sadly lacks. Von Balthasar remarks, "A spontaneity that refused to be receptive would be a power without love."[125] The key is that receptivity elevates rather than drags down consciousness. Von Balthasar comments, "Increased spontaneity thus brings increasingly perfect receptivity. To put it in other terms: Increased self-determination implies a correlative increase in the opportunity and the capacity to let oneself be

120. Ibid.
121. Ibid., 42–43.
122. Ibid., 43.
123. Ibid., 44.
124. Ibid., 45.
125. Ibid., 46.

determined by another."[126] *Pace* Nietzsche, "self-determination" and self-surrender are correlative.

Von Balthasar makes clear that what Nietzsche missed is love. According to von Balthasar, the freest spirit "resolves in the freedom of love to let itself be freely determined in love," and the result of this self-surrender in love is knowledge.[127] In knowledge, receptivity (or self-surrender to the impress of the other) opens up the knower to "every gift of this Thou as a new, truly enriching wonder."[128] Love delights in receiving gifts from the beloved. Act and potency go together here; according to von Balthasar, our very potency is intrinsic to our highest actuality. He speaks of an "active potency," an "openness to any truth that might show itself" and a desire to be informed by more truth.[129] Indeed, for finite knowers, any increase in knowledge reveals an ever-greater enlargement of the domain of yet unknown truth.

Von Balthasar argues that one can move from the identity of being and consciousness in oneself—since consciousness "attains the measure of being and can apply it to the object"—to the existence of *absolute* self-conscious being, God (or Truth).[130] Drawing implicitly upon Augustine, he notes that the light of consciousness or the light of truth participates "in an objective, ultimately infinite and absolute, measure."[131] The measuring consciousness is itself measured by God. What we know in an "immediate" way is our own contingency, which discloses our causal dependence upon God. Our acts of knowing themselves involve dependence both upon God, as the source of our light, and upon the objects that manifest themselves to us. Von Balthasar concludes by suggesting that the diversity of knowers in the world, each open to each other "in their reciprocal disponibility" and each communi-

126. Ibid., 48.
127. Ibid.
128. Ibid.
129. Ibid., 49.
130. Ibid., 51.
131. Ibid.

cating "the truth that God has granted them as a share in his own infinite truth," mirrors in a finite mode "the infinite openness of God's truth."[132] Self-surrendering openness and communion in love are the heart of truth.

Treating the status of objects (including self-conscious objects and nonrational ones), von Balthasar observes that they can be knowable only because they are already "measured," already intelligible, in the mind of God. God's knowledge, the divine ideas, is "the model and exemplar that establishes the being [of every object] and determines all of its relations."[133] Von Balthasar has divine providence in view, since God eternally knows the relationships of everything, how each thing fits in its historical development with all other things. The full truth of worldly things, therefore, can be known only by God in light of his whole plan. Emphasizing that things develop historically toward the fullness of the divine idea of them, von Balthasar comments that "things are always more than themselves, and their constantly self-surpassing transcendence opens ultimately onto an idea that is, not the things themselves, but God and their measure in God."[134]

Here again we find the significance of self-surrender: insofar as God is the infinite subject who knows us, we as "objects" become ourselves by surrendering ourselves to God's idea of us, which von Balthasar describes as an "openness to God's all-fulfilling truth."[135] Self-opening or self-surrendering receptivity pertains not only to the subject but also to the object vis-à-vis truth. When we seek to know objects—especially other persons—we must seek to know them in the way in which God knows them. Von Balthasar's conclusion in this regard stands at complete variance with Nietzsche and yet has affinities with

132. Ibid., 55.
133. Ibid., 57.
134. Ibid., 59.
135. Ibid.

Nietzsche's view that a "Superman" can judge the truth of others (though, crucially, von Balthasar trades self-sufficient power for self-surrendering love). As von Balthasar states, "Only a man who has learned to renounce his own self-concocted judgments and norms and, in the most intimate association with God, to look at the world, as it were, through God's eyes may (assuming God commissions and empowers him for the task) grant objects their truth and tell them what they both are and should be in the sight of the Absolute."[136]

For von Balthasar, therefore, the subject receives and the object reveals; each surrenders to the other, in an "adventure of knowledge" in which each finds a fulfillment that neither can anticipate in advance.[137] Each side fulfills itself by "going out of itself," by self-surrender.[138] Von Balthasar goes so far as to deny that objects of knowledge are "unaffected by being known."[139] He holds that without cognitive subjects to perceive them, nonrational things such as trees cannot be all that they are; for example, their color and sound would make no impression. In terms of God's full idea of trees, trees complete themselves through rational creatures, just as soil completes itself through trees (and so on). The full truth of a tree, just as the full truth of a person, requires not simply the object (the tree) but also a subject that knows the tree. Truth is accomplished in a relationship of self-surrendering. "Nature" does not stand already completed over against a knowing subject. Put otherwise, "appearances" have real importance. Von Balthasar here opposes "naïve realism," which sharply separates the object from any knowing subject.[140]

He also makes clear that rational subjects need objects in order to fulfill themselves, since a subject "is unformed [*unge-*

136. Ibid., 61.
137. Ibid., 62.
138. Ibid.
139. Ibid., 63.
140. Ibid., 65.

bildet] until it finds itself performing the work of knowledge."[141]
It is not that the subject can wait to decide whether or not to interact with the world. On the contrary, the world already is engaging the subject, prior to the subject's rational awakening. Not
autonomous isolation but receptivity is the original stance of the
person. The maturation of the subject in true freedom depends
upon undertaking the labor of judgments of truth.

Against (implicitly) René Descartes, von Balthasar makes
clear that truth is not acquired by an isolated ego who thereby
gains more and more contact with the world; on the contrary, the
subject, upon attaining to rationality, immediately "finds itself
in the midst of a veritable babel of objects expressing themselves
and offering it their truth."[142] Explicitly against the Nietzschean view that knowledge flows from the "will to power," von
Balthasar points out that "not dominion, but service is primary
in knowledge" and that "the first lesson that existence teaches
the subject is the lesson of self-abandonment ... not domination
in the pursuit of interest."[143] For von Balthasar, the subject who
seeks truth will find it "in the measure that it [the subject] serves
in an attitude of self-forgetfulness."[144] This is because of the way
in which knowledge requires the subject to open itself freely to
the objects that are insistently revealing themselves to it with a
force like "hammer strokes," objects that enable the subject to
fulfill itself in a personal manner as its consciousness becomes
"more and more in-formed by the truth of the world."[145]

Von Balthasar reflects upon the "sensorium" and the subject's power to achieve a unity of perception and to express
the intellectual meaning of images received by the senses. He
comments that self-consciousness has the wondrous ability
synthetically to unite experience. He emphasizes once more the

141. Ibid., 67.
142. Ibid., 69.
143. Ibid., 70–71.
144. Ibid., 71.
145. Ibid.

"two-sidedness" of activity and receptivity in knowing truth. From a different angle, he returns to the role of love in the subject's action of knowing truth about the object that unveils itself. He states, "In the creative mirror of the subject, the object sees the image of what it is and of what it can and is meant to be. This creative act of the subject is no longer a mere attitude of justice but much rather an act of *love*."[146] He speaks of the subject seeking, in justice, "to help the object attain its truth," and he urges that this act is more than justice and should therefore be attributed to a "natural love" (as distinct from a free spiritual love).[147] He brings forward even more strongly the view that truth has its root in self-surrender in love, in the will to love. He states, "If the subject is originally and constitutively delivered over to this defenseless abandonment, which it exercises and ... ratifies in every act of knowledge, then an ontological root necessarily underlies the surrender [*Hingabe*] that rises to the nobility of love when the subject recapitulates it at the level of conscious freedom."[148]

For von Balthasar, it follows that the subject's creative work of knowing participates analogically in God's own productive knowing of truth, since the subject draws the object "into the properly spiritual sphere, thus giving it the opportunity to unfold therein."[149] The measure of consciousness, when measuring the being of an object of knowledge, does so inevitably by holding it before the "mirror" of the divine measure and bringing it into the realm of "the loving gaze of [divine] mercy."[150]

Freedom, Consciousness, Love

The next section of *Truth of the World* is devoted to discussion of the freedom of the object and of the subject, under the heading

146. Ibid., 77–78.
147. Ibid., 78.
148. Ibid.
149. Ibid.
150. Ibid.

"Truth as Freedom." Von Balthasar states that although truth "is given only in a cognitive act," truth "reaches into the sphere of freedom" because it involves "a spiritual event" of the free finite subject.[151] Certainly, in the human person, the spirit's openness is a given of its nature. Yet, it remains the case that the spirit's free "Yes" to its nature, through "definite expressions of loving self-abandonment," brings about truth.[152]

Can one really speak of the "freedom" of an object of knowledge? Von Balthasar argues that the answer is yes, in part because of the mysterious depths and wondrousness of each and every being. Even nonrational beings have a mysterious inner reality that no finite intellect can exhaust conceptually. Thus, human knowledge should not be separated into a rationalistic or mechanistic knowledge of nonrational things and an intuitive knowledge of the humanities; this would be a double error. Logic, judgment, and understanding go together in every act of knowing. Even with regard to knowledge of nonrational things, von Balthasar speaks of "a never-ending attempt to woo the core of the material world, which is not directly available to sense perception"—as for example the effort to apprehend "the ultimate essence of matter."[153] The point is not that the material world is unknowable, but rather that even when we know it, it always remains far richer than our knowledge can grasp. This is true even in the case of rocks, but is clearly evident in plants, since, as von Balthasar says, "no scientific research will ever be able to explain what the vital principle is in itself."[154]

Von Balthasar's main opponent in this section is a mechanistic view of things. We should have wonder and awe in the face of every existing thing. Once we are dealing with living things, this fact becomes plain. He states, "Even on the lowest level of

151. Ibid., 79.
152. Ibid., 80.
153. Ibid., 85.
154. Ibid., 86.

life, the living entity already irradiates such plenitude and power from the hidden core of its interiority that we should fall back, blinded, before every one of its outward forms."[155] The mystery of life is both hidden, in its profound mystery and superabundance, and unveiled in its clear outward appearances, which can be accessed and studied. Von Balthasar also discusses animal life. Animals, he notes, are no mere "reflex mechanisms"; though we will never be able to apprehend what animal perception and emotions feel like internally, we know that they have language, even if not "the freedom to express themselves when and how they wish" outside of "a predetermined natural language."[156]

In addressing the subjectivity of animals, von Balthasar arrives once again at the central point that truth is a matter of self-surrendering love. In all cases, we can know another thing only by allowing it to be *other*, by accepting the real limitations of our knowledge. Von Balthasar comments that "the knower must acknowledge these limits imposed by the other's self-being by letting go of the other's self. Genuine community in the truth can be built only on the foundation of this basic resignation. Without this renunciation there can be no reciprocal gift-giving; without this distance there can be no proximity of minds."[157] This point flows across von Balthasar's entire trilogy; it pertains analogously to the Trinity and to all creatures.

Humans possess self-consciousness. Von Balthasar describes this difference from other animals by stating that for humans the "inner dimension is not only luminous, as it is in the case of the animal, but also light for itself."[158] We have real self-possession; we can choose when and how to speak; we can freely tell the truth or lie. In humans, "being coincides with consciousness in self-consciousness, thus becoming its own object."[159] We reflect

155. Ibid., 86.
156. Ibid., 90, 92.
157. Ibid., 90.
158. Ibid., 93.
159. Ibid.

upon ourselves with marvelous freedom, since our consciousness can encompass and reflect upon our whole being. This fact makes truth (about ourselves) "a free, personal reality."[160] We share it with others as our personal testimony, and it is received in "faith" by those who trust us.[161] Von Balthasar's account of testimony helpfully articulates its dynamic. When we know ourselves by turning away from objects and reflecting intentionally upon our own interiority, we do not obtain a perfect knowledge of ourselves in such a way as to be self-sufficient knowers. Furthermore, our "spirit's self-possession is inseparable from the primary self-dispossession entailed in its dependence upon external objects."[162] This means that we become ourselves by openness and receptive service to others. We are also bound to our senses' natural "expressive language," thereby participating "in two forms of interiority."[163]

Von Balthasar accepts the divinely revealed existence of angels, though he points out that their form of interiority must be radically different from ours. He denies that the power of their intelligence makes everything clear to them and thereby deprives them of true personality, since they would have nothing to learn or share. He concludes by reiterating that creaturely contingency reveals the Creator, and specifically reveals the Creator's freedom. In a brief discussion of "The Mystery of Being," he warns against disjoining "being" and "value," a disjunction that he diagnoses as a bitter fruit of the mechanistic mentality, which supposes that there are such things as "naked facts."[164] Things are "unique, dense with mystery, and worthy of being loved."[165] He adds a defense of the distinction between essence and existence, pointing out that "even if we could grasp every aspect of a partic-

160. Ibid., 94.
161. Ibid., 96.
162. Ibid., 98.
163. Ibid., 98–99.
164. Ibid., 103.
165. Ibid., 104.

ular essence, its *reality* would still be an ungraspable, blinding majesty," "the burning core of the mystery of being itself."[166] But there can be no adequate discussion of "existence" that is not also the analysis of a particular essence.

Von Balthasar provides a brief examination of "The Freedom of the Subject." He wishes to underscore that the subject is constrained by the way that objects are. But he notes that the subject has the freedom to choose which objects to attend to. Even when its senses are overwhelmed by a particular object, the free subject can think of something else. This brings him to the central insight that "at every point the will is already involved in the act of knowledge itself."[167] Indeed, not only the will's choice of objects but also the very dynamism toward knowledge indicates the primacy of the will. Von Balthasar states, "Only when the will has already been set in motion does knowledge follow after to perform its own work."[168]

Developing his Nietzschean critique of Nietzsche, he observes that "knowledge can be explained only by and for love," on the grounds that the object's "will to disclose itself and the knowing subject's will to open itself in receptive listening are but two forms of a single self-gift that manifests itself in these two modes."[169] Knowledge requires mutual self-surrendering, whether natural or free. At bottom, therefore, "love is inseparable from truth. It is no more possible to conceive of a truth without love than it is to have a cognition without will."[170] We do not first, rationalistically, produce a truth and then love it. On the contrary, in every truth we already find love, not least because truth always touches upon the mystery of being and is never "a sheer fact."[171]

166. Ibid., 106.
167. Ibid., 110.
168. Ibid., 111.
169. Ibid.
170. Ibid.
171. Ibid.

Von Balthasar reflects further upon the point that the lover, who surrenders himself or herself fully to the object and is maximally attuned to its unveiling, will be the one who sees most deeply into the truth of the object. He affirms that "because the full truth can be attained only in love, only the lover can have the real eye for it."[172] The lover is selflessly attentive toward the person who speaks his or her word of truth. Von Balthasar recognizes, of course, that non-lovers can attain some insight. But he goes so far as to say that "truth originates from love" and even that love is "more comprehensive than truth" and "is the ground that accounts for truth and enables it to be."[173] He underlines the primordial role of personal receptivity and self-surrender (or "radical disponibility") in the relational act of knowing.[174] When we are seeking truth, we need to be willing to receive the full word of the other by "letting go" of our ideas so as to be sure that we truly hear, welcome, and do justice to what the other is saying. This self-surrender for the sake of the other stands as "an act of love" or, at least, as "a manifestation of a primordial love."[175] At the same time, von Balthasar grants that "we cannot say that love was on the scene before truth and that love can be conceived without truth."[176]

Influenced by his perspective as a spiritual director, von Balthasar adds that a lover can at times see, in an unveiled object, things that could not otherwise be seen—and therefore that it is in the eyes of the lover that the object truly and fully *becomes* itself, in its ideality. Von Balthasar has in view the connection to the divine gaze and the divine ideas, by which God raises us to what we should be, but he also has in view the way that a human lover can see something in a beloved that inspires the beloved to grow toward his or her fullness. In addition, von Balthasar likely

172. Ibid., 112.
173. Ibid.
174. Ibid., 113.
175. Ibid.
176. Ibid., 112.

has Christian eschatology implicitly in view when he declares, "Love treats what should not be as it deserves, as something that has absolutely no lawful title to being and whose punishment is simply to have its existence overlooked."[177] He describes a knowledge that covers or veils, in the name of perceiving what can be. Not all truth about a person should endure forever. When another person directs attention to one's ideal self—which in the end can be identified "only in the light of God"—this may inspire hope-filled repentance and growth.[178]

Von Balthasar also speaks about our duty to testify and bear witness to truth, according to a proper discernment of the kinds of self-opening (to others' truth) and self-disclosure (of our own truth) that are required of us. Once more, he highlights his Nietzschean critique of Nietzsche, though without mentioning him by name. In the discernment of how to share and receive truth, he posits a fundamental opposition between "egoism" (surely Nietzsche's highest value) and "love." He insists that it is the latter that "contains the measure of every concrete application of the truth," whereas "egoism ... cannot have knowledge of the truth in the full sense of the word."[179] Certainly, Nietzsche's writings have no room for the enthusiastic claim that "genuine love is at the source of truth, and when this source begins to flow as love, it cannot help generate truth. Love is the selfless communication of what is mine and the selfless welcoming of the other in myself."[180] Once more von Balthasar explicitly extols self-surrender as the principle of life and truth: "Self-communication is a genuine revelation of my unique being when its ultimate raison d'être is to give myself away [*Hingabe*] in love for its own sake."[181]

He grants that loveless rationalists can hit upon some truths and communicate truths, even in a way that bears some fruit in

177. Ibid., 117.
178. Ibid., 120.
179. Ibid., 122.
180. Ibid., 123.
181. Ibid.

the work of others. But he argues that their systems cannot, in the end, do anything but serve destructive, life-negating falsehood. By contrast, when a truth-seeking love includes adherence to some formal errors, even the errors do not negate the overall contribution to truth. This does not mean that von Balthasar approves of such errors. On the contrary, love often involves correcting errors, even to the point of a seemingly "pitiless unveiling" in the service of justice.[182] But love knows when such an unveiling is or is not appropriate. Love may refuse to unveil a particular truth, or love may unveil only a part of the truth with a "*reservatio mentalis*," but its principle must always be a "measureless readiness to give oneself away" rather than personal convenience or advantage.[183] Love will ensure that no narrow part of the truth is allowed to make itself into the whole or to close itself off to the whole. Love, with its appreciation for fullness, will be more eager to hear and acknowledge another's truth than to insist upon its own. Love is "even ready to renounce its own partial standpoint for the sake of this totality" of truth, since the truth of the whole is more important than even a personally cherished (and fully true) partial truth.[184] As befits his emphasis on self-surrender, von Balthasar holds that this "renunciation of partial truth for love's sake is thus a supreme form of the revelation of truth."[185]

In this discussion, in accord with his role as spiritual director, von Balthasar contrasts hypnosis (which he distrusts but does not reject absolutely) with cardiognosis, in which God gives one person insight into another's soul for the purpose of the advancement of love. He concludes this section, "Thanks to its movement of self-surrender, love is given a flood of truth," opening into ever-new vistas of truth, always going beyond what we can put into words.[186]

182. Ibid., 124.
183. Ibid., 127.
184. Ibid., 129.
185. Ibid., 130.
186. Ibid.

Truth as Mystery of Communion

The point that love's truth is always ever greater sets the stage for the next section of *Truth of the World*, on "Truth as Mystery." This section treats sense images, universality and particularity, the phenomenon of the expression of the word (in speech and as the internal "word" of the mind), and intersubjective dialogue in love, as well as the personal circumstances and personal character that shape truth. It ends with further reflection on mystery, on veiling and unveiling, on trust and love, and on the intrinsic relationship of truth to the other transcendentals.

The central contention of the section is that "the truth of being can no more be without an indwelling mystery than being can be exhaustively unveiled to the eye of the intelligence. By its very essence, being is always richer than what we see and apprehend of it."[187] Thus, mystery is *intrinsic* to all truth. The more we know truth, the more we know the mystery in truth. This fits with the fact that truth is personally generated, through "the subject's loving surrender."[188] Far from being dry facts, real truth is filled with mystery and freedom, as the "free" manifestation of being.

With regard to sense images, von Balthasar presents a rich portrait of how they simulate a "world" through their abundance and their patterns. He recognizes that taken by themselves, without a guiding intelligence, they would be "senseless"; in their profusion we could not find a center, an order.[189] After all, sense images are not themselves beings. The mind "always already perceives in the images a perspectival depth that they do not possess of themselves and draws out of them a total form that is more than the bare outline of the naked appearance."[190] Von Balthasar warns against trying to go behind the images or ap-

---

187. Ibid., 131.
188. Ibid., 132.
189. Ibid., 133.
190. Ibid., 134.

pearances to find the actual essence, as though the images were not important. Such rationalism and idealism end up, at best, in the false notion that "pure changefulness is being's enduring essence, pure unreality is the form of its existence."[191] In fact, truth requires the appearances, since the image or appearance is the "revelation" of the "very being that does not itself appear."[192] The key is to understand the nature of signification. As von Balthasar says, "The whole world of images that surrounds us is a single field of significations. Every flower we see is an expression, every landscape has its significance, every human or animal face speaks its wordless language."[193] He adds that for this reason beauty and truth are intimately joined, and indeed "beauty is the aspect of truth that cannot be fit into any definition but can be apprehended only in direct intercourse with it."[194] In every thing, there is always more to be revealed.

In this regard, von Balthasar warns against the temptation of the aesthete, namely, the temptation to remain on the surface of the abundant revelation of images rather than to inquire with further depth into *what* is signified. What is signified is the being and essence of things. Beings reveal themselves through the language of images or appearances; this belongs to what it means to be a being. The image, in revealing the essence, does not negate itself but does exercise (as it were) a "renunciation ... by which it waives any claim to be a reality existing and important for its own sake."[195] Once more we encounter the theme of self-surrender as crucial to truth. Von Balthasar argues that the essence also engages in a self-surrender due to the fact that it can manifest itself only through the image and therefore must surrender "its autonomous, uncommunicated being-for-itself."[196] Von Balthasar sums

191. Ibid., 137.
192. Ibid.
193. Ibid., 140.
194. Ibid., 142.
195. Ibid., 147.
196. Ibid., 149.

up: "This truth, then, has the precise form of a reciprocal surrender between essence and image, ground and appearance."[197]

For its part, the knowing subject also has to undergo a renunciation: specifically, a "renunciation of the immediacy of sense perception" so as to undertake conceptual reflection.[198] I need not recount every aspect of von Balthasar's account of intellectual "abstraction" of the concept, or of the relationship of the universal and particular, which "mutually presuppose each other."[199] In order to show the irreducible mystery of the universal and particular, he reflects upon what it means to be an individual human: both a member of a species with a shared essence or nature, *and* a radically unique person. Turning to the "word" (interior concept and outward expression), von Balthasar shows how the word serves the hidden reality or depth of the sensible sign. He therefore suggests that "the word is able to reveal much more by effacing itself in service than by emphasizing itself in dominion."[200] He comments upon the various modes of expression, including artistic expression, and he discusses the way in which one's "official language" (for example, German) shapes one's thought and seemingly renders it less free or less personal.[201] He describes the freedom of one's internal or mental word. He notes that "if consciousness has laid hold of itself as be-ing, it is in principle capable of opening itself to all being."[202] From this it follows that the human spirit, in its uniqueness, is already self-transcendent.

To share ourselves with others, we must undertake a "free self-surrender"; the "egotist would have no joy in his own truth."[203] We become ourselves in communion with others, in the dialogue

197. Ibid., 150.
198. Ibid.
199. Ibid., 154.
200. Ibid., 160.
201. Ibid., 161.
202. Ibid., 166.
203. Ibid., 172.

of I and Thou. This means that truth, as a dialogic reality, involves both being and becoming. In light of truth's intersubjective grounds, von Balthasar reiterates that "the sense of truth of a whole is *love*," in which the "*logos* of being becomes *dialogos*."[204] Truth involves communication, sharing, communion. In this communion of truth, we receive the testimony of others with a necessary "element of faith and trust."[205] Von Balthasar points out, "As soon as love is seen to be the sense of truth, this demand for faith will no longer appear rigid or irrational."[206] Interpersonal testimony, through which we communicate truth, requires a measure of trust. This trust is not uncritical; on the contrary, we expect that "the subject will prove by its life, its action, and, if necessary, its suffering that its whole being stands behind what it says."[207] Von Balthasar is obviously looking toward Christology here, but his point holds for ordinary interpersonal knowing of truth. He insists that in actual life "truth, as a free deed, has become entirely an ethical matter."[208] Recall that for Nietzsche (whom von Balthasar does not mention in this passage), truth is "self-determination" and "eternally vital word," whereas for von Balthasar—attuned to love—truth is "self-determination and dialogue" and "eternally vital word and surrender."[209]

Thus, von Balthasar strongly affirms the individual or personal dimension of truth, the way in which truth is "determined by freedom, by personality and situation."[210] At the same time, he recognizes (and here again is a critical difference from Nietzsche) that nothing can "produce itself in an absolute creation by an absolute act of the will," an act of "total freedom" marked by "indifference to all possibilities."[211] Such a path is simply not

204. Ibid., 175.
205. Ibid., 176.
206. Ibid.
207. Ibid., 177.
208. Ibid., 178.
209. Ibid., 179.
210. Ibid., 181.
211. Ibid., 180.

possible. Subjective freedom and objective nature are inseparable in the production of meaning and truth. After all, not only
subrational things such as molecules and plants have natures,
but "even man has a 'nature'—not just insofar as he participates
in subspiritual nature, but also insofar as he is spirit."[212] Yet von
Balthasar wishes to emphasize that natures do not impose a
universal truth that could sum everything up, even about molecules and plants. Subrational things, too, have a history, and
this history is more than what one could deduce from their natures, though the latter are obviously crucial too. His fundamental point is that the truth of a contingent historical event, or of
"historical life," is not less than that of an abstract universal,
even though the former does require "a *ratio* that itself conforms
to the prerequisites and preconditions of personality."[213] Here he
likely has in view the historical life (and death and resurrection)
of Jesus, and he also explicitly notes the connection between historical truth and the mystery of divine providence.

He reflects upon the diversity of standpoints and their inte-
gration. He judges that, given the presence of at least some truth
in almost every standpoint, "systems of thought that do nothing
but polemically contrast their differences are dispiriting tokens
of narrow-mindedness, whereas those that overcome the narrow-
ness of limited standpoints by positive opening to more encompassing standpoints liberate and edify."[214] Clearly, we always
will judge things from our own standpoint; we do not have ac-
cess to "a total standpoint," since in receiving any truth we will
always receive it from our personal angle.[215] Here von Balthasar
explicitly agrees with Nietzsche: we must "consider things more
personally, with more decision, with a greater acceptance of responsibility," while also attempting "to look at them through the

212. Ibid., 181.
213. Ibid., 182, 184.
214. Ibid., 187.
215. Ibid.

perspective of many other persons."[216] Subjectivity is not an opponent of truth; there is no "sphere of general, impersonal ideal
contents that is somehow more encompassing than persons."[217]
Personal decision, responsibility, and even willingness to suffer
pertain to truth. Humility, too, pertains to truth: we must entrust
ourselves "to the gift of existence, knowing that this gift will always be infinitely more than what an intellect could expect or a
heart long for."[218]

Von Balthasar reflects upon the distinction of existence and
essence, arguing that it grounds the phenomenon of time—and
also that it mirrors the reality of intradivine distinction. Time,
therefore, is not negative vis-à-vis eternity. Time involves presence (a reflection of divine presence), and it also means tending
toward the future, toward something more. In addition, it means
transitoriness, and therefore the radical preciousness, or serious-
ness, of each moment. Situatedness in time does not adversely
affect truth, but rather gives truth its value and requires us constantly to seek the truth that we know. We never grasp it once
and for all in its totality; we know it even as we need to seek
it, due to "the ever-transcending breadth and plenitude of existing things themselves."[219] When we seek to find and express
truth in concrete social situations, we must do so with a willingness to sacrifice our personal standpoint and with a love that is
"capacious enough to see and to acknowledge others' truth, as
long as it really is truth."[220] Von Balthasar points out that "the
totality of truth's concrete situations is what is called *history*."[221]
He observes that it is not "historical relativism" to hold that "we
cannot grasp the truth of history unless we accompany its immanent process"; it does not negate the universal truth obtained

216. Ibid. See also the thought of Martin Heidegger.
217. Ibid., 189.
218. Ibid., 191.
219. Ibid., 202.
220. Ibid., 203.
221. Ibid., 204.

by an Aristotle to know that his thought bears the traces of his epoch.[222]

Von Balthasar presses further into the mystery of being, its "unveiled veiling."[223] He explores interpersonal truth as a "will to unveiling" and a "will to *trust*"—here, as always, implicitly contrasted with Nietzsche's will to power.[224] At the same time, he reiterates that interpersonal truth also includes "creative *forgetting* and overlooking."[225] He adds that love, as a power, is absolute only in God. He connects truth to goodness and beauty, observing that the "ground of being" is none other than "groundlessly self-giving love," which "simply pours itself out."[226] Thus, "all truth is reducible" to and irradiates "the mystery of love," with its "simultaneity of self-being and self-outpouring," its "unbegrudging self-abandonment" and "groundless grace."[227]

Truth and Theophany

In the final section of *Truth of the World*, von Balthasar discusses "Truth as Participation." He does so under four subheadings: "Participation and Revelation"; "Finitude and Infinity"; "In God's Safekeeping"; and "Confession." I will summarize this material briefly. All of it has to do with "worldly truth's relation to the sustaining ground from which it emerges: eternal truth."[228] In "Participation and Revelation," a key point is that "infinite consciousness ... functions as the condition of the possibility even of finite subjects."[229] For my purposes, it is not necessary to follow all the moves of von Balthasar's argument in this regard. He notes, in accord with the viewpoint of many Thomists, that "God is necessarily affirmed concomitantly, whether explicitly or not, in every

222. Ibid., 205.
223. Ibid., 208.
224. Ibid., 212.
225. Ibid., 215.
226. Ibid., 220, 222.
227. Ibid., 223–25.
228. Ibid., 227.
229. Ibid., 228.

cognition of truth," since truth requires a divine ground.[230] For von Balthasar, the contingency of finite things reveals not only the necessity of God but the infinite freedom of God. The mystery of God, in turn, grounds the mystery of every creaturely being. Creatures "participate" in God, and God manifests or reveals himself in creatures. The world is a vast theophany.

The world is so redolent of divine plenitude, however, that we have the tendency to deify or make idols of creatures. To manifest the Creator properly, the creature must surrender itself to God; when creatures claim to be absolute truth, truth vanishes entirely. In this regard, von Balthasar addresses the "divine ideas" one more time, noting that they are not a bridge between God and the world, because they are simply "God's sovereignly free apportionment of truth."[231] Nothing limits God's freedom, which is indeed infinite necessity because "God is freely what he necessarily is and necessarily what he freely is."[232] Thus, the divine truth utterly transcends creaturely truth, even if creatures participate in and are intended to be conformed to God. Von Balthasar also notes that divine freedom and eternity do not crush creaturely freedom and time. On the contrary, creaturely time has its intense meaning precisely because it "is a participation in, and revelation of, the eternal moment," a point that implicitly contradicts Nietzsche's myth of eternal return or recurrence.[233] For von Balthasar, the reason for the intense meaning of creaturely time consists in the fact that God's eternity has intense meaning, intense urgency—and that in every moment, every situation, God reveals himself anew.

Taking up "Finitude and Infinity," von Balthasar first recalls his earlier point that creaturely knowing involves "delimitation" and thereby finitude.[234] He examines knowing as analysis and

230. Ibid., 230.
231. Ibid., 240.
232. Ibid.
233. Ibid., 243.
234. Ibid., 245.

synthesis, and he shows that there is no possibility of human thought moving progressively toward the infinitude of God's knowledge. Similarly, he points out that "even in the act of knowing, the subject never becomes as fully present to itself as it is in itself."[235] Since bringing essence and existence fully together in creatures is also impossible, no ahistorical systematization of truth is possible either. Is the pursuit of worldly truth then worthwhile? Von Balthasar answers strongly in the affirmative, on the grounds that the truth of the world is ultimately theophanic, as suggested already by "the mind's all-transcending movement, its yearning to know and to lay hold of the truth as a whole."[236] On various grounds, von Balthasar shows that human reason "is already in contact with the infinite," even to the point that in a real sense "every judgment made by a finite intellect proves that there is a God."[237]

In implicit answer to Nietzsche and others, von Balthasar critiques the contemporary trend toward "irrationalism and 'vitalism'."[238] Such philosophies are understandable if the only alternative is rationalism. But as he remarks, "It is not as if 'life', understood in opposition to rational knowledge of the truth, were the factor that continually transcends reason's always finite acquisitions."[239] The self-transcending factor is not "life" but reason itself. It follows that more life is found in more truth. I note that Nietzsche came close to this point but could not reach it. He set in opposition "a theoretical, rational truth of thought" and "a practical, vital, and irrational truth of life."[240] He thought that this would restore philosophy's health and the world's health, at least after the world had bridged the calamity of transitioning away from truth. But von Balthasar considers that philosophies

235. Ibid., 248.
236. Ibid., 252.
237. Ibid., 253.
238. Ibid.
239. Ibid., 253–54.
240. Ibid., 254.

that understand truth to be practical and vital life, as Nietzsche does, are "atrophied" and corrupt rather than vibrant. With an implicit but clear reference to Nietzsche, von Balthasar states that "if you measure the advantages and disadvantages of truth for life by the criterion of life itself, either you mean to tell the truth about life, and, therefore, to declare that even life has real truth or else you cast your lot among the animals that vegetate in their drives without knowledge or responsibility."[241] If Nietzsche meant to do the former, as it often seems he does, then he must hold that "life has real truth" and therefore that truth exists. If Nietzsche meant to do the latter, and this sometimes seems to be the case, then his urgent call to the responsibility to become Supermen is shown to be absurd.

Von Balthasar concludes that when philosophy rejects God and "infinite truth," the two options are absurdity or a sterile rationalism that has no foundation. He thinks that it is no wonder that sterile rationalism gets rejected, since it can be only "disadvantageous for life," and he thinks it is no wonder that thinkers (such as, implicitly, Nietzsche) go "to the opposite extreme of glorifying a life without truth," absurd though this move is on philosophical grounds.[242] Recognizing the existence of God's "eternal truth" constitutes the only sane path forward.[243]

In "In God's Safekeeping," von Balthasar first states that "absolute being is absolute being-for-itself."[244] This might seem to undermine the theme of self-surrender, but his point is that "absolute being" differs infinitely from creaturely being. Only God is God, and we do not know what it is to be God. God is not like anything we know, since God is utterly transcendent. God's revelation places us at his disposal, not him at our disposal. We do not have disposal over any of God's creatures, since we must

241. Ibid., 254. See Friedrich Nietzsche, *On the Advantage and Disadvantage of History for Life*, trans. Peter Preuss (Indianapolis, Ind.: Hackett, 1980).

242. Von Balthasar, *Truth of the World*, 254.

243. Ibid.

244. Ibid., 255.

serve other creatures in order to know them in their mystery. We can make no claim upon God on the basis of our thirst for knowledge. Rejecting talk of a dynamism or appetite that needs God to fill it, and strongly warning against inscribing "an already given supernatural revelation into the dynamism of natural reason," von Balthasar argues that the relationship of nature and grace can be apprehended only when we appreciate that the creature's most fundamental stance is not a dynamism but a "readiness to serve," given that receptivity is the fundamental ground of knowledge.[245] The dynamism to know builds upon this fundamental receptivity. Everything comes to the rational creature as sheer gift. God does not owe us his truth.

Indeed, von Balthasar emphasizes that any claim to a right to unconditional knowledge is a falsification of who we really are and a marker of original sin. We can seek knowledge only because God calls us to his service; we can measure only because God measures us; we can possess ourselves only because God possesses us. We do not even wish, on our own, to know everything. As von Balthasar observes, "Love ... delights in receiving the measure of knowledge from the hand of the beloved."[246] Thus our knowledge of the self-revealing God comes about freely because of God's decision, not because of us. Von Balthasar argues repeatedly that before we know anything else, we have "implicit knowledge" of our creatureliness vis-à-vis the infinite horizon and source of being and truth.[247] In submitting to God, therefore, we are fulfilling our rational nature, which contains a call to service: receptive faith and trust characterize all true creaturely knowing.

Von Balthasar turns once more to the divine ideas, in light of the insight that the gap between what we are and our "archetype" in God is unbridgeable for the creature but is bridgeable for God.

---

245. Ibid., 257–58.
246. Ibid., 264.
247. Ibid., 260.

God's "creative gaze" can justify and sanctify the creature, and thereby can make the creature into God's idea of him or her.[248] Indeed, it is God's idea that stands unchangeable and that has efficacy; "the creature has truth in itself only insofar as God constantly lifts it out of its own nothingness into the sphere of the Divine Being and the divine truth."[249] God views the creature in its current state with justice, but this justice is encompassed within his love, the love by which he will ensure that justice is fulfilled and that more than justice is accomplished. Thus, however alienated the creature might presently be, the creature is "*kept safe in this archetype*."[250] God's truth works through the creature's truth in such a way that the latter is dependent utterly upon the former. When the creature recalls God and looks to God's truth, the creature "knows that it is kept safe in the archetype as its true reality, and it places confident faith in this creative idea present in God."[251] When the creature does this, it attains to the attitude that truly unites it with God: absolute self-surrender, "the primordial attitude of abandonment [*Hingabe*]."[252]

The final brief subheading is titled "Confession." If Nietzsche is onto something about the link between truth and the will to greater life—and I have made clear, I hope, that von Balthasar thinks he is[253]—Nietzsche mistakenly thinks of greater life and truth in terms of power rather than in terms of self-surrendering love. Since God is love, greater life and truth are love. Indeed, since God is not on the same ontological level as humans, "God's subjectivity grounds and undergirds all self-consciousness from within (*Deus interior intimo meo*)."[254] This means that the more

248. Ibid., 265.
249. Ibid., 266.
250. Ibid., 267.
251. Ibid.
252. Ibid.
253. See also the thought of Maurice Blondel, whose influence upon von Balthasar I have noted above. I have not flagged all the numerous places where Blondel and Heidegger, in different ways, have influenced von Balthasar's approach.
254. Ibid., 268.

God is present to us in his truth, the more our will to life—which (when it is true) is self-surrendering love—grows within us as the conscious truth of our being. Von Balthasar emphasizes that God's presence does not overpower our freedom or the mystery of our being. Rather, our mystery, when we freely "unveil" ourselves in an attitude of open confession before the God who sees all, enters into the ever-greater mystery of God. Furthermore, we must freely choose that God's truth be accomplished in us. The will to self-surrender, not the will to power, is again the key to truth: "The creature's will is open to be disposed of according to God's will," and God is glorified by "the creature's free self-surrender, its bringing him, together with its being and its unconcealment, its love."[255] Part of this free embrace of truth as the will to self-surrender consists in seeing our neighbor from the perspective of God's archetypal truth, God's self-surrendering redemptive love for sinners.

Von Balthasar concludes that *Theo-Logic*, the truth of God and the truth of the world, is found ultimately in "the mystery of God himself: the mystery of groundless surrender."[256] In arriving at this conclusion, he accepts the traditional order of being, knowing, and loving. But he also, even more insistently, reverses this order: "The love that stands at the end of the sequence as the goal of its unfolding stands, in another perspective, at its beginning as the basic impulse underlying it."[257] The ground of everything is this basic impulse; as von Balthasar puts it, "The very existence of truth, of eternal truth, is grounded in love."[258] The lesson of the *Theo-Logic* is that the truth of God and of the world is not the will to power but the will to self-surrendering love, whose glorious light calls forth our adoration.

255. Ibid., 270.
256. Ibid., 272.
257. Ibid.
258. Ibid.

Conclusion

In *Pattern of Redemption*, Edward Oakes sets forth three key thinkers whom von Balthasar was attempting to overcome in his trilogy. The first one named by Oakes is Immanuel Kant (who is contrasted with Goethe, a contemporary of Hegel). The second one is Georg W. F. Hegel. And the third one is Friedrich Nietzsche.

In each case, Oakes focuses on the profound contrast between von Balthasar and these three preeminent modern German thinkers. Oakes argues that von Balthasar overcomes the errors of these three thinkers by reclaiming a realist metaphysics and the analogy of being. As Oakes puts it, "When looking at German culture from Kant and Goethe through Hegel and on to Nietzsche, what we can see is *the culmination of the collapse of the distinction between God and the world*."[259] Oakes presents von Balthasar as the great contemporary defender of the analogy of being in theology, against the tremendously influential incursions of German idealist philosophy culminating in Nietzsche's nihilism.

At the same time, Oakes also stresses that von Balthasar "saw his own work as making a clearing for love."[260] That strikes me as exactly right. In the *Theo-Logic*, von Balthasar aims to combat any account of truth that grounds it elsewhere than in the will to self-surrendering love. In doing so, he finds an unusual ally in Nietzsche, since Nietzsche too sought to combat (idealist) rationalism and since Nietzsche saw truth as fundamentally the will to greater life. At the same time, Nietzsche's focus on the self's expansion through the will to power and health could not be more mistaken. Von Balthasar urges that the structure of knowing actually reveals that truth requires self-surrender (indeed, mutual self-surrender between subject and object) and self-renunciation at every turn.

259. Oakes, *Pattern of Redemption*, 92–93.
260. Ibid., 298.

Do lovers have the ability to know more about the world and about God? Surely the answer is yes. If one lacks love for what one is seeking to know, one cannot avoid attending to it in a rationalistic manner and attempting to use it for one's own purposes. Of course, one must also have a firm foundation in study. But the lover will go deeper into the truth of the subject matter.

Yet, is love really at the root of truth in the way that von Balthasar says? To my mind, all the particular judgments that he makes do not need to be correct. His overall argument is that self-surrender plays a crucial role in knowing truth. This strikes me as accurate and salutary. It accords with John's teaching that "he who does not love does not know God; for God is love" (1 Jn 4:8). It explains how it is that the "truth" makes us "free" (Jn 8:32) and also why Satan, who hates God with all his being, has "no truth in him" (Jn 8:44). It fits with Paul's teaching that of faith, hope, and love, "the greatest of these is love" (1 Cor 13:13). It fits with Jesus' naming of the Holy Spirit, who is the bond of love in the Trinity, the "Spirit of truth" (Jn 14:6 and elsewhere).

Admittedly, Paul can envision a scenario in which one might possess great knowledge—real truth—but lack love. Paul states in this vein, "If I have prophetic powers, and understand all mysteries and all knowledge, and if I have all faith, so as to remove mountains, but have not love, I am nothing" (1 Cor 13:2). James, too, suggests that the demons, who lack love, have extensive knowledge of truth: "Even the demons believe—and shudder" (Jas 2:19). But I find that von Balthasar's emphasis on self-surrender (and thus on self-surrendering love) as utterly vital to truth, and indeed as the very truth of the triune God, stands on fundamentally solid ground. Quoting from the preface of the *Roman Catechism* produced to sum up Catholic teaching after the Council of Trent, the prologue of the *Catechism of the Catholic Church* places its whole teaching of truth under the principle of love, as the motive and goal of learning: "The whole concern of doctrine and its teaching must be directed to the love that never

ends. Whether something is proposed for belief, for hope or for
action, the love of our Lord must always be made accessible, so
that anyone can see that all the works of perfect Christian virtue
spring from love and have no other objective than to arrive at
love."[261] Like Augustine, Aquinas, and many others, the *Catechism of the Catholic Church* attests that "the desire for God is
written on the human heart," and this desire is none other than
a desire for truth: "Only in God will he find the truth and happiness he never stops searching for."[262]

Von Balthasar concludes the three volumes of his *Theo-Logic*
with the following sentences: "Through the Son's glory we
glimpse the abyss of the invisible Father's love-glory in the Holy
Spirit's twofold love. Born of the Spirit as we are, we exist in the
fire of love in which Father and Son encounter each other; thus,
together with the Spirit, we simultaneously bear witness and
give glory to this love."[263] Nothing farther from Nietzsche's perspective could be imagined—although Nietzsche did have a highly exalted sense of his own vocation. In Nietzsche, all depends
upon triumphant self-will; in von Balthasar, all depends upon
the glory of the self-surrendering love of the Father, Son, and
Holy Spirit, who enable us to participate in and glorify this triune
self-surrendering love. Every aspect of our knowing is, in some
way, caught up in the self-surrender that we analogously reflect
as images of the Trinity. The truth of reality is self-surrendering
love.

261. *Catechism of the Catholic Church*, 2nd ed. (Vatican City: Libreria Editrice
Vaticana, 1997), §25; quoting the *Roman Catechism*, Preface, §10.
262. *Catechism of the Catholic Church*, §27.
263. Von Balthasar, *The Spirit of Truth*, 448.

Epilogue

In his 1950 encyclical *Humani Generis*, Pope Pius XII warned against the effort to express dogma by means of "the concepts of modern philosophy, whether of immanentism or idealism or existentialism or any other system."[1] The pope was right to warn against these philosophies. No one who (as Nicholas J. Healy says about von Balthasar) steadily "keeps his gaze fixed on the great mystery of God's being 'all in all'" and who at the same time affirms that the world has "a genuine existence that is other than God" can fail to sharply criticize Kantian immanentism, Hegelian idealism, and Nietzschean existentialism.[2]

On the other hand, there is a way to take insights from these three preeminent modern thinkers, even while critiquing their thought. The benefit of this approach consists both in obtaining the insights themselves and in making clear that Catholic theology is able to sift these modern philosophies and to separate the wheat from the weeds. These hugely influential modern philosophers can contribute something to Catholic thought even while the deepest elements of their thought—Kant's locking us in the immanent box of the mind's categories, Hegel's suggestion that the world is simply the dialectical unfolding of "absolute spirit," Nietzsche's proclamation of a Superman based on the will to power—are utterly rejected.

1. Pius XII, Encyclical Letter *Humani Generis*, N.C.W.C. translation (Boston: Pauline Books and Media, n.d.), §15.

2. Nicholas J. Healy, *The Eschatology of Hans Urs von Balthasar: Being as Communion* (Oxford: Oxford University Press, 2005), 21.

As I see it, von Balthasar undertakes just such a task in order
to retrieve and proclaim the fullness of the Gospel to the modern world. He does so in a deeply Ignatian manner, as befits his
Jesuit priestly formation. Adrian Walker insightfully identifies
Ignatius as "in some sense the father of Balthasar's theology"
because of his emphasis on "Christian obedience" as "the preference of God's will to one's own."[3] Todd Walatka points out that
"one would be hard-pressed to find any central Ignatian theme
that does not exert significant influence on Balthasar's theological vision," and Ben Quash comments that even after leaving the
Jesuit order, von "Balthasar remained an Ignatian to his core."[4]
As Jacques Servais has noted, von Balthasar "discerns a threefold center in the method of the *Exercises*: election, indifference,
and obedience."[5] "Election" explains the radically theocentric
character of von Balthasar's theology, including the centrality
of Christ and the Holy Spirit. "Indifference" describes Ignatius's
handing over of his entire life, his whole being, for God to use as
God wills. "Obedience" constitutes the self-surrendering form of

3. Adrian Walker, "Every Thought Captive to Christ: How Balthasar Changed My
Mind about Faith and Philosophy," in *How Balthasar Changed My Mind: 15 Scholars
Reflect on the Meaning of Balthasar for Their Own Work*, ed. Rodney A. Howsare and
Larry S. Chapp, 259–78 (New York: Crossroad, 2008), at 276.

4. Todd Walatka, *Von Balthasar and the Option for the Poor: Theodramatics in
the Light of Liberation Theology* (Washington, D.C.: The Catholic University of America Press, 2017), 86; Ben Quash, "Drama and the Ends of Modernity," in Lucy Gardner, David Moss, Ben Quash, and Graham Ward, *Balthasar at the End of Modernity*,
139–72 (Edinburgh: T&T Clark, 1999), at 151.

5. Jacques Servais, SJ, "Balthasar as Interpreter of the Catholic Tradition," trans.
Sylvester Tan, in *Love Alone Is Credible: Hans Urs von Balthasar as Interpreter of
the Catholic Tradition*, vol. 1, ed. David L. Schindler, 191–208 (Grand Rapids, Mich.:
Eerdmans, 2008), at 200. For the crucial influence of Ignatius of Loyola upon von
Balthasar, see also Servais, *Théologie des Exercices spirituels. H. U. von Balthasar
interprète saint Ignace* (Brussels: Culture et Vérité, 1996); Matthew A. Rothaus Moser,
Love Is Understanding: Hans Urs von Balthasar's Theology of the Saints (Minneapolis,
Minn.: Fortress Press, 2016), 1–23; Werner Löser, SJ, "The Ignatian *Exercises* in the
Work of Hans Urs von Balthasar," in *Hans Urs von Balthasar: His Life and Work*, ed.
David L. Schindler, 103–20 (San Francisco: Ignatius Press, 1991); Ben Quash, "Igna-
tian Dramatics: First Glance at the Spirituality of Hans Urs von Balthasar," *The Way*
38, no. 1 (1998): 77–86.

each person's mission in the obedient Christ, through the Holy Spirit. The triune God who elects us is himself self-surrendering love, and we are called to the self-surrender found in "indifference" and to the love found in "obedience." Von Balthasar's vision of self-surrendering love as the beautiful form, the drama, and the truth of all reality—keeping in mind that God is always infinitely greater than we can conceive—explains his 1941 letter to Karl Rahner in which he states that his goal is "to let the Christian reality radiate from its inmost center, and, thus, in such an irrefutable way that the beacons shine towards the exterior and penetrate into the darkest underbrush before the Church."[6]

In summarizing the first volume of each part of the trilogy, I brought to the fore the richness of von Balthasar's sources and the depth and range of his insights and conversations. Readers of von Balthasar's trilogy find benefit from his differentiation between theological aesthetics and aesthetic theology, his account of apologetics and "seeing the form" of Christ, his understanding of the mediation of divine revelation in scripture and the church, his insights into biblical exegesis, his retrieval of the spiritual senses, his insights into the strengths and weaknesses of post–Vatican II theological approaches, his appreciation for the "world stage" in understanding human history as a drama of divine and human self-surrendering love, his account of the tension between "I" and its roles, his analysis of subject and object in terms of mutual self-surrender, his insistence upon the mystery inherent to beings, his valuation of the divine ideas, and so much more. One may disagree—even quite strongly—with certain ways in which von Balthasar speculatively develops particular philosophical or doctrinal points, but this should not obscure the enormous gift of von Balthasar's reflections on the revelation in Christ of triune self-surrendering love as the true meaning of life (divine and human).

---

6. See K. H. Neufeld, *Die Brüder Rahner. Eine Biographie* (Freiburg: Herder, 1994), 183; cited in Servais, "Balthasar as Interpreter of the Catholic Tradition," 198.

Not surprisingly, von Balthasar's admirers include many of
the greatest theologians of our time. Writing during the period
of the publication of the *Theological Aesthetics*, his friend Henri de Lubac rejoiced in von Balthasar's achievement: "Classical
antiquity, the great European languages, the metaphysical tradition, the history of religions, the diverse exploratory adven-
tures of contemporary man and, above all, the sacred sciences,
St. Thomas, St. Bonaventure, patrology (all of it)—not to speak
just now of the Bible—none of them is not welcomed and made
vital by this great mind."[7] De Lubac adds that von Balthasar's
theology shines crucial light upon the meaning of the Second
Vatican Council.

Pope John Paul II, in presenting the International Paul VI
Prize to von Balthasar in 1984, described him as "the only prominent contemporary Catholic theologian who has dared to undertake—on his own—the tremendous venture of a theological
Summa, one whose conceptual unity and impressive scale give it
the right to be placed in the line of the other great syntheses that
have marked the pace of western theology."[8] Joseph Ratzinger,
observing that von Balthasar had accepted the cardinalate from
John Paul II but died prior to being installed as a cardinal, comments that "what the Pope intended to express by this mark of
distinction and of honor remains valid: no longer only private
individuals but the Church itself, in its official responsibility,
tells us that he is right in what he teaches of the Faith, that he
points the way to the sources of living water—a witness to the
word which teaches us Christ."[9]

7. Henri de Lubac, SJ, *The Church: Paradox and Mystery* (Staten Island, N.Y.:
Ecclesia Press, 1969), 105; cited in Servais, "Balthasar as Interpreter of the Catholic
Tradition," 193.

8. Istituto Paolo VI, Premio Internazionale Paolo VI 1984, *Notiziario*, n. 8 (May
1984) (Brescia: 1984), 25; cited in Servais, "Balthasar as Interpreter of the Catholic
Tradition," 192. See also Brendan Leahy, "John Paul II and Hans Urs von Balthasar,"
in *The Legacy of John Paul II*, ed. Gerald O'Collins and Michael Hayes, 31–50 (New
York: Continuum, 2008).

9. Joseph Ratzinger, "Homily at the Funeral Liturgy of Hans Urs von Balthasar,"

Similarly, in his *Last Testament*, Pope Emeritus Benedict XVI praises von Balthasar's theology profusely. He proclaims that in it "the theology of the Fathers was present, a spiritual vision of theology, which is genuinely developed out of faith and contemplation, which goes down to the depths and is new at the same time too. Thus it wasn't just academic stuff, with which one ultimately can do nothing."[10] He makes clear that he remains completely "enraptured" by von Balthasar's "synthesis of erudition, genuine professionalism and spiritual depth."[11] He explains that he and von Balthasar shared the same "inward intention, the vision as such," even if he (Ratzinger/Benedict) could not "keep up with his [von Balthasar's] erudition" and did not take an interest in the mystical theology of Adrienne von Speyr.[12]

I share Pope Emeritus Benedict's enraptured response to von Balthasar's theological vision, erudition, and spiritual depth. Yet, I have written a number of books in which—without it ever being the focus of the book—I have paused to criticize von Balthasar's position on various points, some minor but others major. Von Balthasar himself, of course, was never shy about criticizing other theologians. Although he, de Lubac, Yves Congar, Ratzinger, Erich Przywara, and Jean Daniélou were trained under the regimen of neo-scholasticism—or perhaps *because* they were thus trained and therefore remembered the oft-inadequate intellectual experience that seminary training can involve (due in part to the inevitably wide range of intellectual abilities among the seminarians)—these *ressourcement* theologians were very critical of the neo-scholastic theology set forth

in *Hans Urs von Balthasar: His Life and Work*, 291–95, at 293; cited in Servais, "Balthasar as Interpreter of the Catholic Tradition," 195.

10. Benedict XVI with Peter Seewald, *Last Testament: In His Own Words*, trans. Jacob Phillips (London: Bloomsbury, 2016), 146.

11. Ibid., 146. See also Benedict XVI, "Hans Urs von Balthasar: Christlicher Universalismus," in *Logik der Liebe und Herrlichkeit Gottes: Hans Urs von Balthasar im Gespräch. Festgabe für Karl Kardinal Lehmann zum 70. Geburtstag*, ed. Walter Kasper, 14–24 (Ostfildern: Matthias-Grünewald-Verlag, 2006).

12. Benedict XVI with Peter Seewald, *Last Testament*, 147.

by many of their teachers. Looking back, we can say that teachers capable of training such scholars, and of preparing them with
the languages and direction needed for mastering the entirety
of the Christian tradition as well as philosophy from the Greeks
onward, must have possessed some intellectual and pedagogical
skills. In fact, a more differentiated reading of the neo-scholastic
theologians of the first forty years of the twentieth century shows
a number of very bright lights, despite the inevitable existence of
flaws in neo-scholastic approaches. Often invoking strong and
sweeping criticisms of neo-scholasticism and post-Tridentine
theology, von Balthasar leaves these figures almost entirely out
of his corpus. Unfortunately, he gives almost no attention to the
contributions of Thomas de Vio Cajetan, Francisco de Vitoria,
Robert Bellarmine, Francisco Suárez, Melchior Cano, John of St.
Thomas, Ambroise Gardeil, and so on.[13]

By the time von Balthasar began serious work on his trilogy, he was in his fifties and the period of neo-scholasticism was
fast approaching its end. Immediately after the Council, neo-
scholasticism vanished for all practical purposes. During the
postconciliar period, he skirmished most notably with Rahner, although he included certain ideas from Rahner in his trilogy, such
as the nonexistence of the intermediate state of the soul separated from the body after death.[14] In his criticisms of Rahner, von
Balthasar was deeply concerned that Rahner and his followers
were placing in doubt the objective reality of divine revelation. As
von Balthasar notes, "Christian belief means the unconditional
resolve to surrender one's life for Christ's sake," but this can be
done only if we today can know, through scripture as interpreted
by the church over the centuries, both the real truth about Christ

13. See the instructive essay by Christopher Ruddy, "*Ressourcement* and the *Enduring* Legacy of Post-Tridentine Theology," in *Ressourcement: A Movement for Renewal in Twentieth-Century Catholic Theology*, ed. Gabriel Flynn and Paul D. Murray,
185–201 (Oxford: Oxford University Press, 2012).

14. See Andrew Hofer, OP, "Balthasar's Eschatology on the Intermediate State:
The Question of Knowability," *Logos* 12, no. 3 (2009): 148–72.

(the incarnate Word, whose death is "the opening-up of the glory of divine love" and is the ever-new foundation of the church) and the real truth about how Christ wills for his followers to live unto salvation.[15]

In his 1987 afterword to a new edition of his *Cordula oder der Ernstfall*, published in English as *The Moment of Christian Witness* and famous for its critique of Rahner, von Balthasar points out that, inspired by Rahnerian thought, the process of "liberal broadening of dogma, of some transformation of its content into a 'non-objective' reality," has resulted in many parish contexts in the rejection by priests, religious, and laity of the truth of the church's life-giving authoritative dogmatic and moral tradition.[16] That von Balthasar's postconciliar critique of Rahner was fundamentally not an exaggeration can be seen in Rahner's *The Shape of the Church to Come*, which was published in German in 1972, six years after von Balthasar's *Cordula* first appeared.[17]

Similarly, von Balthasar did not hesitate to disagree with other contemporaries, even while gladly appropriating various elements of their thought. For example, he repeatedly disagreed with the way that de Lubac articulated the natural desire for the

15. Hans Urs von Balthasar, *The Moment of Christian Witness*, trans. Richard Beckley (San Francisco: Ignatius Press, 1994), 27.

16. Ibid., 148. See (now-Bishop) Robert Barron's remembrance of his thoroughly Rahnerian training in seminary and in his S.T.L. program, in his "A Reflection on Christ, Theological Method, and Freedom," in *How Balthasar Changed My Mind*, 9–25. For a view that ultimately sides with Rahner, see Karen Kilby, "Balthasar and Karl Rahner," in *The Cambridge Companion to Hans Urs von Balthasar*, ed. Edward T. Oakes, SJ, and David Moss, 256–68 (Cambridge: Cambridge University Press, 2004). See also Rowan Williams, "Balthasar and Rahner," in *The Analogy of Beauty: The Theology of Hans Urs von Balthasar*, ed. John Riches, 11–34 (Edinburgh: T&T Clark, 1986). Williams grasps the heart of von Balthasar's concern regarding anthropocentric theology when Williams observes, "Balthasar's dread is the Inquisitorial claim to love humanity more than its maker does—the most comprehensible and sympathetic of all blasphemies—and that is why, for him, revelation is a radical assault on what we know of love, or of liberty, or of hope" (ibid., 34).

17. Karl Rahner, SJ, *The Shape of the Church to Come*, trans. Edward Quinn (New York: Seabury Press, 1974).

supernatural.[18] Less surprisingly, he disagreed with Jürgen Molt-
mann and René Girard, while giving significant and respectful
attention to their proposals.

In addition, von Balthasar disagreed repeatedly with almost
all of his saintly patristic and medieval interlocutors, though he
also drew heavily upon them in positive ways. In his well-known
1939 article "The Fathers, the Scholastics and Ourselves," he argues that the Church Fathers were plagued by Neoplatonist dis-
dain for the particular and this-worldly, and he suggests that the
medievals too suffered under the same burden. In his view, contemporary theology—if it can negotiate the problems connected
with the modern anthropocentric turn, problems characteristic
of Kant, Hegel, and Nietzsche—has the potential to be the apex
of Christian theology so far.[19]

At various places in his corpus, von Balthasar has good
things to say about Augustine's theology, but he repeatedly and
sharply criticizes Augustine's theology of grace and predestina-
tion. He remarks negatively about the *City of God*, "It is a constant astonishment to find how much *The City of God*, which laid
the foundations of Western philosophy of history, is an essentially unhistorical work, original and creative only in those places
where it abstracts the eternally unchanging existential conditions of historical existence from the historical process."[20] Regarding Irenaeus, about whom he is generally more positive than
he is about Augustine, he has this to say: "Irenaeus' *Scriptural interpretation* of the saving economy of the Old and New Covenants
is based ... wholly on the wording of the texts and on their literal
correspondence.... This exegesis ... impedes and obstructs the

18. This point is made in D. Stephen Long, *Saving Karl Barth: Hans Urs von Balthasar's Preoccupation* (Minneapolis, Minn.: Fortress Press, 2014).

19. See, in English translation, Hans Urs von Balthasar, "The Fathers, the Scholastics and Ourselves," *Communio* 24, no. 2 (1997): 347–96.

20. Hans Urs von Balthasar, *The Glory of the Lord: A Theological Aesthetics*,
vol. 2, *Studies in Theological Style: Clerical Styles*, trans. Andrew Louth, Francis
McDonagh, and Brian McNeil, CRV, ed. John Riches (San Francisco: Ignatius Press,
1984), 143.

achievement of the very aim implicit in the structure of the system, a historical understanding of revelation."[21] In his Trinitarian theology, he often parts ways sharply with Augustine and the medievals. Regarding medieval theology, he raises the concern that "High Scholasticism ... made the mistake of thinking that it had to give an appropriate answer to every question, however untheological."[22] He criticizes Aquinas regularly, including in developing his theology of the cross, where he bemoans that in Aquinas "there is no emphasis whatsoever on Christ's abandonment by God as the center of the Passion."[23] At the same time, as should be clear from the above chapters, he also draws a large number of positive contributions from Aquinas, as well as from the Fathers and from numerous medieval doctors. I do not wish to leave the erroneous impression that he is always criticizing, let alone that he criticizes his great predecessors without love and respect. But he is quite willing to criticize whenever he finds a point of difference.

Reception and Criticism

Joseph Fessio once remarked to me in conversation that one could not truly appreciate von Balthasar's achievement if one differed from von Balthasar on the cross and Trinity, most notably the places in the trilogy that read as a string of quotations

---

21. Ibid., 90. For a reading of von Balthasar within Irenaean categories, however, see Kevin Mongrain, *The Systematic Thought of Hans Urs von Balthasar: An Irenaean Retrieval* (New York: Crossroad, 2002). Mongrain states, "I am not attempting to demonstrate that von Balthasar's theology is in fact Irenaean. That claim would require a comparative analysis of von Balthasar and Irenaeus's texts. Rather, I am arguing that von Balthasar *thinks* his theology is Irenaean. In other words, he consciously identifies Irenaeus's thought as the purest expression of the patristic consensus and builds the theology of his trilogy around it" (ibid., 16). I agree that von Balthasar favors Irenaeus among the Fathers, but I do not think that he "builds the theology of his trilogy" around his understanding of Irenaeus's thought.

22. Hans Urs von Balthasar, *Theo-Drama: Theological Dramatic Theory*, vol. 4, *The Action*, trans. Graham Harrison (San Francisco: Ignatius Press, 1994), 458.

23. Ibid., 264.

from the mystical theology of von Speyr.[24] This struck me as an odd claim, given von Balthasar's speculative willingness to set forth experimental positions and his own practice of strongly criticizing the tradition even while affirming it. Can one be a "Balthasarian," highly appreciative of the achievement of von Balthasar, if one criticizes central aspects of von Balthasar's theology? Another way to state this question is to ask how great the tension must be between those who receive inspiration from von Balthasar and those who do not. Are the former primarily those who accept all of the particular positions of von Balthasar's Trinitarian theology and his Christology? Or is it possible, as I hope, for "Balthasarian" theologians to have a more varied form of engagement with von Balthasar's work and insights?[25]

Since von Balthasar stays grounded in "Christianity's scandal of particularity" and in the magisterial tradition (allowing for speculative efforts to develop doctrine, efforts that are proper for a theologian of his ability), I think that von Balthasar rightly felt free to criticize sharply the Fathers, Aquinas, and many other sainted theologians. The same, however, should hold for the reception of von Balthasar's achievement among those who share his faith commitments. Thus, a "Balthasarian"—one who is "enraptured" with von Balthasar's achievement—should be able to praise von Balthasar's critique of Kant while wishing that he had given more place to historical apologetics, to praise his critique of Hegel while wishing that Hegel's argument about God

24. Note that although I include von Balthasar among the *ressourcement* theologians (a term that I am using interchangeably with "nouvelle théologie"), I recognize that he at times distanced himself from this theological perspective, even if his debts to Henri de Lubac were enormous. See Edward T. Oakes, SJ, "Balthasar and *Ressourcement*: An Ambiguous Relationship," in *Ressourcement*, ed. Gabriel Flynn and Paul D. Murray, 278–88; Rudolf Voderholzer, "Die Bedeutung der sogenannten "Nouvelle Théologie" (insbesondere Henri de Lubacs) für die Theologie Hans Urs von Balthasars," in *Logik der Liebe und Herrlichkeit Gottes*, ed. Walter Kasper, 204–28.

25. Note that the question is not posed only to Balthasar's students and disciples but also to his critics. Arguably, the extremes mirror one another as mutually opposed forms of excess.

containing his own contradiction had not led von Balthasar to
speak of a form of alienation in the Trinity, and to praise his critique of Nietzsche while thinking that truth and love should be
distinguished more firmly.

Such issues regarding the reception of von Balthasar's
achievement have become pressing, not least due to the increas-
ing intensity and confidence of criticism that has arisen in recent
years with respect to von Balthasar's theology. In two books,
for example, Lyra Pitstick has sharply criticized von Balthasar's
doctrine of Holy Saturday. In my view, she goes much too far; for
example, she terms von Balthasar "a *reputably* Catholic theologian."[26] But I think it true that von Balthasar's doctrine of Holy
Saturday is mistaken and that other great theologians have done
a much better job of understanding this reality of faith. Karen Kilby's *Balthasar: A (Very) Critical Introduction* has also stirred up
tense responses. Describing von Balthasar as "a creative and important thinker from whom there is a great deal to be learned," she
affirms the "impressive richness of Balthasar's thought" and finds
that "much of his work is original, stimulating, and fruitful," but
she nevertheless warns that "there is also something that should
make us wary of looking to him as a general theological model, or
as the great voice of tradition in our time" or "*the* great Catholic
theologian of the twentieth century."[27] Her fundamental critique
is that his mode of presenting theological arguments leads him
implicitly (and, she suggests, unconsciously) to posit himself
as the director of the whole theological symphony, rather than
as simply one voice within it. She states, "Balthasar frequently
writes as though from a position above his materials—above tra-

26. Alyssa Lyra Pitstick, *Light in Darkness: Hans Urs von Balthasar and the Catholic Doctrine of Christ's Descent into Hell* (Grand Rapids, Mich.: Eerdmans, 2007),
345. See also Pitstick, *Christ's Descent into Hell: John Paul II, Joseph Ratzinger, and
Hans Urs von Balthasar on the Theology of Holy Saturday* (Grand Rapids, Mich.: Eerdmans, 2016).

27. Karen Kilby, *Balthasar: A (Very) Critical Introduction* (Grand Rapids, Mich.:
Eerdmans, 2012), 2.

dition, above Scripture, above history—and also, indeed, above his readers. He frequently seems to presume, to put the point in its sharpest and most polemical form, a God's eye view."[28]

Responses to Kilby from experts on von Balthasar have largely been negative. But in my opinion, she has hit upon a weakness of von Balthasar's, and her concerns are at their most persuasive when she observes critically that "the way in which Balthasar brings together reflection on the immanent Trinity and reflection on the world's horrors involves, in the end, an introduction of elements from the latter into the former, elements of darkness into the divine light."[29] Kilby has in view especially the fourth and fifth volumes of the *Theo-Drama*, and she echoes concerns that Pitstick and numerous others have raised, including me and most recently Thomas Joseph White in his *The Incarnate Lord*.[30] I think that von Balthasar's achievement remains a major one even if we grant that, at times, in the content that he gave to particular doctrines, he significantly overreached. After prais-

28. Ibid., 13. Kilby's concerns fit with those raised by Karl Rahner early on, as Kilby (an expert on Rahner's theology) recognizes. See also, for perspectives that extend these concerns in liberationist directions, Philip Endean, SJ, "Von Balthasar, Rahner, and the Commissar," *New Blackfriars* 79, no. 923 (January 1998): 33–38; Gerard F. O'Hanlon, SJ, "The Jesuits and Modern Theology: Rahner, von Balthasar, and Liberation Theology," *Irish Theological Quarterly* 58, no. 1 (1992): 25–45; Thomas G. Dalzell, SM, "Lack of Social Drama in Balthasar's Theological Dramatics," *Theological Studies* 60, no. 3 (1999): 457–75. For feminist theological concerns arising within the engagement of von Balthasar's work, see Susan Ross, "Women, Beauty, and Justice: Moving Beyond von Balthasar," *Journal of the Society of Christian Ethics* 25, no. 1 (2005): 79–98; Michelle Gonzalez, "Hans Urs von Balthasar and Contemporary Feminist Theology," *Theological Studies* 65, no. 3 (2004): 566–95; Lucy Gardner and David Moss, "Something like Time; Something like Sexes: An Essay in Reception," in *Balthasar at the End of Modernity*, 69–137; Jennifer Newsome Martin, "The 'Whence' and the 'Whither' of Balthasar's Gendered Theology: Rehabilitating Kenosis for Feminist Theology," *Modern Theology* 31, no. 2 (2015): 211–34; Tina Beattie, "A Man and Three Women: Hans, Adrienne, Mary and Luce," *New Blackfriars* 79, no. 924 (1998): 97–103; Corrine Crammer, "One Sex or Two? Balthasar's Theology of the Sexes," in *The Cambridge Companion to Hans Urs von Balthasar*, 93–112. See also Frederick Christian Bauerschmidt, "Theo-Drama and Political Theology," *Communio* 25, no. 3 (1998): 532–52.

29. Kilby, *Balthasar*, 122.

30. Thomas Joseph White, OP, *The Incarnate Lord: A Thomistic Study in Christology* (Washington, D.C.: The Catholic University of America Press, 2015).

ing von Balthasar's achievement, Walatka rightly urges that we should "adopt a non-idolatrous view of Balthasar's thought" even while celebrating "his wealth of insights and theological contributions."[31] Quite appropriately—especially in light of what we have seen of the trilogy's constructive critique of Kant, Hegel, and Nietzsche—Walatka praises von Balthasar's opposition to "a promethean rejection of humanity's natural dependence upon God" and von Balthasar's affirmation of "the particularity of Jesus Christ as the irreplaceable site of God's revelation."[32]

Revisiting an Internecine Struggle

Recent sharp criticisms of some of von Balthasar's theological positions, especially when these criticisms come from theologians with expertise in Aquinas, have touched a nerve among some experts in von Balthasar who consider that theological neo-scholasticism should have come to an end by now—a position that mirrors the old neo-scholastic view that *ressourcement* theology should be eliminated.[33] Arguably, the terrible mid-twentieth-century clash between the *ressourcement* theologians, including von Balthasar, and their neo-scholastic teachers was inevitable, given that both sides were supremely confident and were convinced that if they did not win, the church's future would be gravely imperiled.[34] Certainly, von Balthasar himself

31. Walatka, *Von Balthasar and the Option for the Poor*, 213.

32. Ibid., 213–14.

33. Von Balthasar's boldly provocative efforts against the regnant neo-scholasticism have been well surveyed by Fergus Kerr, OP, "Foreword: Assessing This 'Giddy Synthesis'," in *Balthasar at the End of Modernity*, 1–13.

34. For example, although in Henri de Lubac's 1949 preface to the second edition of *Corpus Mysticum* he argues unpersuasively that the first edition (published in 1939) was misunderstood as a critique of high scholasticism, his confident and indeed urgent opposition to neo-scholastic theology shines quite strongly throughout the book. See for example de Lubac, *Corpus Mysticum: The Eucharist and the Church in the Middle Ages: Historical Survey*, trans. Gemma Simmonds, CJ, with Richard Price and Christopher Stephens, ed. Laurence Paul Hemming and Susan Frank Parsons (London: SCM Press, 2006), 226–30.

felt this way and sought to do whatever he could to raze the neo-scholastic bastions, as in his 1952 *Schleifung der Bastionen: Von der Kirche in Dieser Zeit.*[35]

The tensions were already bubbling in the 1930s.[36] In 1937, Marie-Dominique Chenu's *Une école de théologie: le Saulchoir* influentially charged neo-scholastic theology with being infected by Wolffian rationalism, thereby linking neo-scholasticism to liberal modernity.[37] Chenu was reprimanded by Rome, and the book was placed on the Index of Forbidden Books in 1942. In the same year, Chenu was dismissed as rector of Le Saulchoir. Ten-

35. See Hans Urs von Balthasar, *Razing the Bastions: On the Church in This Age*, trans. Brian McNeil, CRV (San Francisco: Ignatius Press, 1993).

36. For background see Jon Kirwan, *An Avant-garde Theological Generation: The Nouvelle Théologie and the French Crisis of Modernity* (Oxford: Oxford University Press, 2018).

37. See the new edition of this work: Marie-Dominique Chenu, OP, *Une école de théologie: le Saulchoir* (Paris: Cerf, 1985). For the direction in which his work (and the punishment that he received) led him, see Chenu, "'Consecratio mundi'," *Nouvelle revue théologique* 86, no. 6 (1964): 608–18, where he proposes that "the distinction between profane and sacred is dissolved" in the light of the incarnation (ibid., 616). He is trying to uphold the integrity and sacredness of God's creation (the natural order, fully taken up by Christ), but the message that all too easily results is that the sphere of the divine mysteries is now the world rather than distinctively the worshipping church. See also the accurate concerns about Chenu's historicizing of dogma and anti-metaphysical bent raised by White, *The Incarnate Lord*, 471–72. White shows how Edward Schillebeeckx, OP, develops some logical implications of Chenu's thought in untenable theological directions, as did Chenu himself (though less directly) in "Vérité évangélique et métaphysique wolfienne à Vatican II," *Revue des sciences philosophiques et théologiques* 57 (1973): 632–40. Linking the neo-scholastics with the philosophy of Christian Wolff has roots in the work of Maurice Blondel and Joseph Maréchal, SJ. See especially Maréchal, *Le Point de Depart de la Metaphysique. Lecons sur le developpement historique du probleme de la Connaissance. Cahier II: Le Conflit du Rationalisme et de l'Empirisme dans la Philosophie moderne, avant Kant* (Bruges: Charles Beyaert, 1923). For Chenu's broader perspective during this period, see also Chenu, "Le sens et les leçons d'une crise religieuse," *Vie Intellectuelle* 13 (1931): 356–80; Chenu, "Position de la théologie," *Revue des sciences philosophiques et théologiques* 25 (1935): 232–57; Chenu, "Aux origins de la 'science moderne'," *Revue des sciences philosophiques et théologiques* 29 (1940): 206–17; Chenu, *La théologie comme science au XIIIe siècle*, 2nd ed. (Paris: Vrin, 1943). See also Blondel, *Le problème de la philosophie catholique* (Paris: Bloud & Gay, 1932). See also Henri de Lubac, SJ, "Sur la philosophie chrétienne: Réflexions à la suite d'un débat," *Nouvelle revue théologique* 63 (1936): 225–53.

sions exploded in 1946 with the publication of Jean Daniélou's "Les orientations présentes de la pensée religieuse," in which he called for the replacement of neo-scholastic theology with a more historical theology that would be truly able to answer the faith-sapping challenges posed by liberal theology ("modernism"). Responding to Daniélou in an article titled "La théologie et ses sources" (1946), Marie-Michel Labourdette argued that any theological mode other than neo-scholastic scientific theology would destroy the objectivity of dogma by inevitably falling into historical relativism and subjectivism. In the same year, de Lubac's *Surnaturel: Études historiques* argued that the Thomistic commentatorial tradition since Cardinal Cajetan had distorted the nature-grace relationship as understood by Aquinas and the Fathers.[38] This publication intensified the battle, since the relationship of nature and grace had been a neuralgic point in the nineteenth-century controversies that led to the early twentieth-century modernist crisis.

Responding to Labourdette's article, a group of Jesuit theologians led by de Lubac (and including von Balthasar) strongly denied being historicist or doctrinally relativist. In their response, they did not back down from Daniélou's rejection of neo-scholastic theology, and they warned against curtailing the freedom of diverse theological schools within the shared commitment to Catholic orthodoxy. In response to this response, Réginald Garrigou-Lagrange published his 1947 "La nouvelle théologie, où va-t-elle?" which stated openly that the path being taken by the Jesuit theologians was a return to modernism. At the same time, Labourdette co-authored with Marie-Joseph Nicolas an article defending Thomistic metaphysics as in accord with being itself and therefore as especially suitable for the theology of history. In

38. Henri de Lubac, SJ, *Surnaturel: Études historiques* (Paris: Cerf, 1946). For historical and theological studies from various perspectives, see *Surnaturel: A Controversy at the Heart of Twentieth-Century Thomistic Thought*, ed. Serge-Thomas Bonino, trans. Robert Williams (Ave Maria, Fla.: Sapientia Press, 2009), especially Étienne Fouilloux's "Henri de Lubac at the Moment of the Publication of *Surnaturel*," 3–20.

addition, Labourdette and Nicolas suggested that since Thomism is the church's philosophy and theology, their *ressourcement* opponents were going too far, notwithstanding the otherwise valid principle of the diversity of theological schools.[39]

39. See Jean Daniélou, SJ, "Les orientations présentes de la pensée religieuse," *Études* 79 (1946): 5–21; Marie-Michel Labourdette, OP, "La théologie et ses sources," *Revue Thomiste* 46 (1946): 353–71; Réginald Garrigou-Lagrange, OP, "La nouvelle théologie, où va-t-elle?," *Angelicum* 23 (1946): 126–45; M.-M. Labourdette, OP, and M.-J. Nicolas, OP, "L'analogie de la vérité et l'unité de la science théologique," *Revue Thomiste* 55 (1947): 417–66. For discussion, see Étienne Fouilloux, "Dialogue théologique? (1946–1948)," in *Saint Thomas au XXe siècle*, ed. Serge-Thomas Bonino, OP, 153–95 (Paris: Saint-Paul, 1994); Aidan Nichols, OP, "Thomism and the Nouvelle Théologie," *The Thomist* 64, no. 1 (2000): 1–19. See also such works as Marie-Rosaire Gagnebet, OP, *La nature de la théologie spéculative* (Paris: Desclée, 1938); Gagnebet, "Le problème actuel de la théologie et la science aristotélicienne d'après un ouvrage recent," *Divus Thomas* 46 (1943): 237–70; Garrigou-Lagrange, "Vérité et immutabilité du Dogme," *Angelicum* 24 (1947): 124–39; Garrigou-Lagrange, "Nécessité de revenir à la definition traditionnelle de la vérité," *Angelicum* 25 (1948): 185–98; Garrigou-Lagrange, "L'immutabilité du dogme selon le concile du Vatican et le relativisme," *Revue Thomiste* 49 (1949): 309–32; Garrigou-Lagrange, "Le relativisme et l'immutabilité du dogme," *Revue Thomiste* 50 (1950): 219–46. It is obvious what Garrigou-Lagrange thought the real issue was. Although he was right that certain of Henri Bouillard's formulations in his understanding of dogma were problematic, he misjudged the intentions of his *ressourcement* opponents, who were equally concerned with combating liberal theology, though from a different direction that sought more direct engagement with historical-critical and ecumenical issues. See also the work of Yves Congar, OP, whose mentor was Chenu: "Autour du renouveau de l'ecclésiologie: la collection 'Unam Sanctam'," *La Vie Intellectuelle* 51 (1939): 9–32; Congar, "Tendances actuelles de la pensée religieuse," *Cahiers du monde nouveau* 4 (1948): 33–50; Congar, *Vraie et fausse réforme dans l'Église* (Paris: Cerf, 1950). Translation of Congar's *Vraie et fausse réforme dans l'Église* was forbidden in 1952, and in 1954 Congar was removed from his teaching position at Le Saulchoir. The bitterness and excess of the debate can be seen in Congar's *True and False Reform*, trans. Paul Philibert (Collegeville, Minn.: Liturgical Press, 2011), 137, where Congar argues that the medieval "schools were created less to prepare ecclesial servants for the people of God or creative thinkers than to produce 'doctors' capable of brilliantly arguing in scholastic disputations with a view to augmenting their number and prestige and perpetuating the scholastic system itself.... Instead of valuing creativity in the principled use of a living tradition and looking at the problems and the data of their own time, rather they imagined an unchanging perfection and tried to set about reproducing it." Unfortunately, numerous examples of such inflamed rhetoric and absurdly unfair overgeneralizations, produced in the heat of controversy and ecclesiastical power plays, can be found on both sides of the debate. For a constructive discussion of neo-scholastic and *ressourcement* engagement with development of doctrine, see Guy Mansini, OSB, "The Development of the Development of Doctrine in the Twentieth Century," *Angelicum* 93, no. 4 (2016): 785–822.

In June 1950, Daniélou was removed from his teaching position at Fourvière, de Lubac was removed from his teaching position at Lyon and from his editorship of *Recherches de science religieuse*, and three of de Lubac's books were ordered to be removed from Jesuit libraries (including *Surnaturel* and *Corpus Mysticum*).[40] This was capped by the publication shortly thereafter of Pope Pius XII's *Humani Generis*, which was widely interpreted as being directed against *ressourcement* theology.[41]

Yet, despite this lengthy history of trench warfare in which each side sought to destroy the other through behind-closed-doors machinations and public interventions, most neo-scholastic theologians and their *ressourcement* counterparts were agreed in being deeply concerned to combat the inroads being made in Catholic regions of Europe by classical liberal theology or modernism.[42] Arguing in 1898 in favor of the spread of liberal theology, the German Protestant thinker Ernst Troeltsch notes happily that the "doctrine of authority and revelation has been deeply affected by

40. Looking back on these events, de Lubac denies that any "legitimate authority of the Church ever took action against me. Having failed to avert the storm, my superior general asked me (not through a formal written order, however) to interrupt my teaching and to inform the cardinal myself that I was doing so. I was, for several years, officially 'on leave' and was myself supposed to choose my personal 'replacement'" (de Lubac, *A Theologian Speaks* [interview by Angelo Scola] [Los Angeles, CA: Twin Circle, 1985], 4).

41. See Joseph A. Komonchak, "Humani Generis and Nouvelle Théologie," in *Ressourcement*, ed. Gabriel Flynn and Paul Murray, 138–56.

42. Here I am differentiating between the *ressourcement* theology advocated by Daniélou, de Lubac, von Balthasar, Congar, Louis Bouyer, Ratzinger, and others, on the one hand, and the more accommodationist approaches of Rahner, Schillebeeckx, and (in his own distinctive way) Chenu, on the other. Whether to term Rahner and Schillebeeckx "*ressourcement* theologians" is a contested issue. For the view that they were such, and that the *ressourcement* movement as a whole was in fact modernist—a position that strikes me as blind to the main purposes of Daniélou, de Lubac, von Balthasar, Congar, Bouyer, Ratzinger et al.—see Jürgen Mettepenningen, *Nouvelle Théologie—New Theology: Inheritor of Modernism, Precursor of Vatican II* (London: T&T Clark, 2010); Mettepenningen, "Truth, Orthodoxy and the *Nouvelle Théologie*: Truth as Issue in a 'Second Modernist Crisis' (1946–1950)," in *Orthodoxy, Liberalism, and Adaptation: Essays on Ways of Worldmaking in Times of Change from Biblical, Historical and Systematic Perspectives*, ed. Bob Becking, 149–82 (Leiden: Brill, 2011).

the spirit of historical criticism, analogy, and relativity. Indeed, it has been almost destroyed."[43] What is no longer possible after Kant and Hegel, says Troeltsch, is the supposition of a real human *need* for "supernatural revelation" or for "the atonement of sins"; such things "are in the first instance purely historical forms which do not lead beyond history."[44] He emphasizes that Christianity, in its scriptures and in its institutional (ecclesiastical) forms, cannot be exempted in any way from the historicist "flux, the conditioning, and the mutability of history."[45]

Much like Kant in his *Religion within the Limits of Reason Alone*, Troeltsch urges that liberal Christianity should colonize and take over the existing Christian churches. For Troeltsch, liberal Christianity rightly eschews dogmatic content or obedience to a divine Word mediated authoritatively by scripture and the church under the guidance of the Spirit. What liberal Christianity possesses, instead, is a confidence in "the divine depth of the human spirit" and in the evolving human consciousness of what constitutes truly liberative praxis.[46]

In 1910, Troeltsch influentially defined "liberal Christianity ... in terms of two characteristics."[47] The first characteristic is that liberal Christianity "replaces the tie to an authoritative church by an inwardness that derives, freely and individually, from the strength of the common spirit of the tradition," with tradition here signifying the "religious life-world" that is ever evolving among Christians in ever-new forms.[48] The second

43. Ernst Troeltsch, "Historical and Dogmatic Method in Theology," in *Religion in History*, trans. James Luther Adams and Walter F. Bense, 11–32 (Minneapolis, Minn.: Fortress Press, 1991), at 31.

44. Ibid., 30.

45. Ibid., 28.

46. Ibid., 27.

47. Troeltsch, "On the Possibility of a Liberal Christianity," in *Religion in History*, 343–59, at 343.

48. Ibid. For an influential contemporary Catholic exemplar of this basic approach, see Terrence W. Tilley, *Inventing Catholic Tradition* (Maryknoll, N.Y.: Orbis Books, 2000).

characteristic is that liberal Christianity "transforms what has been the basic idea of historic Christianity, namely, the idea of a miraculous salvation of a human race suffering from the mortal infection of sin, into the idea of a redemptive elevation and liberation of the person through the attainment of a higher personal and communal life from God."[49] Troeltsch thereby historicizes Christianity and identifies its truth with the emergence of new forms of liberative praxis (political and economic movements) that deepen and enrich our personal and communal life. These evolving forms are not rooted in or bound by an authoritative Word of God, dogma, or faith in redemption from sin and death won by Jesus Christ.

With regard to liberative praxis, Troeltsch urges that "the ultimate goal of individual action is thus a kind of personhood filled with the import of eternity, and the ultimate goal of communal action is a kingdom of divine love which overcomes the law (*Recht*), coercion, and the struggle for existence."[50] What he means by this is obviously broad enough to be filled in differently as the zeitgeist changes. Note that Troeltsch's goal is not to destroy Christianity but to "save Christianity"; though in his supposed act of saving it, its character as divine revelation in Christ Jesus, overcoming original sin and transforming us in self-surrendering love, is lost.[51] For Troeltschian Christians, divine revelation as mediated by scripture no longer can be believed. As Friedrich Schleiermacher put it in his early work *On Religion: Speeches to Its Cultured Despisers*, "Every holy writing is merely a mausoleum of religion, a monument that a great spirit was there that no longer exists.... [H]ave you not often felt this holy longing as something unknown? Become conscious of the

---

49. Troeltsch, "On the Possibility of a Liberal Christianity," 343–44. For an influential contemporary Catholic exemplar of such an approach, see Jon Sobrino, SJ, *No Salvation Outside the Poor: Prophetic-Utopian Essays* (Maryknoll, N.Y.: Orbis Books, 2008).

50. Troeltsch, "On the Possibility of a Liberal Christianity," 352.

51. Ibid., 359.

call of your innermost nature, I beseech you, and follow it."[52]

It is not too difficult to perceive that this standpoint is in fact where many Christians in the West are now, and so it is no wonder that Christianity is dwindling in the West. This standpoint assumes that scripture is merely a "mausoleum" of various human attempts to gesture toward the non-cognizable divine mystery from within particular cultural contexts, rather than being the revelation of God's personal and covenantal words and deeds addressed to the mind and heart. The inevitable result is loss of faith.

In the late nineteenth century, Pope Leo XIII reinvigorated neo-scholastic philosophy in order to combat such Kant-inspired "modernism" through the reassertion of philosophical realism, not least in apologetics. Early twentieth-century popes added a strong layer of ecclesiastical authority to the fight against liberal theology. For their part, the *ressourcement* theologians, among them von Balthasar, de Lubac, Daniélou, Congar, and Ratzinger, sought to combat liberal theology by entering more deeply and dialogically into the problems that historical research and modern philosophy pose for Christian faith. As exemplified by von Balthasar's trilogy, their work argued that Christ and the fullness of Catholic faith are still in fact the answer, while granting that positive things can be learned from modernity. At the Second Vatican Council, the *ressourcement* theologians sought to focus the church on the full mystery of Jesus Christ, while at the same time committing the church to engagement with the world, ecumenism, religious freedom, Jewish-Christian and interreligious dialogue, openness to historical-critical biblical scholarship, deepened collaborations between laity and clergy, appreciation of bishops (as distinct from the pope), and a properly historical understanding of development of doctrine.[53]

52. Friedrich Schleiermacher, *On Religion: Speeches to Its Cultured Despisers*, 2nd ed., trans. and ed. Richard Crouter (Cambridge: Cambridge University Press, 1996), 50.

53. For further discussion, see my *An Introduction to Vatican II as an Ongoing Theological Event* (Washington, D.C.: The Catholic University of America Press,

After the Second Vatican Council, however, liberal Christian thought moved firmly to the cutting edge of Catholic theology. This new direction informed such popular books as *Do We Need the Church?* and *The Shape of the Church to Come*, among countless others.[54] Von Balthasar's work was hardly read in the 1970s. In the postconciliar period, the neo-scholastic theologians faded away altogether, and the *ressourcement* theologians either shifted their perspective (as did Edward Schillebeeckx and Hans Küng) or were sidelined by their religious orders and by the theological academy. In 1969, de Lubac published a work titled *L'Église dans la crise actuelle*, which warned strongly against the ongoing relativizing and historicizing of Christ and dogmatic truth, a concern that he had begun to express as early as 1964.[55] Von Balthasar in 1966 published his sharp warning against liberal Rahnerian theology, *Cordula oder der Ernstfall* (noted above).[56] Immediately after the Council, Rahner, Schillebeeckx, Küng, and others took over the new postconciliar journal *Concilium*, with which Congar remained involved, although his perspective soon seemed rather old-fashioned.[57] Von Balthasar,

2017). See also the essays in *The Reception of Vatican II*, ed. Matthew L. Lamb and Matthew Levering (Oxford: Oxford University Press, 2017).

54. See Richard P. McBrien, *Do We Need the Church?* (New York: HarperCollins, 1969).

55. De Lubac, *L'Église dans la crise actuelle* (Paris: Cerf, 1969).

56. Von Balthasar, *Cordula oder der Ernstfall* (Einsiedeln: Johannes Verlag, 1966). Acquaintance with books and articles published by major theologians in the years 1966–1967 shows that Pope Paul VI's encyclical *Humanae Vitae*, though controversial, was not in any way at the root of the broader situation.

57. Congar's postconciliar standpoint has been debated, the key question being whether after the Council he continued to uphold, as enduring cognitive givens through which the church hands on the revealed truth of the gospel, dogmatic truth about the divine mysteries. The alternative is to conceive of the definitively proclaimed truths of faith and morals as reversible in their cognitive core—reversible because while these definitive dogmatic truths may have been authentic expressions of or guideposts to the church's authentic experience in a past epoch, the church can now be prompted by the Spirit to reverse them in accord with the authentic experience and needs of different epochs. This alternative is advocated by liberal theology (or "modernism"). One finds it in various forms in numerous postconciliar works, including Edward Schillebeeckx, OP, *Church: The Human Story of God*, trans.

de Lubac, Ratzinger, Daniélou, Louis Bouyer, and others founded the journal *Communio*, which, despite their theological acumen and their renown in the years prior to the Council, was perceived as conservative, even reactionary.

Fessio tells the story of traveling to Europe as a young Jesuit doctoral student during the early postconciliar period, only to find de Lubac completely alone, viewed as outdated and irrele-

---

John Bowden (New York: Crossroad, 1993), and Terrence W. Tilley, *Inventing Catholic Tradition* (Maryknoll, N.Y.: Orbis Books, 2000). After the Council, influenced especially by Jean-Pierre Jossua, OP, in his "Immutabilité, progres ou structurations multiples des doctrines chrétiennes," *Revue des sciences philosophiques et théologiques* 52 (1968): 173–200, Congar argues: "One is no longer able to maintain in so naïve and optimistic a manner as before (Marin-Sola!) an understanding of a continuous linear development of an 'implicit' content in dogmatic statements. While it is true that the faith of the Church remains the same and that it inspires one same life in Christ, history makes us attend to a series of rereadings. At the level of formulation and of a certain systematization, we find that successive structurings employ intellectual resources linked to complex historical conjectures, containing a true deposit [*donné réel*] that has been given once for all to the faithful (Jude 3)" (Congar, "The Ecumenical Value and Scope of Some Hermeneutical Principles of Saint Thomas Aquinas," trans. Andrew Jacob Cuff and Innocent Smith, OP, *Pro Ecclesia* 26 [2017]: 186–201, at 196). This seems clear enough, but Congar's position becomes less clear when he adds, "The identity is not to be sought in the conceptual material but in the vision, the signification, in short the *intentio*, in the integrity and relative equilibrium of the elements or essential values of reality. Newman, under the name of 'development,' spoke modestly of a 'preservation of type' and of a 'continuity of principles.' ... Not only theology, but the fact of dogmatization represents *an effort* to express the reality of the faith. Saint Thomas gave the following as a definition of the *articulus fidei*, that is, of dogma: 'Perceptio veritatis tendens in ipsam,' a perception of truth that aims at the Truth itself. It is a formulation enlivened by an intention, a tendency, an ambition. Consequently, there always exists a distance between the expressed result of this tension-tendency and the reality itself. In this way, one will be able to have multiple expressions of the same tendency, 'tendens in ipsam.' ... It is necessary to see that articulations can translate imperfect perceptions of the same reality but communicate the same 'tendens in ipsam'" (ibid., 196, 200–1). It appears to me that Congar is underestimating the importance of the "conceptual material," since without some cognitive or conceptual "identity" or core continuity, a mere identity in "*intentio*" or spirit will produce divergent cognitive claims in different epochs and will result in the reversal of definitive church teaching on faith and morals (thus once and for all relativizing such teaching as unable to hand on cognitively the truth of the gospel). Arguably, Congar's points here can (and, in the context of his work, should) be understood in a less historicist manner, as in Andrew Meszaros, *The Prophetic Church: History and Doctrinal Development in John Henry Newman and Yves Congar* (Oxford: Oxford University Press, 2016), especially chap. 5.

vant by the young Jesuits. Fessio ended up doing his dissertation under Ratzinger on the topic of von Balthasar's ecclesiology,
with de Lubac's encouragement. From the opposite perspective,
Jon Sobrino, then a young Jesuit from Spain, recalls that in this
period he and his fellow Jesuit students "went through Kant and
Hegel, through Marx and Sartre.... To put it bluntly, we began
questioning the God we had inherited from our pious Central
American, Spanish, and Basque families. We delved into exeget-
ical criticism and Bultmann's demythologizing, into the legacy of
modernism and the relativism of the church."[58]

In sum, despite their agreement in opposing liberal theology, the neo-scholastics and the *ressourcement* theologians fought
each other to the bitter end over the specific modes proper to
theology.[59] After the reversal of fortunes at the Second Vatican
Council, it was the *ressourcement* theologians' turn to be the old-
er generation, overwhelmed by the liberationist political theologies of the late 1960s and generally deeply dismayed by the neo-
modernist ascendancy in the Catholic theological academy.[60]
In this period, as Bernard Lonergan remarked, many Catholics
experienced a state of "almost complete disorientation" or "endless relativism," and many Catholic theologians came to wonder

58. Jon Sobrino, SJ, "Introduction: Awakening from the Sleep of Inhumanity,"
trans. Dimas Planas, in *The Principle of Mercy: Taking the Crucified People from the
Cross*, 1–11 (Maryknoll, N.Y.: Orbis Books, 1994), at 2.

59. Neo-scholastic and *ressourcement* theologians can agree with Junius Johnson, an expert on von Balthasar's thought, in identifying "the central theological
topics" as the Trinity, Christology, and grace. Johnson adds that "from these mid-
points, theology will expand to include a doctrine of creation (including angelology,
demonology, anthropology, and theology of nature), a theology of history, and other
such things." See Junius Johnson, *Christ and Analogy: The Christocentric Metaphysics of Hans Urs von Balthasar* (Minneapolis, Minn.: Fortress Press, 2013), 4.

60. For von Balthasar's responses to liberation theology in its German and Span-
ish forms (in addition to the response found in the first volume of his *Theo-Drama*),
see for example von Balthasar, *Engagement with God*, trans. R. John Halliburton (San
Francisco: Ignatius Press, 2008); von Balthasar, "Liberation Theology in the Light of
Salvation History," trans. Erasmo Leiva, in James Schall, SJ, *Liberation Theology in
Latin America: With Selected Essays and Documents*, 131–46 (San Francisco: Ignatius
Press, 1982).

"whether the dogmas [of the Catholic Church] are permanently relevant."[61]

The collision ended by carrying off both neo-scholasticism and *ressourcement* theology from the theological faculties of Catholic universities for more than a generation. Even now that new adherents of Thomistic theology and *ressourcement* theology have emerged (a process which began in earnest in the 1990s, after a quarter century of nearly complete desuetude), each side still often casts the blame for the debacle on the other side. Thus, for some contemporary experts on von Balthasar, the neo-scholastic mode of distinguishing nature and grace by positing a hypothetical state of "pure nature" is responsible for eroding piety and culture during five long post-Tridentine centuries until Catholic theology, after Vatican II, finally collapsed. By contrast, for some contemporary Thomists, the neo-scholastic mode of distinguishing nature and grace kept Catholicism alive during the same five long post-Tridentine centuries until, when this distinction was finally overthrown after the Council, Catholic theology collapsed.

When two sides that agree with each other in their fundamental faith commitments (and whose members in fact are often friends and allies) blame *each other* for the prevalence of classical liberal theology in the Catholic theological academy, then something has gone badly wrong. Classical liberal theology has roots in the Renaissance's discovery of historical consciousness and has many other nontheological roots as well. There is no need for neo-scholastic and *ressourcement* Christians to anathematize each other as though either side were to blame for large numbers of modern people thinking that the positions of Schleiermacher and Ernst Troeltsch—and of Kant, Hegel, and Nietzsche—are correct. No matter how many people were influenced by neo-Thomistic or *ressourcement* positions on nature

61. Bernard Lonergan, SJ, "Doctrinal Pluralism," in *Philosophical and Theological Papers 1965–1980*, ed. Robert C. Croken and Robert M. Doran, 70–104 (Toronto: University of Toronto Press, 2004), at 75, 97.

and grace, the liberal impulse goes much deeper than this eru-
dite debate among schools. Viewed reasonably and with proper
balance, the basic projects of neo-scholasticism and *ressourcement* can be complementary, even if they remain quite distinct
and even if much mutual criticism will fruitfully take place.

If Catholic theology is to recover in our day and to be able
once again to strongly affirm the enduring truth and faithful mediation of divine revelation, what is needed is a *rapprochement*
between the two sides. Along this salutary path, Anne Carpenter, whose love for von Balthasar's theology is evident, remarks
that "a theo-poetic ought not serve as the sole style of theological
speculation because it was never meant to serve as such.... So,
too, metaphysical rigor ought to be maintained in theological efforts, but this does not make explicit metaphysical discussion
necessary in every work of theology."[62] Similarly gesturing toward a *rapprochement*, another expert on von Balthasar, Michele Schumacher, has commented that "Balthasar's theology
... might well be served by a thorough questioning of all that
is in (at least apparent) contradiction with certain aspects of
Christian doctrine. This theology might, in other words, be ren-
dered more credible by being ... 'purified' (to borrow from the
Catechism) of certain images or concepts that might lead to mis-
understanding."[63] Schumacher thinks that much of von Speyr's
controversial contributions to von Balthasar's theology could,
through such a process, be interpreted or explained more clearly
than von Balthasar managed to do, so as to render her ideas more
clearly congruent with prior Catholic thought.

In accord with these steps toward *rapprochement*, other
young theologians have been retrieving resources from the
neo-scholastic and baroque periods that should now once again

62. Anne M. Carpenter, *Theo-Poetics: Hans Urs von Balthasar and the Risk of Art
and Being* (Notre Dame: University of Notre Dame, 2015), 185.
63. Michele M. Schumacher, *A Trinitarian Anthropology: Adrienne von Speyr and
Hans Urs von Balthasar in Dialogue with Thomas Aquinas* (Washington, D.C.: The
Catholic University of America Press, 2014), 388.

take their proper part in the theological symphony.[64] Although von Balthasar generally ignored the theologians of the period 1550–1950, we should now fully restore them—without denying the inevitable presence of deficiencies—to the Catholic theological symphony promoted by von Balthasar.

Von Balthasar speculated that the vocation of Catholics in the modern world may well be to "accompany mankind on its way to the scaffold" in an increasingly inglorious hiddenness, through an ever-greater configuration to "the kenotic obedience of the Son of God."[65] I suspect that von Balthasar may well be proven right in the decades to come. But this perspective, rooted not in pessimism but rather in Christ's teaching that "if they persecuted me, they will persecute you" (Jn 15:20), did not prevent von Balthasar from urgently striving to enliven and renew the church's proclamation of the beauty, goodness, and truth of the triune God who created the cosmos, who is infinite self-surrendering love, who revealed himself to us preeminently in the crucified Christ, and who calls us to take up our cross and to follow him for the sake of the whole world. Von Balthasar proclaimed this wondrous self-surrendering love in his trilogy by undertaking a wide range of theological, philosophical, and literary conversations and by offering a Kantian critique of Kant (*Theological Aesthetics*), a Hegelian critique of Hegel (*Theo-Drama*), and a Nietzschean critique of Nietzsche (*Theo-Logic*).

In the ongoing critical and appreciative reception of von Balthasar's achievement, let us follow von Balthasar's example. The tragic warfare among theologians who are committed to the inbreaking of divine revelation (salvation from sin and death) in Christ Jesus, over against the reductive immanentism of classi-

64. See, for example, Reginald M. Lynch, OP, *The Cleansing of the Heart: The Sacraments as Instrumental Causes in the Thomistic Tradition* (Washington, D.C.: The Catholic University of America Press, 2017).

65. Hans Urs von Balthasar, *In the Fullness of Faith: On the Centrality of the Distinctively Catholic*, trans. Graham Harrison (San Francisco: Ignatius Press, 1988), 20, 26.

cal liberal theology in its Protestant and Catholic forms, must stop if Catholic theology is to recover its health and purpose. The important thing today is that those who have been enraptured by von Balthasar's achievement *and* those who find his theology deficient but share in his fundamental faith commitments come together with mutual respect for the purpose of proclaiming to the whole world *L'amour de Dieu et la croix de Jésus*—the love of God and the cross of Jesus, to cite the title of a notable 1929 book by Réginald Garrigou-Lagrange.[66] Only thus will the reception of von Balthasar's achievement "bear much fruit" (Jn 15:8) in our day.

66. Réginald Garrigou-Lagrange, OP, *L'amour de Dieu et la croix de Jésus* (Paris: Cerf, 1929).

BIBLIOGRAPHY

Albus, Michael. *Die Wahrheit ist Liebe: Zur Unterscheidung des Christlichen nach Hans Urs von Balthasar.* Freiburg: Herder, 1976.

Avenatti de Palumbo, Cecilia Inés. *La literatura en la estética de Hans Urs von Balthasar: Figura, drama y verdad.* Salamanca: Secretariado Trinitario, 2002.

Barbarin, Philippe. *Théologie et sainteté: Introduction à Hans-Urs von Balthasar.* Paris: Parole et Silence, 2017.

Barrett, Melanie Susan. *Love's Beauty at the Heart of the Christian Moral Life: The Ethics of Catholic Theologian Hans Urs von Balthasar.* Lewiston, N.Y.: Edwin Mellen, 2009.

Barron, Robert. "A Reflection on Christ, Theological Method, and Freedom." In Howsare and Chapp, *How Balthasar Changed My Mind*, 9–25.

Bätzing, Georg. *Die Eucharistie als Opfer der Kirche.* Einsiedeln: Johannes Verlag, 1992.

Bauerschmidt, Frederick Christian. "Theo-Drama and Political Theology." *Communio* 25, no. 3 (1998): 532–52.

Beattie, Tina. "A Man and Three Women: Hans, Adrienne, Mary and Luce." *New Blackfriars* 79, no. 924 (1998): 97–103.

Beaudin, Michel. *Obéissance et solidarité. Essai sur la christologie de Hans Urs von Balthasar.* Montreal: Fides, 1989.

Benedict XVI. "Hans Urs von Balthasar: Christlicher Universalismus." In Kasper, *Logik der Liebe und Herrlichkeit Gottes*, 14–24.

———. *Last Testament: In His Own Words.* With Peter Seewald. Translated by Jacob Phillips. London: Bloomsbury, 2016.

Bieler, Martin. "Die Kleine Drehung: Hans Urs von Balthasar und Karl Barth im Gespräch." In Kasper, *Logik der Liebe und Herrlichkeit Gottes*, 318–38.

Blondel, Maurice. *Le problème de la philosophie catholique.* Paris: Bloud and Gay, 1932.

———. *The Letter on Apologetics* and *History and Dogma.* Translated by Alexander Dru and Illtyd Trethowan. Grand Rapids, Mich.: Eerdmans, 1994.

Bonino, Serge-Thomas, OP, ed. *Surnaturel: A Controversy at the Heart of Twentieth-Century Thomistic Thought*. Translated by Robert Williams. Ave Maria, Fla.: Sapientia Press, 2009.

Carpenter, Anne M. *Theo-Poetics: Hans Urs von Balthasar and the Risk of Art and Being*. Notre Dame: University of Notre Dame, 2015.

Catechism of the Catholic Church. 2nd ed. Vatican City: Libreria Editrice Vaticana, 1997.

Chenu, Marie-Dominique, OP. "Le sens et les leçons d'une crise religieuse." *Vie Intellectuelle* 13 (1931): 356–80.

———. "Position de la théologie." *Revue des sciences philosophiques et théologiques* 25 (1935): 232–57.

———. "Aux origins de la 'science moderne'." *Revue des sciences philosophiques et théologiques* 29 (1940): 206–17.

———. *La théologie comme science au XIIIe siècle*. 2nd ed. Paris: Vrin, 1943.

———. "'Consecratio mundi'." *Nouvelle revue théologique* 86, no. 6 (1964): 608–18.

———. "Vérité évangélique et métaphysique wolfienne à Vatican II." *Revue des sciences philosophiques et théologiques* 57 (1973): 632–40.

———. *Une école de théologie: le Saulchoir*. Paris: Cerf, 1985.

Congar, Yves, OP. "Autour du renouveau de l'ecclésiologie: la collection 'Unam Sanctum'." *Vie Intellectuelle* 51 (1939): 9–32.

———. "Tendances actuelles de la pensée religieuse." *Cahiers du monde nouveau* 4 (1948): 33–50.

———. *Vraie et fausse réforme dans l'Église*. Paris: Cerf, 1950.

———. *True and False Reform*. Translated by Paul Philibert. Collegeville, Minn.: Liturgical Press, 2011.

———. "The Ecumenical Value and Scope of Some Hermeneutical Principles of Saint Thomas Aquinas." Translated by Andrew Jacob Cuff and Innocent Smith, OP. *Pro Ecclesia* 26 (2017): 186–201.

Crammer, Corrine. "One Sex or Two? Balthasar's Theology of the Sexes." In *The Cambridge Companion to Hans Urs von Balthasar*, edited by Edward T. Oakes, SJ, and David Moss, 93–112. Cambridge: Cambridge University Press, 2004.

Dahlke, Benjamin. *Karl Barth, Catholic Renewal, and Vatican II*. London: Bloomsbury, 2012.

Dalzell, Thomas G., SM. *The Dramatic Encounter of Divine and Human Freedom in the Theology of Hans Urs von Balthasar*. Bern: Peter Lang, 1997.

———. "Lack of Social Drama in Balthasar's Theological Dramatics." *Theological Studies* 60, no. 3 (1999): 457–75.

Danet, Henriette. *Gloire et croix de Jésus-Christ: L'analogie chez H. Urs von Balthasar comme introduction à sa christologie*. Paris: Desclée, 1987.

Daniélou, Jean, SJ. "Les orientations présentes de la pensée religieuse."
    Études 249 (1946): 5–21.
de Lubac, Henri, SJ. "Apologétique et théologie." Nouvelle revue
    théologique 57 (1930): 361–78.
———. "Sur la philosophie chrétienne: Réflexions à la suite d'un débat."
    Nouvelle revue théologique 63 (1936): 225–53.
———. Surnaturel: Études historiques. Paris: Cerf, 1946.
———. The Church: Paradox and Mystery. Staten Island, N.Y.: Ecclesia
    Press, 1969.
———. L'Église dans la crise actuelle. Paris: Cerf, 1969.
———. A Theologian Speaks. Interview by Angelo Scola. Los Angeles,
    Calif.: Twin Circle, 1985.
———. Theological Fragments. Translated by Rebecca Howell Balinski.
    San Francisco: Ignatius Press, 1989.
———. Corpus Mysticum: The Eucharist and the Church in the Middle
    Ages: Historical Survey. Translated by Gemma Simmonds, CJ, with
    Richard Price and Christopher Stephens. Edited by Laurence Paul
    Hemming and Susan Frank Parsons. London: SCM Press, 2006.
Denny, Christopher D. A Generous Symphony: Hans Urs von Balthasar's
    Literary Revelations. Minneapolis, Minn.: Fortress Press, 2016.
Dickens, W. T. Hans Urs von Balthasar's Theological Aesthetics: A Model
    for Post-Critical Biblical Interpretation. Notre Dame: University of
    Notre Dame Press, 2003.
Dieser, Helmut. Der gottähnliche Mensch und die Gottlosigkeit der Sünde:
    Zur Theologie des Descensus Christi bei Hans Urs von Balthasar.
    Trier: Paulinus, 1998.
Dockwiller, Philippe. Le temps du Christ: Coeur et fin de la théologie de
    l'histoire selon Hans Urs von Balthasar. Paris: Cerf, 2011.
Dulles, Avery, SJ. A History of Apologetics. San Francisco: Ignatius Press,
    2005.
Endean, Philip, SJ. "Von Balthasar, Rahner, and the Commissar." New
    Blackfriars 79, no. 923 (January 1998): 33–38.
Fessio, Joseph, SJ. The Origin of the Church in Christ's Kenosis: The
    Ontological Structure of the Church in the Ecclesiology of Hans Urs von
    Balthasar. Regensburg: Pustet, 1974.
Fichte, Johann Gottlieb. Fichte: Early Philosophical Writings. Edited and
    translated by Daniel Breazeale. Ithaca, N.Y.: Cornell University Press,
    1988.
Fouilloux, Etienne. "Dialogue théologique? (1946–1948)." In Saint Thom-
    as au XXe siècle, edited by Serge-Thomas Bonino, OP, 153–95. Paris:
    Saint-Paul, 1994.
Fout, Jason A. Fully Alive: The Glory of God and the Human Creature in
    Karl Barth, Hans Urs von Balthasar and Theological Exegesis of Scrip-
    ture. London: Bloomsbury, 2015.

Furnal, Joshua. *Catholic Theology after Kierkegaard*. Oxford: Oxford University Press, 2016.

Gagnebet, Marie-Rosaire, OP. *La nature de la théologie spéculative*. Paris: Desclée, 1938.

———. "Le problème actuel de la théologie et la science aristotélicienne d'après un ouvrage récent." *Divus Thomas* 46 (1943): 237–70.

Gardeil, Ambroise, OP. *La crédibilité et l'apologétique*. 4th ed. Paris: Gabalda, 1928.

Gardner, Lucy, and David Moss. "Something like Time; Something like Sexes: An Essay in Reception." In Gardner, Moss, Quash, and Ward, *Balthasar at the End of Modernity*, 69–137.

Gardner, Lucy, David Moss, Ben Quash, and Graham Ward. *Balthasar at the End of Modernity*. Edinburgh: T&T Clark, 1999.

Garrigou-Lagrange, Réginald, OP. *De revelatione per Ecclesiam catholicam proposita*. 2 vols. 3rd ed. Rome: F. Ferrari, 1929.

———. *L'amour de Dieu et la croix de Jésus*. Paris: Cerf, 1929.

———. "La nouvelle théologie, où va-t-elle?" *Angelicum* 23 (1946): 126–45.

———. "Vérité et immutabilité du Dogme." *Angelicum* 24 (1947): 124–39.

———. "Nécessité de revenir à la définition traditionnelle de la vérité." *Angelicum* 25 (1948): 185–98.

———. "L'immutabilité du dogme selon le concile du Vatican et le relativisme." *Revue Thomiste* 49 (1949): 309–32.

———. "Le relativisme et l'immutabilité du dogme." *Revue Thomiste* 50 (1950): 219–46.Gawronski, Raymond, SJ. *Word and Silence: Hans Urs von Balthasar and the Spiritual Encounter between East and West*. Grand Rapids, Mich.: Eerdmans, 1995.

Gesthuisen, J. *Das Nietzsche-Bild Hans Urs von Balthasars; Ein Zugang zur Apokalypse der deutschen Seele*. Rome: Gregorian University Press, 1986.

Göbbeler, Hans-Peter. *Existenz als Sendung: Zum Verständnis der Nachfolge Christi in der Theologie Hans Urs von Balthasars. Unter besonderer Berücksichtigung der Gestalt des Priestertums und von Ehe und Familie*. St. Ottilien: EOS Verlag, 1997.

Gonzalez, Michelle. "Hans Urs von Balthasar and Contemporary Feminist Theology." *Theological Studies* 65, no. 3 (2004): 566–95.

Guerriero, Elio. *Hans Urs von Balthasar*. Milan: Edizioni Paoline, 1991.

Haas, Alois M. "Hans Urs von Balthasars Nietzschebild: Eine Problemskizze." In Kasper, *Logik der Liebe und Herrlichkeit Gottes*, 146–62.

Healy, Nicholas J. *The Eschatology of Hans Urs von Balthasar: Being as Communion*. Oxford: Oxford University Press, 2005.

Hegel, Georg W. F. *Aesthetics: Lectures on Fine Art*. Vol. 1. Translated by T. M. Knox. Oxford: Oxford University Press, 1975.

———. *Aesthetics: Lectures on Fine Art.* Vol. 2. Translated by T. M. Knox. Oxford: Oxford University Press, 1975.

———. *Phenomenology of Spirit.* Translated by A. V. Miller. Oxford: Oxford University Press, 1977.

———. *Elements of the Philosophy of Right.* Edited by Allen W. Wood. Translated by H. B. Nisbet. Cambridge: Cambridge University Press, 1991.

———. *The Philosophy of History.* Translated by J. Sibree. Buffalo, N.Y.: Prometheus Books, 1991.

———. *Lectures on the Philosophy of Religion.* Vol. 3, *The Consummate Religion.* Translated by R. F. Brown, P. C. Hodgson, and J. M. Stewart, with H. S. Harris. Edited by Peter C. Hodgson. Oxford: Clarendon Press, 2007.

Henrici, Peter, SJ. "The Philosophy of Hans Urs von Balthasar." In Schindler, *Hans Urs von Balthasar: His Life and Work*, 149–67.

Hofer, Andrew, OP. "Balthasar's Eschatology on the Intermediate State: The Question of Knowability." *Logos* 12, no. 3 (2009): 148–72.

Holzer, Vincent. *Hans Urs von Balthasar, 1905–1988.* Paris: Cerf, 2012.

Howsare, Rodney A. *Hans Urs von Balthasar and Protestantism: The Ecumenical Implications of His Theological Style.* London: T&T Clark International, 2005.

———. *Balthasar: A Guide for the Perplexed.* New York: T&T Clark International, 2009.

Howsare, Rodney A., and Larry S. Chapp, eds. *How Balthasar Changed My Mind: 15 Scholars Reflect on the Meaning of Balthasar for Their Own Work.* New York: Crossroad, 2008.

Ide, Pascal. *Une théologie de l'amour. L'amour, centre de la* Trilogie *de Hans Urs von Balthasar.* Brussels: Lessius, 2012.

———. *Une théo-logique du don. Le don dans la* Trilogie *de Hans Urs von Balthasar.* Leuven: Peeters, 2013.

Johnson, Junius. *Christ and Analogy: The Christocentric Metaphysics of Hans Urs von Balthasar.* Minneapolis, Minn.: Fortress Press, 2013.

Jossua, Jean-Pierre, OP. "Immutabilité, progres ou structurations multiples des doctrines chrétiennes." *Revue des sciences philosophiques et théologiques* 52 (1968): 173–200.

Kant, Immanuel. *Religion with the Limits of Reason Alone.* Translated by Theodore M. Greene and Hoyt H. Hudson. New York: Harper and Row, 1960.

———. *Grounding for the Metaphysics of Morals.* 3rd ed. Translated by James W. Ellington, Indianapolis, Ind.: Hackett, 1993

———. "The End of All Things" (1794). In *Religion and Rational Theology*, edited by Allen W. Wood and G. di Giovanni, 221–31. Cambridge: Cambridge University Press, 1996.

———. *Critique of Pure Reason*. Translated and edited by Paul Guyer and Allen W. Wood. Cambridge: Cambridge University Press, 1998.

———. *Critique of Judgement*. Translated by James Creed Meredith. Edited by Nicholas Walker. Oxford: Oxford University Press, 2007.

Kasper, Walter, ed. *Logik der Liebe und Herrlichkeit Gottes: Hans Urs von Balthasar im Gespräch: Festgabe für Karl Kardinal Lehmann zum 70. Geburtstag*. Ostfildern: Matthias-Grünewald-Verlag, 2006.

Kerr, Fergus, OP. "Foreword: Assessing This 'Giddy Synthesis.'" In Gardner, Moss, Quash, and Ward, *Balthasar at the End of Modernity*, 1–13.

Kilby, Karen. "Balthasar and Karl Rahner." In *The Cambridge Companion to Hans Urs von Balthasar*, edited by Edward T. Oakes, SJ, and David Moss, 256–68. Cambridge: Cambridge University Press, 2004.

———. *Balthasar: A (Very) Critical Introduction*. Grand Rapids, Mich.: Eerdmans, 2012.

Kirwan, Jon. *An Avant-garde Theological Generation: The Nouvelle Théologie and the French Crisis of Modernity*. Oxford: Oxford University Press, 2018.

Klaghofer-Treitler, Wolfgang. *Gotteswort im Menschenwort: Inhalt und Form von Theologie nach Hans Urs von Balthasar*. Innsbruck: Tyrolia, 1992.

Komonchak, Joseph A. "Humani Generis and Nouvelle Théologie." In *Ressourcement: A Movement for Renewal in Twentieth-Century Catholic Theology*, edited by Gabriel Flynn and Paul D. Murray, 138–56. Oxford: Oxford University Press, 2012.

Labourdette, M.-M., OP. "La théologie et ses sources." *Revue Thomiste* 46 (1946): 353–71.

Labourdette, M.-M., OP, and M.-J. Nicolas, OP. "L'analogie de la vérité et l'unité de la science théologique," *Revue Thomiste* 55 (1947): 417–66.

Lamb, Matthew L., and Matthew Levering, eds. *The Reception of Vatican II*. Oxford: Oxford University Press, 2017.

Leahy, Breandán [Brendan]. *The Marian Principle in the Church according to Hans Urs von Balthasar*. New York: Peter Lang, 1996.

———. "John Paul II and Hans Urs von Balthasar." In *The Legacy of John Paul II*, edited by Gerald O'Collins and Michael Hayes, 31–50. New York: Continuum, 2008.

Levering, Matthew. *An Introduction to Vatican II as an Ongoing Theological Event*. Washington, D.C.: The Catholic University of America Press, 2017.

Lochbrunner, Manfred. *Hans Urs von Balthasar als Autor, Herausgeber und Verleger: Fünf Studien zu seinen Sammlungen (1942–1967)*: Würzburg: Echter Verlag, 2002.

———. *Hans Urs von Balthasar und seine Philosophenfreunde: Fünf Doppelporträts*. Würzburg: Echter Verlag, 2005.

————. *Hans Urs von Balthasar und seine Literatenfreunde: Neun Korrespondenzen.* Würzburg: Echter Verlag, 2007.

————. *Hans Urs von Balthasar und seine Theologen-kollegen: Sechs Beziehungsgeschichten.* Würzburg: Echter Verlag, 2009.

Lonergan, Bernard, SJ. "Doctrinal Pluralism." In *Philosophical and Theological Papers 1965–1980*, edited by Robert C. Croken and Robert M. Doran, 70–104. Toronto: University of Toronto Press, 2004.

Long, D. Stephen. *Saving Karl Barth: Hans Urs von Balthasar's Preoccupation.* Minneapolis, Minn.: Fortress Press, 2014.

López, Antonio. *Gift and the Unity of Being.* Eugene, Ore.: Cascade, 2013.

Lösel, Steffen. *Kreuzwege: Ein ökumenisches Gespräch mit Hans Urs von Balthasar.* Paderborn: Schöningh, 2001.

Löser, Werner, SJ. "The Ignatian *Exercises* in the Work of Hans Urs von Balthasar." In Schindler, *Hans Urs von Balthasar: His Life and Work*, 103–20.

Lynch, Reginald M., OP. *The Cleansing of the Heart: The Sacraments as Instrumental Causes in the Thomistic Tradition.* Washington, D.C.: The Catholic University of America Press, 2017.

Mansini, Guy, OSB. "The Development of the Development of Doctrine in the Twentieth Century." *Angelicum* 93, no. 4 (2016): 785–822.

Marchesi, Giovanni. *La cristologia di Hans Urs von Balthasar: La figura di Gesù Cristo espressione visibile di Dio.* Rome: Gregorian University Press, 1977.

————. *La cristologia trinitaria di Hans Urs von Balthasar: Gesù Cristo pienezza della rivelazione e della salvezza.* 2nd ed. Brescia: Queriniana, 2003.

Maréchal, Joseph. *Le Point de Depart de la Metaphysique: Lecons sur le developpement historique du probleme de la Connaissance.* Cahier II, *Le Conflit du Rationalisme et de l'Empirisme dans la Philosophie moderne, avant Kant.* Bruges: Charles Beyaert, 1923.

Marshall, Bruce D. "The Church, the Modern World, and the Spirit of Vatican II." *Nova et Vetera* 15, no. 4 (2017): 999–1012.

Martin, Jennifer Newsome. *Hans Urs von Balthasar and the Critical Appropriation of Russian Religious Thought.* Notre Dame: University of Notre Dame Press, 2015.

————. "The 'Whence' and the 'Whither' of Balthasar's Gendered Theology: Rehabilitating Kenosis for Feminist Theology." *Modern Theology* 31, no. 2 (2015): 211–34.

McInroy, Mark. *Balthasar on the Spiritual Senses: Perceiving Splendour.* Oxford: Oxford University Press, 2014.

McIntosh, Mark A. *Christology from Within: Spirituality and the Incarnation in Hans Urs von Balthasar.* Notre Dame: University of Notre Dame Press, 1996.

Meszaros, Andrew. *The Prophetic Church: History and Doctrinal Development in John Henry Newman and Yves Congar.* Oxford: Oxford University Press, 2016.

Mettepenningen, Jürgen. *Nouvelle Théologie—New Theology: Inheritor of Modernism, Precursor of Vatican II.* London: T&T Clark, 2010.

———. "Truth, Orthodoxy and the *Nouvelle Théologie*: Truth as Issue in a 'Second Modernist Crisis' (1946–1950)." In *Orthodoxy, Liberalism, and Adaptation: Essays on Ways of Worldmaking in Times of Change from Biblical, Historical and Systematic Perspectives*, edited by Bob Becking, 149–82. Leiden: Brill, 2011.

Miller, Colin. "Ivan Illich, Catholic Theologian (Part I)." *Pro Ecclesia* 26, no. 1 (2017): 81–110.

Moga, Ioan. *Kirche als Braut Christi zwischen Kreuz und Parusie: Die Ekklesiologie Hans Urs von Balthasars aus orthodoxer Sicht.* Münster: LIT, 2010.

Mohr, Daniela. *Existenz im Herzen der Kirche: Zur Theologie der Säkularinstitute in Leben und Werk H. Urs von Balthasars.* Würzburg: Echter Verlag, 2000.

Mongrain, Kevin. *The Systematic Thought of Hans Urs von Balthasar: An Irenaean Retrieval.* New York: Crossroad, 2002.

Moser, Matthew A. Rothaus. *Love Itself Is Understanding: Hans Urs von Balthasar's Theology of the Saints.* Minneapolis, Minn.: Fortress Press, 2016.

Murphy, Francesca. *Christ the Form of Beauty: A Study in Theology and Literature.* Edinburgh: T&T Clark, 1995.

———. "Truth Grounded in Love: Hans Urs von Balthasar's *Theo-Logic* and Christian Pedagogy." In Howsare and Chapp, *How Balthasar Changed My Mind*, 123–34.

Murphy, Michael Patrick. *A Theology of Criticism: Balthasar, Postmodernism, and the Catholic Imagination.* Oxford: Oxford University Press, 2008.

Murphy, William F., Jr. "Thomism and the *Nouvelle Theologie*: A Dialogue Renewed?" *Josephinum Journal of Theology* 18, no. 1 (2011): 4–36.

Nebel, Gerhard. *Das Ereignis des Schönen.* Stuttgart: Klett, 1953.

Neufeld, K. H. *Die Brüder Rahner: Eine Biographie.* Freiburg: Herder, 1994.

Nichols, Aidan, OP. *The Word Has Been Abroad: A Guide through Balthasar's Aesthetics.* Washington, D.C.: The Catholic University of America Press, 1998.

———. *No Bloodless Myth: A Guide through Balthasar's Dramatics.* Washington, D.C.: The Catholic University of America Press, 2000.

———. "Thomism and the Nouvelle Théologie." *The Thomist* 64, no. 1 (2000): 1–19.

——. *Say It Is Pentecost: A Guide through Balthasar's Logic*. Washington, D.C.: The Catholic University of America Press, 2001.

——. *Scattering the Seed: A Guide through Balthasar's Early Writings on Philosophy and the Arts*. Washington, D.C.: The Catholic University of America Press, 2006.

——. *A Key to Balthasar: Hans Urs von Balthasar on Beauty, Goodness, and Truth*. Grand Rapids, Mich.: Baker Academic, 2011.

Niemeyer, Christian. *Nietzsche verstehen: Eine Gebrauchsanweisung*. Darmstadt: Lambert-Schneider-Verlag, 2011.

Nietzsche, Friedrich. *The Will to Power*. Translated by Walter Kaufmann and R. J. Hollingdale. Edited by Walter Kaufmann. New York: Random House, 1967.

——. *Thus Spoke Zarathustra*. Translated by R. J. Hollingdale. New York: Penguin, 1969.

——. *On the Advantage and Disadvantage of History for Life*. Translated by Peter Preuss. Indianapolis, Ind.: Hackett, 1980.

——. *On the Genealogy of Morals* and *Ecce Homo*. Edited by Walter Kaufmann. New York: Vintage Books, 1989.

——. *The Gay Science: With a Prelude in German Rhymes and an Appendix of Songs*. Translated by Josefine Nauckhoff and Adrian Del Caro. Edited by Bernard Williams. Cambridge: Cambridge University Press, 2001.

——. *Twilight of the Idols* and *The Anti-Christ*. Translated by R. J. Hollingdale. New York: Penguin, 2003.

Norris, Thomas. "The Symphonic Unity of His Theology: An Overview." In *The Beauty of Christ: An Introduction to the Theology of Hans Urs von Balthasar*, edited by Bede McGregor, OP, and Thomas Norris, 213–52. Edinburgh: T&T Clark, 1994.

Oakes, Edward T., SJ. *Pattern of Redemption: The Theology of Hans Urs von Balthasar*. New York: Continuum, 1994.

——. "Balthasar and *Ressourcement*: An Ambiguous Relationship." In *Ressourcement: A Movement for Renewal in Twentieth-Century Catholic Theology*, edited by Gabriel Flynn and Paul D. Murray, 278–88. Oxford: Oxford University Press, 2012.

Oakes, Kenneth. "Gathering Many Likenesses: Trinity and Kenosis." *Nova et Vetera* (forthcoming).

Oettler, Dietrich. *Sauerteig der Einheit: Der Beitrag der Theodramatik Hans Urs von Balthasars für die evangelisch-katholische Oekumene nach der Gemeinsamen Erklärung zur Rechtfertigungslehre*. Würzburg: Echter, 2011.

O'Hanlon, Gerald F., SJ. "The Jesuits and Modern Theology: Rahner, von Balthasar, and Liberation Theology." *Irish Theological Quarterly* 58, no. 1 (1992): 25–45.

O'Regan, Cyril. *Gnostic Return in Modernity*. Albany, N.Y.: SUNY Press, 2001.

———. "Balthasar and Gnostic Genealogy." *Modern Theology* 22, no. 4 (2006): 609–50.

———. "I Am Not What I Am Because of … " In Howsare and Chapp, *How Balthasar Changed My Mind*, 151–71.

———. *Theology and the Spaces of Apocalyptic*. Milwaukee, Wisc.: Marquette University Press, 2009.

———. "Hans Urs von Balthasar and the Unwelcoming of Heidegger." In *Grandeur of Reason: Religion, Tradition, and Universalism*, edited by Conor Cunningham and Peter Candler, 264–98. London: SCM, 2010.

———. *The Anatomy of Misremembering: Von Balthasar's Response to Philosophical Modernity*. Vol. 1, *Hegel*. New York: Crossroad, 2014.

———. "Heidegger and Christian Wisdom." In *Christian Wisdom Meets Modernity*, edited by Kenneth Oakes, 37–57. London: Bloomsbury, 2016.

Pitstick, Alyssa Lyra. *Light in Darkness: Hans Urs von Balthasar and the Catholic Doctrine of Christ's Descent into Hell*. Grand Rapids, Mich.: Eerdmans, 2007.

———. *Christ's Descent into Hell: John Paul II, Joseph Ratzinger, and Hans Urs von Balthasar on the Theology of Holy Saturday*. Grand Rapids, Mich.: Eerdmans, 2016.

Pius XII. *Humani Generis*. N.C.W.C. translation. Boston, Mass.: Pauline Books and Media, n.d.

Prevot, Andrew L. "Dialectic and Analogy in Balthasar's 'The Metaphysics of the Saints.'" *Pro Ecclesia* 26, no. 3 (2017): 261–77.

Quash, Ben. "Ignatian Dramatics: First Glance at the Spirituality of Hans Urs von Balthasar." *The Way* 38, no. 1 (1998): 77–86.

———. "Drama and the Ends of Modernity." In Gardner, Moss, Quash, and Ward, *Balthasar at the End of Modernity*, 139–71.

Rahner, Karl, SJ. *The Shape of the Church to Come*. Translated by Edward Quinn. New York: Seabury Press, 1974.

Ratzinger, Joseph. "Homily at the Funeral Liturgy of Hans Urs von Balthasar." In Schindler, *Hans Urs von Balthasar: His Life and Work*, 291–95.

Reifenberg, Peter. "Blondel and Balthasar—eine Skizze." In Kasper, *Logik der Liebe und Herrlichkeit Gottes*, 176–203.

Reno, R. R. "The Paradox of Hans Urs von Balthasar." In Howsare and Chapp, *How Balthasar Changed My Mind*, 172–90.

Riches, Aaron, and Sebastián Montiel. "On Re-membering *Geist*: Hegelian Hauntotheology and O'Regan's *Anatomy of Misremembering*." *Modern Theology* 32, no. 2 (2016): 268–78.

Riches, John, ed. *The Analogy of Beauty: The Theology of Hans Urs von Balthasar*. Edinburgh: T&T Clark, 1986.

Rosenberg, Randall S. *The Givenness of Desire: Concrete Subjectivity and the Natural Desire to See God*. Toronto: University of Toronto Press, 2017.

Ross, Susan. "Women, Beauty, and Justice: Moving beyond von Balthasar." *Journal of the Society of Christian Ethics* 25, no. 1 (2005): 79–98.

Rousselot, Pierre, SJ. *The Eyes of Faith*. Translated by Joseph Donceel, SJ. New York: Fordham University Press, 1990.

Ruddy, Christopher. "*Ressourcement* and the *Enduring* Legacy of Post-Tridentine Theology." In *Ressourcement: A Movement for Renewal in Twentieth-Century Catholic Theology*, edited by Gabriel Flynn and Paul D. Murray, 185–201. Oxford: Oxford University Press, 2012.

Saint-Pierre, Mario. *Beauté, bonté, vérité chez Hans Urs von Balthasar*. Paris: Cerf, 1998.

Schillebeeckx, Edward, OP. *Church: The Human Story of God*. Translated by John Bowden. New York: Crossroad, 1993.

Schindler, D. C. *Hans Urs von Balthasar and the Dramatic Structure of Truth: A Philosophical Investigation*. New York: Fordham University Press, 2004.

Schindler, David L., ed. *Hans Urs von Balthasar: His Life and Work*. San Francisco: Ignatius Press, 1991.

———. "Modernity and the Nature of a Distinction: Balthasar's Ontology of Generosity." In Howsare and Chapp, *How Balthasar Changed My Mind*, 224–58.

———. "Modernity and the Nature of a Distinction: Balthasar's Ontology of Generosity." In *Ordering Love: Liberal Societies and the Memory of God*, 350–82. Grand Rapids, Mich.: Eerdmans, 2011.

Schleiermacher, Friedrich. *On Religion: Speeches to Its Cultured Despisers*. 2nd ed. Translated and edited by Richard Crouter. Cambridge: Cambridge University Press, 1996.

Schulz, Michael. *Hans Urs von Balthasar begegnen*. Augsburg: Sankt-Ulrich-Verlag, 2002.

———. "Die Logik der Liebe und die List der Vernunft: Hans Urs von Balthasar und Georg Wilhelm Friedrich Hegel." In Kasper, *Logik der Liebe und Herrlichkeit Gottes*, 111–33.

Schumacher, Michele M. *A Trinitarian Anthropology: Adrienne von Speyr and Hans Urs von Balthasar in Dialogue with Thomas Aquinas*. Washington, D.C.: The Catholic University of America Press, 2014.

Sciglitano, Anthony C., Jr. "Leaving Neo-Scholasticism Behind: Aspirations and Anxieties." *Josephinum Journal of Theology* 18, no. 1 (2011): 216–39.

———. *Marcion and Prometheus: Balthasar against the Expulsion of Jewish Origins from Modern Religious Dialogue*. New York: Crossroad, 2014.

Scola, Angelo. *Hans Urs von Balthasar: A Theological Style*. Grand Rapids, Mich.: Eerdmans, 1995.

Servais, Jacques, SJ. *Théologie des Exercices spirituels: H. U. von Balthasar interprète saint Ignace*. Brussels: Culture et Vérité, 1996.

———. "Balthasar as Interpreter of the Catholic Tradition." Translated by Sylvester Tan. In *Love Alone Is Credible: Hans Urs von Balthasar as Interpreter of the Catholic Tradition*. Vol. 1. Edited by David L. Schindler. Grand Rapids, Mich.: Eerdmans, 2008.

Sobrino, Jon, SJ. "Introduction: Awakening from the Sleep of Inhumanity." Translated by Dimas Planas. In *The Principle of Mercy: Taking the Crucified People from the Cross*, 1–11. Maryknoll, N.Y.: Orbis Books, 1994.

———. *No Salvation Outside the Poor: Prophetic-Utopian Essays*. Maryknoll, N.Y.: Orbis Books, 2008.

Spiegelhalter, Eva-Maria. *Objektiv Evident? Die Wahrnehmbarkeit der Christusgestalt im Denken Hans Urs von Balthasars und Hansjürgen Verweyens*. Freiburg: Herder, 2013.

Steck, Christopher W., SJ. *The Ethical Thought of Hans Urs von Balthasar*. New York: Crossroad, 2001.

Steinhauer, Hilda. *Maria als dramatische Person bei Hans Urs von Balthasar: Zum marianischen Prinzip seines Denkens*. Innsbruck: Tyrolia, 2001.

Thompson, John. "Barth and Balthasar: An Ecumenical Dialogue." In *The Beauty of Christ: An Introduction to the Theology of Hans Urs von Balthasar*. Edited by Bede McGregor, OP, and Thomas Norris, 171–92. Edinburgh: T&T Clark, 1994.

Tilley, Terrence W. *Inventing Catholic Tradition*. Maryknoll, N.Y.: Orbis Books, 2000.

Troeltsch, Ernst. "Historical and Dogmatic Method in Theology." In *Religion in History*, translated by James Luther Adams and Walter F. Bense, 11–32. Minneapolis, Minn.: Fortress Press, 1991.

———. "On the Possibility of a Liberal Christianity." In *Religion in History*, translated by James Luther Adams and Walter F. Bense, 343–59. Minneapolis, Minn.: Fortress Press, 1991.

Turek, Margaret M. *Towards a Theology of God the Father: Hans Urs von Balthasar's Theodramatic Approach*. New York: Peter Lang, 2001.

Uehling, Theodore Edward, Jr. *The Notion of Form in Kant's Critique of Aesthetic Judgment*. The Hague: Mouton, 1971.

van Erp, Stephan. *The Art of Theology: Hans Urs von Balthasar's Theological Aesthetics and the Foundations of Faith*. Leuven: Peeters, 2004.

Voderholzer, Rudolf. "Die Bedeutung der sogenannten 'Nouvelle Théologie' (insbesondere Henri de Lubacs) für die Theologie Hans Urs von Balthasars." In Kasper, *Logik der Liebe und Herrlichkeit Gottes*, 204–28.

von Balthasar, Hans Urs. *Apokalypse der deutschen Seele: Studien zu einer Lehre von letzten Haltungen*. Vol. 1, *Der deutsche Idealismus*. Salzburg: A. Pustet, 1937.

——. *Apokalypse der deutschen Seele: Studien zu einer Lehre von letzten Haltungen*. Vol. 2, *Im Zeichen Nietzsches*. Salzburg: A. Pustet, 1939.

——. *Apokalypse der deutschen Seele: Studien zu einer Lehre von letzten Haltungen*. Vol. 3, *Die Vergöttlichung des Todes*. Salzburg: A. Pustet, 1940.

——. *Thomas von Aquin: Besondere Gnadengaben und die zwei Wege des menschlichen Lebens: Kommentar zur Summa Theologica II-II, 171–182*. Vol. 23 of Die Deutsche Thomas-Ausgabe. Edited by H. M. Christmann. Vienna: Pustet, 1958.

——. *Cordula oder der Ernstfall*. Einsiedeln: Johannes Verlag, 1966.

——. *Heart of the World*. Translated by Erasmo S. Leiva. San Francisco: Ignatius Press, 1979.

——. *The Glory of the Lord: A Theological Aesthetics*. Vol. 1, *Seeing the Form*. Translated by Erasmo Leiva-Merikakis. Edited by Joseph Fessio, SJ, and John Riches. San Francisco: Ignatius Press, 1982.

——. "Liberation Theology in the Light of Salvation History." Translated by Erasmo Leiva. In James Schall, SJ, *Liberation Theology in Latin America: With Selected Essays and Documents*, 131–46. San Francisco: Ignatius Press, 1982.

——. *Convergences: To the Source of the Christian Mystery*. Translated by E. A. Nelson. San Francisco: Ignatius Press, 1983.

——. *The Glory of the Lord: A Theological Aesthetics*. Vol. 2, *Studies in Theological Style: Clerical Styles*. Translated by Andrew Louth, Francis McDonagh, and Brian McNeil, CRV. Edited by John Riches. San Francisco: Ignatius Press, 1984.

——. *Truth Is Symphonic: Aspects of Christian Pluralism*. Translated by Graham Harrison. San Francisco: Ignatius Press, 1987.

——. *In the Fullness of Faith: On the Centrality of the Distinctively Catholic*. Translated by Graham Harrison. San Francisco: Ignatius Press, 1988.

——. *Theo-Drama: Theological Dramatic Theory*. Vol. 1, *Prolegomena*. Translated by Graham Harrison. San Francisco: Ignatius Press, 1988.

——. *The Glory of the Lord: A Theological Aesthetics*. Vol. 4, *The Realm of Metaphysics in Antiquity*. Translated by Brian McNeil, CRV, Andrew Louth, John Saward, Rowan Williams, and Oliver Davies. Edited by John Riches. San Francisco: Ignatius Press, 1989.

——. *The Glory of the Lord: A Theological Aesthetics*. Vol. 7, *Theology: The New Covenant*. Translated by Brian McNeil, CRV. Edited by John Riches. San Francisco: Ignatius Press, 1989.

——. *The Glory of the Lord: A Theological Aesthetics*. Vol. 5, *The Realm of Metaphysics in the Modern Age.* Translated by Oliver Davies, Andrew Louth, Brian McNeil, CRV, John Saward, and Rowan Williams. Edited by Brian McNeil, CRV, and John Riches. San Francisco: Ignatius Press, 1991.

———. *Light of the World: Brief Reflections on the Sunday Readings.* Translated by Dennis D. Martin. San Francisco: Ignatius Press, 1993.

———. *My Work: In Retrospect.* San Francisco: Ignatius Press, 1993.

———. *Razing the Bastions: On the Church in This Age.* Translated by Brian McNeil, CRV. San Francisco: Ignatius Press, 1993.

———. *The Moment of Christian Witness.* Translated by Richard Beckley. San Francisco: Ignatius Press, 1994.

———. *Our Task: A Report and a Plan.* Translated by John Saward. San Francisco: Ignatius Press, 1994.

———. *Theo-Drama: Theological Dramatic Theory.* Vol. 4, *The Action.* Translated by Graham Harrison. San Francisco: Ignatius Press, 1994.

———. "The Fathers, the Scholastics and Ourselves." *Communio* 24, no. 2 (1997): 347–96.

———. *Theo-Logic: Theological Logical Theory.* Vol. 1, *Truth of the World.* Translated by Adrian J. Walker. San Francisco: Ignatius Press, 2000.

———. *Epilogue.* Translated by Edward T. Oakes, SJ. San Francisco: Ignatius Press, 2004.

———. *Love Alone Is Credible.* Translated by D. C. Schindler. San Francisco: Ignatius Press, 2004.

———. *Theo-Logic: Theological Logical Theory.* Vol. 2, *Truth of God.* Translated by Adrian J. Walker. San Francisco: Ignatius Press, 2004.

———. *Theo-Logic: Theological Logical Theory.* Vol. 3, *The Spirit of Truth.* Translated by Graham Harrison. San Francisco: Ignatius Press, 2005.

———. *Engagement with God.* Translated by R. John Halliburton. San Francisco: Ignatius Press, 2008.

Walatka, Todd. *Von Balthasar and the Option for the Poor: Theodramatics in the Light of Liberation Theology.* Washington, D.C.: The Catholic University of America Press, 2017.

Walker, Adrian. "Every Thought Captive to Christ: How Balthasar Changed My Mind about Faith and Philosophy." In Howsare and Chapp, *How Balthasar Changed My Mind,* 259–78.

White, Thomas Joseph, OP. "The Precarity of Wisdom: Modern Dominican Theology, Perspectivalism, and the Tasks of Reconstruction." In *Ressourcement Thomism: Sacred Doctrine, the Sacraments, and the Moral Life,* edited by Reinhard Hütter and Matthew Levering, 92–123. Washington, D.C.: The Catholic University of America Press, 2010.

———. *The Incarnate Lord: A Thomistic Study in Christology.* Washington, D.C.: The Catholic University of America Press, 2015.

Wicks, Jared, SJ. "A Note on 'Neo-Scholastic' Manuals of Theological

Instruction, 1900–1960." *Josephinum Journal of Theology* 18, no. 1 (2011): 240–46.

Williams, Rowan. "Balthasar and Rahner." In Riches, *The Analogy of Beauty: The Theology of Hans Urs von Balthasar*, 11–34.

Zimmerman, Robert. "Kant: The Aesthetic Judgement." In *Kant: A Collection of Critical Essays*, edited by Robert Paul Wolff, 385–408. London: Macmillan, 1968.

INDEX

The Achievement of Hans Urs von Balthasar: An Introduction to His Trilogy
was designed in Meta Serif with Hypatia Sans display type and composed by
Kachergis Book Design of Pittsboro, North Carolina. It was printed on
60-pound Natural Eggshell and bound by McNaughton & Gunn
of Saline, Michigan.